The Kind *of* Life *It's* Been

LLOYD ROBERTSON

The Kind of Life It's Been

A MEMOIR

To Susan Best Wishes

Enjoy!

HARPERCOLLINS PUBLISHERS LTD

To Father, George, who guided,
and
Life partner, Nancy, who sustained

Contents

The Awakening

I<small>T WAS A CLASSIC CANADIAN WINTER DAY IN SOUTHERN</small> Ontario: bright sunshine, cold and crisp, with the hard-packed snow crackling underfoot on the edge of the sidewalks. January 16, 1946: my hometown of Stratford, Ontario, was decked out for a major event. The Union Flag of the British Empire, better known as the Union Jack, adorned storefronts, hung from balconies and was clasped tightly in the hands of the majority who turned out. There was merriment in the air; for the more thoughtful, there was also a sense of history. This, after all, was the day our little community was welcoming the boys home—the dads, brothers, relatives and neighbours who had fought in the Perth Regiment during the Second World War. This was their parade; they were survivors of that cataclysmic chapter of the twentieth century, and our town had been a part of it, sharing in both the pain and the glory.

As an eager and excited youngster on the cusp of my twelfth birthday, I scrambled for a good viewing position. My father was too old to have fought in the war, but I was aware of many other dads who had, and some who had made the supreme sacrifice. So for everyone in Stratford, this was the place to be on this day. My friends and I found a perfect location, hanging on to the supports of a platform put in place for the broadcasters at CJCS, the local radio station. When the bands and soldiers swung into view and the commentators began to describe the scene, I was swept up in the excitement of the moment and that buoyant feeling that stayed with me on big broadcast occasions for all of my life: I was there at the centre of something important, something bigger than myself and of interest to the wider community. It's hard to say whether some tiny seed was planted in my consciousness that day—there was no blinding revelation, no dropping of the penny. I just remember being fascinated by the voices of the two commentators as they painted vivid pictures of the marchers and the joyous crowds. Ken Dougan, one of the two announcers, possessed a powerful, deep baritone voice. He was floored when, many years later while working with him at the CBC in Ottawa, I was able to relate the story of that winter day in Stratford.

I look back on that January afternoon as the beginning of my awakening to a new realization: radio could transport me into a different world. I became fascinated with all of the voices on the local radio station and could identify every one of them when they started to speak. They became my heroes. Other kids may have been wowed by Superman, hockey's Howie Meeker or movie star Humphrey Bogart, but for me, it was the collection of personalities that spoke to me through my hometown radio station.

I was soon among the enthusiastic groupies of CJCS, located above the beer parlour in the Windsor Hotel. Somehow I talked my way into becoming a regular visitor. It bothered some of the announcers that this bratty kid wanted to sit in the studio with them and watch while they went through their daily routines of news, sports and weather and, with the requisite amount of mock enthusiasm, rolled the records of the big bands of the day— "All right everybody, let's swing and sway with Sammy Kaye." It cramped their style when they wanted to slip downstairs for a beer, rant about the boss or invite a girlfriend up for a Sunday afternoon liaison. Eventually, the station manager told me he had to ask me to leave and would I please stay away for a while. I had no choice but to comply.

He couldn't have known, as I certainly didn't, that I'd be back working there in a few years. I simply transferred my thirst for radio elsewhere. Fortunately, for as long as I can remember, I'd been blessed with a good voice that attracted attention wherever I went, and that perhaps gave me the confidence to be a little more forward than I should have been at times. At Shakespeare Public School (all Stratford schools were named after Shakespeare and his characters) I approached the principal, E.R. Crawford, an authoritarian figure with a soft heart, and told him I would like to help with the morning announcements over the internal public address system. He agreed, and I soon found myself alternating on those daily "shows" with a cheery, apple-cheeked girl by the name of Annetta Young. Until my arrival, Annetta had these slots all to herself, but if she was jealous, she never showed it; in fact, she was helpful. It could be seen as my first lesson in professional decorum.

At home, I was an avid fan of the great variety shows of the postwar years hosted by Fred Allen and Jack Benny and Canadians Wayne and Shuster. There were also the Saturday night hockey broadcasts of Foster Hewitt and the news with Lorne Greene, long before he left for Hollywood and a rapid ascent to stardom in the early TV series *Bonanza*.

The radio also provided an escape from a dreary home life. My father, George, was sixty years old when I was born. By the time I was five, he was retired on a tiny pension from his job as a machinist's helper at the Canadian National Railway's locomotive repair shops in Stratford. During my early years, he became ill with a series of stomach disorders, which caused him much pain and were accompanied by loud retching and vomiting during the night. Those were the sounds that echoed through the house in the small hours, causing much nervousness and concern to a young boy. As I peered out fearfully through my slightly opened bedroom door, I watched my poor mother, Lilly, run back and forth in the dimly lit upstairs hallway, wringing her hands, not knowing how to cope. She was tortured by immense problems of her own from a string of mental and emotional disorders: anxiety neuroses, deep paranoia and extreme obsessive-compulsive behaviour. She would stand for hours in the kitchen, drying a single dish while rocking back and forth, lost in her own reveries. Her muffled cries could be heard in the night, and for days on end she wouldn't emerge from her bedroom. It all meant she was hospitalized much of the time while I was young, and when at home her erratic behaviour and dark moods cast a gloomy pall over the household. She constantly warned against playing with certain boys because their parents were out to harm us, or, from her insecurities of being born a gardener's daughter on estates in England, she chided me: "You should know your place" and "You're getting too big for your britches." The visits to the psychiatric hospital in St. Thomas, Ontario, are forever etched in my mind: the images of the poor souls who stood frozen in catatonic states in the hallways or walked along babbling to themselves in strings of loud incoherence, the occasional anguished cries and screams from patients behind locked doors who were dealing with their own demons in the deepest recesses of their imaginings. All of this left me with a lifelong commitment to try to help in every way possible to uncover the mysteries of mental illness.

During my mother's occasional periods at home, her anxieties kept us suspended in turmoil. Her constant suspicions that neighbours were spying on us frayed any friendly relationships we might have had. Since she was totally stymied by how to handle a small child, before I was old enough to go to school she would leave me in my room all morning, until my father recognized what was happening and arranged to have someone look in on me. Eventually, the frustrated psychiatrists, with no medication available to help them, recommended a prefrontal lobotomy, a popular operation of the day, long since discredited, that was used to calm frenetic psychotics or others who were deemed untreatable. In the 1975 movie *One Flew Over the Cuckoo's Nest*, Randle McMurphy receives a lobotomy to discipline him. The procedure was introduced to North America in 1935 and was "refined" by U.S. clinical neurologist Walter Freeman. He developed the "ice pick method" (named for the shape of the principal medical instrument used), and it sounds brutal and abusive: the "pick" was hammered in above the eyeball after the patient was rendered unconscious through electroshock, then another tool was inserted to—in theory, at least—uncouple the brain's emotional centre from the seat of the intellect. Freeman, who was seen as a trailblazer of the era, performed the operation on John F. Kennedy's sister, Rosemary, which left her in a vegetative state the rest of her life. The reactions in others, like my mother, were not so severe, but all underwent behavioural change.

The best description for my mother following her lobotomy can be found in Sylvia Plath's 1963 novel *The Bell Jar*, in which a lobotomized young woman is described as being in a state of "perpetual marble calm." That's exactly how I remember my mother later in her life, with her large eyes staring out from behind big glasses, and I knew she was not capable of making any kind of real connection to her son. The operation hadn't taken away the paranoia but had drained her of any dimension of emotional response. Her condition has haunted me all of my life. I believed she loved me from those occasional times we were able to connect in earlier years, but as I grew older I realized the protective barrier I had thrown up to close myself off from her had cramped my emotional development as well. It was a long time before I could bring myself to be truly intimate with anyone, and, like any child who grows up with a deeply disturbed parent, I was constantly on the lookout for any symptoms in my own behaviour that might signal emotionally entrenched demons. While I admit to occasional bouts of anxiety, they have never seemed more severe than what the average person endures from time to time.

Because of my parents' illnesses, I was shunted around as a youngster between neighbours and relatives. And there were plenty of half-brothers and half-sisters. My father had eight children from his first wife. As a widower in his fifties, he married my mother, an attractive Englishwoman who had moved in to keep house for him. This pairing brought two more children—my brother, Gordon, nine years my senior, and me, the youngest of the lot. My father was proud of his Scottish heritage; his grandfather had emigrated with his family from Blairgowrie, Perth, Scotland, and settled in Ontario's Perth County, near Mitchell, around 1850. All of the offspring fanned out from there, with my father moving from the farm to Stratford to take advantage of the burgeoning age of steam when that city became a major centre for the repair of locomotives. We grew up with the familiar chug-chug of the steam engines as they shunted around the "shops" in the centre of town. We became acquainted with the various shapes and sizes of the massive machines as they belched steam, spun their wheels and blew those attention-getting whistles, from the low moans to the piercing blasts that would shatter the calm of a lazy afternoon. While I was always fascinated by the engineer, who usually had his elbow stuck out the window in good weather, and was delighted on one occasion to have been invited, as a youngster, to climb up into the big machine, I had no inclination to pursue a career on the railroad. This was just as well, as diesel was about to replace steam and the little city on the Avon River was about to undergo dramatic change.

Obviously, I saw very little of my mother, and any meaningful relationship with her was impossible anyway. So any upbringing I was to have was left to my ailing father. Given his physical limitations, we never played soccer or basketball, but that didn't matter. To me he was a philosopher-king, and I treasured the time we were able to spend together. My dad had only a grade-school education, but he was wise in the ways of the world. He had an entrepreneurial streak that saw him purchase a row of aging terrace houses during the Great Depression. We lived in one of the five, but my father never made much money out of the enterprise. He allowed families who were down on their luck to stay in some of the others rent free, month after month. "I'll pay you next time, George" was a constant refrain through the years. When it came time to sell, there wasn't much profit for him. His generous nature may have come from the way he looked at life. He believed there was a spiritual dimension to our every-day affairs, and while he wasn't ardently religious, he insisted I accompany him to church on Sundays, read the Bible with him and use the golden rule as a marker for life when dealing with others. It isn't easy to "do unto others as you would have them do unto you," but I still believe it's the best way to build civility into everyday affairs. Most admirable was my father's attitude toward my mother. He demonstrated total compassion in deal-ing with her mental illness. I was embarrassed and ashamed that someone so close to us should have such a problem. Those were times when the stigma surrounding mental and emotional prob-lems was much more pronounced. My father reminded me she couldn't have done anything to prevent her condition and I was to regard her the same way as any other person with a serious incapacity. It helped me to deal with my own conflicting feelings, but total acceptance of his approach still took a while.

While most people cautioned against discussing religion and politics, they were always fodder for good talk with my father. He was a rabidly partisan supporter of the Liberal Party. To him, that great Liberal icon Mackenzie King could do no wrong. He was scornful of the Conservatives, whom he described as "Tory top hats" and ridiculed their leaders, from R.B. Bennett through John Bracken to George Drew. As for the CCF, now the NDP, he subscribed to former Prime Minister Louis St. Laurent's dic-tum that they were simply "Liberals in a hurry." I was to realize later that my father's dialectic, while highly entertaining, wasn't a good example for a son who was heading for a career in broad-cast journalism, where being even-handed about politics is a first principle. Nonetheless, he was the first to spark my lifelong interest in politics and current affairs.

I was also lucky to fall in with the right crowd in high school. Since I was involved in public speaking and debating contests and was in many of the school plays, I gravitated naturally to a group with the same interests, and these boys became the centre of my universe. There was Waldo Ryerson, a bright young man and provocative thinker who looked to be headed for a great future; Frank Walsh, whose mischievous sense of humour was always bubbling and whose father's gas station served as our hangout on many Friday and Saturday nights; Derek Blackburn, son of the collegiate music director and the reigning high-school heart-throb; and Art Burt, stepson of the owner of radio station CJCS. They were all from the right side of the tracks in a city bisected socially by the CN repair shops. Our times together allowed me to soak up the thinking of boys who came from more sophisticated backgrounds than my own. Interestingly, they never discriminated against me because I came from the "other" side and humble beginnings. If I could hold my own, I was allowed to participate. They provided me entry to a wider world.

Our gang was a ginger group around the school. We formed a barbershop quartet to entertain at assemblies and dances, a few of us played in the band that opened every school day with the national anthem ("God Save the King"—"O Canada" was not yet the official anthem). We were always present for forums and debates to argue stridently, and often speciously, for or against whatever ideas or theories were being discussed. It was the late forties and early fifties. The war was over, fascism was dead or dying, communism under the Soviet Union's Joe Stalin looked menacing, and democratic socialism was coming into vogue in Europe. Canada was set to play an ever more important role on the world stage. It was a heady time for kids on the brink of adulthood.

While having a good time and doing well at high school, I was still expected to bring in some money at home. My father's pension was too small to support us, and the food would often run out at the end of the week, leaving us with only eggs, a few slices of bread for toasting, and ketchup. It's a combination I still enjoy.

The dismal home finances meant I was always on the lookout for after-school and weekend work. There were odd jobs to be had as early as I can remember. I helped out the Canada Bread man on his daily rounds; he could sit in the wagon and watch the horse and give me a few nickels and dimes to run into the customers with the cakes and pastries. I later delivered for a small grocery store called the Dufferin Market, and it was there I learned about financial responsibility the hard way. The pay was four dollars and fifty cents a week to deliver groceries and stock shelves. One December day, the front wheel of my bike slipped on a patch of black ice and down I went, spilling everything out of the carrier, smashing a Javex bottle and ruining about twelve dollars' worth of goods. The store owner told me to make it a life lesson while I worked off the price of the groceries over the next few weeks.

Later, in my teen years, I landed a coveted downtown position with Reward Shoes. The company owned a chain of stores around the country. My friends and I regarded this as a dream job. Imagine, an eager young man with an eye for a good ankle who would be consistently visited for fittings by a string of Stratford's young lovelies. There was some truth in that, but it was mostly youthful stargazing.

My own romantic interest had covered the spectrum from blondes to brunettes and redheads but was beginning to centre on Nancy Barrett, a classically beautiful high school honour student with movie star looks that were just beginning to blossom. She had shown mild interest when I asked to borrow her dictionary in French class. Nancy came from a more upscale section of the city than I, but her father, like my own, was a working man for the CNR. Finally, I plucked up my courage and asked her to be my date for the biggest annual event of the school year, the "At Home" dance at the end of the term.

Nancy didn't show much enthusiasm but politely said she'd get back to me. A few days later, and again with not much enthusiasm, she agreed. I found out much later she had been waiting for my tall, dashing friend Derek to ask her out, and when he decided to take a pass on the dance, she accepted me as the consolation prize. As it turned out, the date was a smashing success for both of us. We were smitten with each other, and while our relationship was on-again, off-again for several years, it became obvious to both that marriage was inevitable. My father was delighted with the arrangement because he had such high regard for Nancy's father. He died before we were married, but he wouldn't have been surprised that it turned out well. He could have predicted Nancy would have strong character and would be successful in navigating the shoals of modern marriage. She became a teacher and eventually established a partnership with a friend in early childhood education. Finding her own path was essential in a marriage where the husband would be away much of the time or working long days on the crazy shift patterns of daily TV news-gathering operations. Fifty years and four wonderful daughters later, we are still together, a milestone of survival for anyone in the media.

Nancy and my high school pals were well aware that my foray into the world of retail would be short lived, even though

I was judged successful enough to be promised a good job in the Reward Shoe chain when school ended. I still yearned for radio and began plotting a return to CJCS. I enlisted the support of my friend Art, stepson of the owner, Frank "Pappy" Squires, to help in my quest. I also asked the school guidance counsellor, Dave Root, to help set up an interview with the station's program director, Alex Smith. The counsellor agreed, but, being a cautious man, told me a radio career might be risky because so few who entered ever got very far: "Only about one in ten million, Lloyd," he said.

Undeterred, I was off for my interview with Smith. He was a tall and courtly gentleman with many years of broadcasting experience in various parts of Canada as an announcer, producer and station executive. If he had been told by his boss to "give this kid a listen," he never let on. He heard me out as I told him of my passion for radio and how I would work hard and not bother him if he would just give me a part-time job—any job to get me inside the station on a regular basis. Smith looked as though he'd heard this line before but, to my everlasting surprise, he came out with a few quiet words that would set the course for my life: "Maybe," he said, "we could try you out as an operator." That meant rolling the records, those old 78-rpm discs, for announcers during the busy commercial periods. But much more than that, it meant I would have a foot in the door of the wonderful world of radio. Smith hired me for after school and Saturday work, saying he couldn't pay much, but he must have known I didn't care about that. To supplement the paltry amount, about seven dollars a week, I would have worked all night at the cement plant in nearby St. Marys if my father had needed more money. Fortunately, it never came to that. I leapt at the radio opportunity and went home walking on a cloud.

In 1951, at the tender age of seventeen, the heavens had opened. I was on my way.

2

Taking the Plunge

MY FATHER COULDN'T UNDERSTAND MY INTEREST IN broadcasting. He was concerned that it might not be secure enough work and dropped hints that I should perhaps consider an apprenticeship in railroading. He would have been delighted if I had taken up a very early suggestion of the Reverend Ferguson Barr, our minister at St. Andrew's Presbyterian Church. He was impressed by my voice, saw me as a success in the pulpit and wanted me to consider a career in the ministry. I thought about it quite seriously for a while, and my first regular girlfriend, the exotically beautiful Joyce, who was determined to marry a minister, also promoted the idea. But I wasn't hearing that necessary call to give all of my life to the church. Knowing he didn't have much choice in the matter, my father resigned himself to letting me go my own way—ultimately, a wise move. As for Joyce, she achieved her objective and married a minister, as I knew she would.

My friends began to develop a fascination with my occasional appointments behind the microphone at CJCS. I vividly remember the first one. After several weeks of learning how to be a competent operator, I was itching for a turn behind the mike.

The local sportscaster, Bill Inkol, had been urging me to take the plunge and do a station break. "Nothing to it, Lloydric," he said. He had decided on that pet name for me. So he took over my controls one day and I settled into the announce booth next door. With my stomach in knots, I carefully pushed down the on-air switch to activate the red light outside the door. At the appointed time I took a deep breath, paused and blurted out "THIS IS CJCS STRA-HERD." To this day, Inkol, who moved on to TV sportscasting, greets me with that station call. Waldo and Derek, who were listening at the time, also had great fun mimicking my mangling of the Classic City's name. I knew instinctively that, having fallen off the horse, I would have to try again. I did, and while there would be more bloopers in years to come, none would ever displace the original—for the enjoyment it gave my friends and the discomfort it brought to me.

Then came a big break: my first actual program. It was called *Musical Personality Time* and was heard every Saturday morning. The first "personality" was bandleader Freddy Martin. I rolled his records and read from his biography—pretty small stuff by today's standards, but I was in seventh heaven. The show was literally handed over to me by announcer Norm Jary, one of the finest people I've met in the business. Norm always wore crisp white shirts and pressed pants. He was headed for a career as a minister before being captured by the radio bug. He was busy, with many different chores at the station, readily admitted my voice was better than his and, rather than regard me as a threat, looked for ways to move me forward. Fortunately, I was able to repay his extraordinary kindness in a few years and we became lifelong friends

Gradually, the impression began to form among the regulars at the station that the kid might have something. The workload and on-air duties increased. The daily routine saw Nancy walk with me from high school to the station. We had become an "item" after the big school prom. There was a fond hand-holding goodbye, and then I would shoot up the stairs to CJCS, which had relocated from its spot over the beer parlour to a bigger space above a menswear store on Ontario Street, the city's main thoroughfare. Monday to Friday I would spin records or roll taped commercials for the announcers, but Saturday night was my own as sole proprietor of the airwaves from eight until sign-off around twelve-thirty. I was the folksy host on *Western Jamboree*, an hour of country music.

My buddies dubbed me "Tex" after that, and even today prominent Toronto lawyer Julian Porter, who found out about the tag through his Stratford connections, hangs the "Tex" nickname on me whenever we meet. The most popular program of the evening was the *Saturday Night Platter Party*. It was a very busy show. Requests were called in, and we would have to scurry and dig through the library of 78-rpm discs to find what had been asked for. I say "we" because I always managed to recruit friends to help. Waldo, Derek, Frank and Art thought it was a lark to handle the phone calls from the many female babysitters who would be calling in for their favourite songs. Sometimes it felt like I was running a dating service for my pals rather than conducting a radio show.

My increased involvement with the radio station coincided with the sharp decline in my schoolwork. Except for my two favourite subjects, English and history, I'd lost interest, and marks of eighties and nineties in Grade 11 crashed into the fifties and below by Grade 12. The problem had become so serious there was a call for me to appear in the principal's office. The tall and dour Donald Scott said, "Shape up, Lloyd, or stand the chance of failing." I managed to finish the year and was allowed a Grade 12 graduation. I have sometimes regretted not trying harder and perhaps going forward to university. The lack of a post-secondary education never impaired my progress in broadcasting, but it would have been a great confidence builder in years to come, when I was to associate with highly educated and scholarly people from several different disciplines. As it was, I became a voracious reader and used every work opportunity to expand my general knowledge base.

The completion of the high school year happened to coincide with the departure of two announcers from the radio station. Could this mean a break for me? As I was stewing about this, Alex Smith suddenly invited me to lunch with him at the Golden Bamboo restaurant, one of the new and popular places on Ontario Street with "fine Chinese and Canadian cuisine," as advertised. I sensed something was coming and was almost shaking in anticipation as he set out his idea. He felt I had shown some promise for on-air work and, in his mild-mannered way, said, "Now, young man, I may be taking a chance here, but I have a good feeling about you, and in offering you a full-time position, I know you will work to improve yourself." My agreement was immediate and I was almost bursting with happiness and enthusiasm. It was a short lunch and couldn't have cost him much.

It was 1952. I was eighteen years old and, as I saw it, the future could be nothing but rosy.

Since there were plenty of program slots, and I was a very eager recruit, I found myself doing a lot of work, probably filling both slots left by the departing announcers. There was the morning show, *Rise & Shine*; the noon run, *Suggestions & Music*, with the "suggestions"—the ads—always swamping the music. The hour also included the main newscast of the day, at twelve-thirty, anchored by Smith himself, and the one everlasting feature from the hour still heard today, *In Memoriam*, the death announcements from the Perth County community. Then, after a couple of hours off, I was back for *Uncle Lloyd's Birthday Club* at five o'clock and the evening news at six-thirty. I also wrote commercials and any local news that would be presented during my shifts. I was paid forty-five dollars a week, not bad for a greenhorn beginner in 1952.

My father admitted he was happy for me, and even my mother, who by this time had gone through the horror of her lobotomy and was at home more often, indicated she liked listening to me on the radio.

The Stratford station was typical of the small-town breed. It was set up to serve the city and all of Perth County in south-western Ontario, except it was hard to pick up its 250-watt signal if you were driving outside the city limits at night. Like all successful smaller radio stations, it had sunk its roots into the community. The station celebrated its seventy-fifth anniversary in 1999 and now has an FM counterpart and a website.

CJCS has had the usual range of characters float through its halls to help dress up its history. Some were brilliant broadcasters with terrible booze problems; there were the errant sons of rich men who were hiding out from fathers who wanted them to be doctors or lawyers; and there was the usual collection of wannabes like myself. Some, like Bill Inkol and Norm Jary, would move forward; others would find different careers. And there were a few professionals who had been around the broadcasting track and were invaluable to people like me. Program director Alex Smith, who coaxed me forward with his gentle prodding, was one of those. John Phillips, the station's production manager, was another.

He was a jaunty Welshman with a ruddy complexion and the air of a person who knew exactly what he was doing. He had arrived at CJCS after helping with the startup of Radio Jamaica. Our first encounter was traumatic. He castigated me for sloppy work during the broadcast of the Kentucky Derby, which the station carried through an affiliation arrangement with the CBC. The network allowed thirty-second and one-minute breaks in the broadcast for local stations to sell their own commercial time. I hadn't yet mastered the art of reading the advertising copy so that it would end at the exact second required before the race announcers started up again. As a result, listeners were hearing my voice extolling the virtues of Boyd's Footwear on Downie Street over top of the network track announcers who were beginning their call of the big race. Phillips chewed me out: "If you're going to be any good in this business, kid, you'd better learn about timing." I learned it, all right—and years later, script assistants in television could count on me to do my best to bring programs out to the split second.

And I was to learn another important professional lesson. This time it had to with making sure I understood what I was talking about before taking the subject to air. Alex Smith's wife, Edith, was a petite, warm and bubbly woman who sold commercial time for the station. Edith and the typewriter could never get along, so she resorted to leaving me handwritten notes about the content of her commercials. I had trouble reading her writing, and on one occasion the problem almost snuffed out my budding career. She had written a commercial for a local auto shop about the dangers of battery powders. I somehow managed to misinterpret the message and began to talk about the wonderful performance you could expect from your car if you'd just put those powders in your battery. The advertiser was understandably upset. Edith spent most of the next week calming him down and yelling obscenities at me, in the midst of purple-faced rages, whenever she saw me. Station owner "Pappy" Squires was so angry he could only bluster that I had committed a "firable" offence. Somehow, I survived, and Edith and I were eventually able to have a good laugh about it.

I was fortunate to be in Stratford and working for the station when the Shakespearean Festival was born. The locals had been very skeptical about this bold artistic venture, but in 1952 construction was underway for a tent theatre in the park on the banks of the Avon River. Finally, there was an air of enthusiasm in the city to replace the brooding sense of economic decline that had prevailed following the closing of the CNR shops a few years earlier.

The festival was the dream of local boy Tom Patterson, who had grown up in the Classic City, with all of its references to William Shakespeare. Most thought it was a nutty idea. How could a bunch of long-haired actors and their pals replace the key industry the city had lost? But Tom, a business journalist with the Canadian publisher Maclean-Hunter, pushed ahead with his proposal for a Stratford-on-Avon in Canada, patterned after its English namesake. Given the financial woes besetting his beloved hometown, he saw an opening. He spent many hours walking the well-trodden lover's lane around the Avon River, plotting his strategy for persuading a reluctant populace. As he told me, "I had to do more than just try to realize a dream I'd had from high school days; I had to have a plan as well." Tom tried to enlist the renowned British actor Laurence Olivier, to no avail. Finally, he arranged to meet another British star, actor and director Tyrone Guthrie. He found an avid listener intrigued by his idea. Guthrie was sold; he started to put together a high-powered team of top actors, designers and directors. Tom's dream was suddenly a reality. I met him often when visiting Stratford through the years, and while he fought a long battle with cancer, his spirit and zest for life never waned. That same spirit is evoked by his statue in front of the main theatre, which places him where he belongs: standing near the banks of the Avon, wrapped in the everlasting appreciation of those who come to visit.

Although there were several financial crises over Festival funding right up to the last minute, the doors would open in July of 1953. My beautiful little hometown, well off the beaten track and, until then, secluded in anonymity, became the centre of a worldwide success story.

My first broadcast assignment involving the Festival was to provide the commentary for the official opening ceremony, which was held at the bandshell on the riverbank. It was basically an outdoor stage fitted with wings on either side, just down the hill from a wide green space that led to the riverbank. The well-worn town landmark was the place where prime ministers and dignitaries often shared the spotlight with the Stratford Boys' Band and Perth County choirs.

Governor General Vincent Massey was there to make the formal declaration that the Stratford Festival was underway. There was a feeling of euphoria in the air as an excited crowd gathered and His Excellency moved toward the microphone at centre stage. John Phillips, who was producing, located me in the wings, just stage left of the governor general. I was carried away with the mood of the occasion as I tried to describe the scene and continued to babble while the Queen's representative, who could hear me quite clearly, waited at the microphone. Finally, he levelled a stare in my direction that left no doubt about his annoyance; I halted in mid-sentence and quickly introduced him. Phillips continued long afterward to chide me about my successful attempt to be recognized by the governor general. Something must have worked, though, because when I returned to the station, "Pappy," who was not known for his largesse, gave me a one-time bonus of twenty-five dollars.

In the week before the plays were launched, I was roaming the theatre for interview material one night and spotted a lone figure on the festival stage. He was pacing back and forth, familiarizing himself with the setting as he went over his lines. Moving closer, I recognized Alec Guinness. A major international star, Guinness had been recruited by the Stratford Festival to give it some instant credibility. He was rehearsing for his lead role in the opening-night presentation of Shakespeare's *Richard III*. Should I approach, or would he be furious with me? Walking softly toward him, I asked for a few moments. He paused briefly, and then his face broke into a smile. "Why, of course," came the response. We sat on the edge of the stage in a darkened theatre, looking out over the rows of empty seats that in a week's time would be filled with an excited opening-night audience. Guinness spoke into the tape recorder's microphone about his life's work. "I started off writing advertising copy, was on a London stage by the time I was twenty, and performed my first Shakespeare with a role in *Hamlet* when I was twenty-two." He was confident of success for the Stratford project. "It's a natural setting—Stratford on Avon, after all." He was so gracious and charming that I thought of him many times afterward whenever a colleague would make the point that the great ones, in theatre, sports, politics or, indeed, in any field of endeavour, are always the most humble.

By the autumn of 1953 I had been a full time employee of CJCS for a year and a half. Friends were confirming my own inclination that it was time to move on. Nancy was off to the University of Western Ontario. Waldo and Derek had also gone on to higher education. The old gang was breaking up. They could never know what they meant to me. In so many ways, these boys had provided a context for my life. They had become an integral part of my extended family.

The energy, the ideas, the sheer fun that always flowed so easily when we were together provided lifetime memories. Derek Blackburn became a teacher and then went into politics. For many years he was the NDP member of Parliament for the constituency of Brant in Ontario. His Fabian socialist ideas had found a natural home. Frank Walsh and Art Burt pursued business careers. The world was Waldo Ryerson's oyster. He was a natural leader and so bright and witty he could have found success in any field. But fate intervened. On a winter night in Stratford, while walking home from his girlfriend's house, he was fatally injured in a hit-and-run accident. His death shook us all. Suddenly we were face to face with the fragile nature of life.

My mother and father had moved into a small apartment in 1953. Their needs were not as great, but I assured them I'd continue to send money, no matter where I ended up.

Life was to change dramatically in the coming months. But the Stratford chapter was over. It had provided an appropriate launching pad for the years that were about to unfold.

3

Biting into the Apple

MOVING ON FROM STRATFORD WAS MUCH HARDER THAN I thought it should be. People in the know had told me I had some unpolished talent, and certainly I had lots of ambition, but no one seemed very interested.

My sights were set on moving to London, Ontario, about an hour west and considered a natural stepping-stone for broadcasters from CJCS. Several had graduated to that city's CFPL, a thriving commercial radio station in a medium-sized market. It was part of the *London Free Press* empire owned by the Walter Blackburn family (no relation to my Stratford pal), which was about to add television to its newspaper and radio enterprises.

I submitted audio tapes to them a couple of times. At first, there was no interest, and then finally came a reply acknowledging that I had some promise but needed more experience. In the relatively small and incestuous world of private radio, managers and program directors are constantly exchanging information about talent, formats and commercial prospects. It's quite possible that someone from London sent my tape over to Guelph, a charming city to the east of Stratford, where a bouncy modern radio station, CJOY, was making its mark in the industry.

After just a few years on the air, it had already sent promising talent out into the larger broadcasting world. There was Gordie Tapp, who went on to become host of the CBC's *Country Hoedown* and a regular for several years on the internationally syndicated *Hee Haw;* Rod Coneybeare, who had a long career as Jerome the Giraffe on the long-running children's show *The Friendly Giant;* and Carl Banas, who became one of Canada's top commercial announcers and the voice of many characters in a variety of TV skits and movies.

I was aware of CJOY's reputation, so when there was a sudden phone call from the program director, Don LeBlanc, he had an eager listener. LeBlanc, whom I came to know as a gentle and very funny man with a real creative gift for radio, started off with the mantra common to small commercial stations: "We can't pay you any more money, but we can make it interesting for you." He had heard that I wanted more work in news, so he offered a role as backup to the station's news director as well as host of the morning show. At that point, he knew he had me, and I knew it too. With all of my friends emptying out of Stratford, I had lots of incentive to find new, if not necessarily greener, pastures, so I jumped at the opportunity. There was also the understandable itch to move away from home and get out into the world.

To my great surprise, my half-brother Irvin showed up from Sault Sainte Marie, Ontario, where he was the chief of police, to drive me the short distance to Guelph. I was touched by his concern and generosity. Of all of the members of the first leg of the family, Irvin was about as close a match for my father as you could find. He was a little taller and larger of frame, but he was just as generous and reliable. My father had become concerned that Irvin might now be voting Conservative; he regarded him as being a member of the elites through his role as a police chief, a title that would usually cause its occupant to be seen as more conservative anyway. Dad questioned me persistently: "What about it, boy? Do you know?" While I came to understand that was indeed the case, I never revealed the news to our dad, who probably would have given Irvin a long lecture, in mock-serious manner, about "your humble beginnings, boy—you should never forget them." I spared Irvin from that and was just enormously appreciative that, in this transitional moment of my life, he had gone so far out of his way to help me get settled. It was obviously important for him to see that his youngest sibling didn't take a wrong step on the first day of his venture out into the wider world. As I listened to him talk about everything from the war in Korea (he felt the West had to "be strong" against the Communists) to the size of the snowbanks in the Soo during the last winter, I reflected on how I could do worse than model myself on this wise, jovial and helpful man. He had the same strength of character as our mutual father and was just as reflective and intelligent.

He took me straight to my first boarding house, one of those large, rambling red-brick homes found on the fringes of the downtown areas in Ontario cities. I was greeted by a white-haired lady and her small, black, yappy Scottie dog. Scottie immediately lunged for my pant leg and was sternly reprimanded by his mistress, who assured me that he would be fine once he got to know me. Irvin said his goodbyes and continued to follow my career over the years; he continuously called other Robertson relatives around the country and would yell into the phone: "Quick! Turn on TV! Lloyd's on!" and then slam down the receiver.

I saw very little of my kindly landlady or the two other boarders, but Scottie kept track of my every move, obviously an assignment he had deemed to come from the lady of the house and one he undertook with deadly seriousness. He and I eventually bonded when he discovered I was the only one prepared to feed him table scraps, something strictly prohibited by the landlady. Given my erratic hours, I often found myself nibbling alone in her spotless kitchen and couldn't resist Scottie's persistent pleadings.

It was about a four-block walk from the boarding house to the station, and it was a trek I made every morning to sign on the station at 6 a.m., always swinging past a hole-in-the-wall restaurant called the One-Minute Lunch, just around the corner off the main square in Guelph, where CJOY (pronounced "see joy") was located. I would order a coffee from a rotund man in a dirty apron who wearily heaved himself to a standing position, poured the steaming black liquid into a cardboard cup and accepted my money with a barely audible grunt.

It was a daily routine until I thought there might be a new and better way to catch a few extra winks, always a valuable commodity for morning broadcasters. I raced to the station first, threw on a long-playing record and, in an arrangement with my sourpuss pal, ran to the One-Minute Lunch, where he would have the coffee ready for me in a cardboard cup and grunt "It's about time" before I zoomed back to the station. All worked well for a couple of weeks, until the morning I heard the door to the radio station lock behind me. The audience was treated to several minutes of the swish-swish of the needle tracing the record's run-out groove after the music had ended before I could rouse the station's engineer to help me with my dilemma. I got away with that one, probably because the kindly, sandy-haired engineer, Jake Milligan, was a patient man who was always too busy dreaming up the next big idea in broadcast technology to bother about an errant morning man.

However, the next episode could have seen me make a quick exit from Guelph. I seriously overslept one morning and didn't get into the station till after seven o'clock. The phones were going crazy, so I lifted all the receivers off their hooks, dropped a record on the turntable ("Pretty Baby" by Doris Day) and started it halfway through. When the music stopped, my voice was heard giving the time and weather as though we'd been on the air for some time. I hoped nobody would know the difference and listeners would think there was just something wrong with their radios. It was a dumb idea, but I was desperate and aware that others had done it—it was an old trick passed down through generations of small-town radio lore. Don LeBlanc, who knew the game, appeared in the studio at the end of the morning show and accused me of faking the sign-on, a very serious matter. I confessed—guilty as charged. He marched me into the front office, where I was set to face the wrath of the station manager, Fred Metcalfe, and the CJOY owner, Wally Slatter. Metcalfe looked furious and proclaimed loudly, "I think we have to order you to pack up your things and get out of here." I was shaking. Fred and Wally had both been in the services during the Second World War and, at this point, Wally intervened. "Look guys," he said. "I hated those early calls during the war years. I know how tough it is on that shift." He turned to me and said, "Lloyd, you have one more chance." I almost slumped to the floor in relief. He had saved my job, and I'd learned an early and critically important lesson: it's never wise to try to bluff your audience.

A few days later, Jake Milligan called me. "Hey, Lloyd, now that you've been spared from getting fired, how would you like to help me out?" Jake was a forward thinker and was intrigued by the promise of cable for carrying television signals to large sections of the Canadian population. At this point, in early 1954, television was just getting started, and a few rooftop antennas were popping up to receive over-the-air signals, but it would be years before cable became a major force. His plan was to test a video and audio signal for a possible community cable operation by running a line from a camera in one room into a link to a TV set in another. Jake's instructions to me were, "Read your radio newscast into the camera I'm hooking up on the third floor, and we'll see what kind of signal we get two floors below." It worked well, and the potential for Jake's experiment was not lost on Fred Metcalfe, who went on to set up a highly successful cable franchise for Maclean-Hunter. It's likely that Jake's ideas for mass signal distribution on cable helped spawn a whole circle of Canadian millionaires, including Ted Rogers in the east and JR Shaw in the west. To my knowledge, Jake never got to be a rich man; he was one of those inventive people who give others the ideas and then blithely move on to their next project. Oh yes, the anchor of the newscast that day didn't go on to gather up cable riches, either.

Doing the morning show and putting newscasts together, as well as presenting them on air, kept me busy, but I was happy to spend extra hours creating big broadcast specials with my radio pals.

Small radio stations develop their own culture around the cast of characters they employ, and, in my case, this being my first position outside my hometown, these people became members of my extended family. Most of them resembled stereotypes familiar to viewers of the various sitcoms about life in radio that have dotted TV schedules over the years. There were the smooth, sly time salesmen, the flirty girls from accounting or the reception desk, the earnest news people, and the wild-and-crazy but often enormously talented disc jockeys who filled the airwaves with occasionally engaging chatter and just as often with woeful banalities. Since many of us were young and single and filled with enthusiasm for what we were doing, we spent a lot of time together and talked endlessly about the broadcast business overall—who was up, who was down, who was in or out, and who was worth watching or who was a waste of time. Lorne Greene, who had been the "voice of doom" on the CBC during the war, was now fronting a daily newscast on CKEY in Toronto. Jack Dennett was a major newscaster on CFRB, where his deep, warm and sincere voice stood in marked contrast to the edgy sound of scrappy writer Gordon Sinclair, who was starting his daily feature broadcasts on the same station. We were also aware that the CBC, with its more serious classical programming, was becoming a major broadcasting force, and we were impressed by the precision and objectivity of its news presenters. It was in Guelph that the lights of the big time in broadcasting began to lure me, but they were still distant constellations.

In the early fifties, the big bands continued to rule the airwaves, with Tommy Dorsey, Woody Herman and Benny Goodman leading the way. There were also such great jazz singers as Ella Fitzgerald and pretty songstresses like Doris Day. Another outstanding icon of the era was Glenn Miller. His story was playing at a local theatre, and I decided we should put together a feature on the great man, his outstanding music and the dramatic story of his stunning loss to the world after he disappeared in action in World War II. Don LeBlanc, who was quick to forgive my morning show fakery, was more than happy to allow me to indulge in what would be my first professional effort as a producer. "Go for it, kid," he said. "You may be a Hollywood star one day, and I'll take the credit."

My colleague on this project was Peter Griffin, another CJOY broadcaster who, as it turned out, would push my career upwards further and faster than I could ever have dreamed possible.

In his own right, Pete, who later gained fame as half of Pete & Geets on various FM stations in Toronto, was to become one of the best and funniest radio talents the country has ever seen. He was a tall, serious-looking man with a perpetually furrowed brow above horn-rimmed glasses, and when those features added a sardonic smile, you knew something was up. His mind was a stirring cauldron of mischief and imaginative ideas. He devised a secret language for all the announcers that had us adding "ves" to every syllable. For example, I would be Lloyves Robves-terves-son. This code meant we could communicate with one another in a way the boss would never understand. It may have been the reason that, on one occasion, we managed to change the entire program schedule of the radio station without management understanding what we'd been jabbering about for days. When the morning show suddenly burst onto the air one day with the new and snappy title of *Clockwatcher,* Wally Slatter came bounding into the studio to demand, "What the hell is going on here?" Griffin also frequently pulled the fiendish trick of leaving all the audio switches open when he signed off at night. As morning man, I would arrive the next day and turn on the transmitter by remote control before actually signing on the station. What followed was always fascinating to those turning their radio dials to find something listenable at six o'clock in the morning. I could be heard flushing the toilet, talking to myself, slamming doors, or committing other loud indiscretions before realizing that my audio board was totally live and everything was going out over the air.

It was Griffin who challenged me to audition for a CBC job. "You've got the pipes for it, Lloydo," he said. At the time, I had a mild interest in the CBC but wasn't panting to work there. I enjoyed the freedom and hurly-burly of private radio, but the prospects of graduating to a national network intrigued me.

Eventually, I gathered up the nerve to apply to Mother Corp., and a date was set for one of the most daunting exercises of my young life: the CBC announcer audition. Of course, I had to make the trek to Toronto to keep my appointment and since, as noted, my salary was minuscule, I took the bus from Guelph to Canada's "Big Apple."

It was only my second or third visit to the city, and on this occasion, since I had to walk the three or four blocks from the bus depot to the CBC headquarters on the storied Jarvis Street, I saw everything in a new light. To me, Toronto was not just big. It was big and exciting, with a rhythmic hustle and a cornucopia of visual delights and exotic enterprise. While I considered myself somewhat worldly, despite not having been outside small-town Ontario, I was taken aback by the brazen nature of my first encounter with one of the city's "working girls." Walking up Jarvis to my appointment in the middle of the afternoon, I was approached by a perky, attractive brunette who was wearing a tight, low-cut sweater that displayed her ample attributes and jeans she had been poured into. She offered a variety of

sexual services on a graduated economic scale and seemed willing to bargain because I looked like "a nice guy." Aware of the
importance of my appointment, and imagining the echoes of
my father's voice warning of the perils of loose women, I stam-
mered something about not being able to participate right then,
but might see her on the way back. It was a dodge she recognized,
but she was very pleasant and told me to be sure to let her know
later about my special business of the day. I didn't run into her
again.

The CBC Radio offices and studios were housed in a ramshackle former girls' school at 354 Jarvis Street. It was certainly
an unimposing presence for Canada's national broadcaster. Once
inside, I met a man who would become a critical influence in my
life over the next several years. W.H. "Steve" Brodie was a former university professor who had become the CBC's Supervisor
of Broadcast Language. He determined how the network should
sound through its announcers, who were described at the time as
the "front windows" of the organization.

Brodie was a short but stalwart man with a faint military
bearing and a professorial, no-nonsense air. He handed me the
audition script, about a dozen typed pages of text and instructions, and gave me twenty minutes to look it over. I began to
perspire just going through it. There was the requisite newscast
to read, but then came poetry as well as introductions to Italian
operas and German lieder concerts. There was a section where
you were given three minutes to talk about yourself, and finally
a list of Canadian place names and commonly misspelled and
misprinted words.

I did pretty well with the newscast. Since the Korean War
was winding down, I was familiar enough with places like

Panmunjom. The ad-lib section on my brief life was no problem, but I was stumped on the list of trick English words by *schism* (pronounced "sizm"), *fustian* (FUH-shen) and *cabal* (ca-BAHL). I badly mangled the Italian and German pronunciations. However, my elegant and beautiful high school French teacher, Maggie Baldwin, would have been proud as I successfully manoeuvred my way past *Le Havre*. Overall, I didn't think I had done very well, and Mr. Brodie wore an inscrutable smile as he ushered me out. I almost ran back to the bus station, and an hour and a half later I was back in Guelph. Pete Griffin was anxious to know about the experience, but I brushed it aside and said I never expected to hear from them, and that was that.

A month later, to my enormous surprise, I received a telegram from Steve Brodie offering a position as a summer relief announcer at the CBC radio outlet in Windsor, Ontario (also known by its call letters, CBE). Should I throw off a steady job for a summer slot? Ultimately, the answer was yes, but not before a stern lecture from Wally Slatter on the dangers of working for the CBC. "You'll be buried in their bloody bureaucracy," he declared. His well-meaning rant and offer of a better position at the station fell on deaf ears, but before leaving I managed to put a word in for my CJCS pal, Norm Jary, who had been so good to me in Stratford. Wally had an opening for a sportscaster, and I knew Norm could do the job. He won the position, moved to Guelph, had a flourishing career and was elected several times as mayor of the Royal City.

For me, it was time to try my wings on a new adventure, and so, in July of 1954, at the tender age of twenty, I began life as a CBC announcer, a role that would shape my character and personality for years to come.

4

Joining Hands with Mother Corp.

THE CBC OFFICES AND STUDIOS IN WINDSOR WERE ON the top floor of a nine-storey building overlooking the Detroit River. In the fifties, Detroit was a bustling, clean and cosmopolitan U.S. metropolis. The ugly race riots were to come thirteen years later and would change the face of the city, leaving the central area to fall into decay for decades afterward. But in the fifties, it had class and style. Detroit loomed like a colossus over the much tinier Windsor, and the allure of its major department stores and glittering nightlife were an irresistible beacon for residents of the Canadian side. The relationship between the two cities was a metaphor for the famous Canada–U.S. elephant-and-mouse comparison. A few years before, and in a stroke of ingenuity, CBC managers and engineers decided Windsor would be a good place to start a radio station that would showcase the Corporation and its Canadian content with a strong signal blasting its way into the northern U.S.

At the CBC offices I was introduced to a tall, friendly bear of a man by the name of John Moore. After the formalities, he said, "Well, you may as well get started" and handed me a pile of 78-rpm records while he explained that the program I would be handling was called *Light and Lyrical,* a blend of melodic semi-classics mixed with Mantovani strings that was broadcast from Windsor over the Trans-Canada Network three weekday mornings. He ushered me through the soundproof doors into the announce booth and punched the talkback button to the control room to introduce me to the operator. He then said, "Good luck. You're on the air in ten minutes." Good grief! I thought he must be kidding—on the air to the network in ten minutes!

The rest, including the very first words I spoke on a national system, is a blur. The music was rolled in groups of three, so I only had to read the script with a few minor adjustments and the show was over. I never spoke to anyone who heard it, and Moore only gave me a pleasant nod when I left the studio. A few minutes later, I was in the record library, talking with announcer Warren Davis, who would become a lifetime colleague, when the doors swung open and the records from *Light and Lyrical* came crashing through, some landing in pieces on the floor and on desks.

Warren calmly said, "Oh yes. You weren't told that you were supposed to pick up your records from the control room when your show is over." One of the operators wanted to show the newcomer how he had to follow the rules.

CBE was a favourite spot on the dial for many Americans. It served up the traditional CBC fare of quality music in classics and jazz as well as excellent radio dramas and local, national and international news—all of it free of commercials. For me, the Windsor experience meant the beginning of an education in the liberal arts for a young man who didn't get beyond Grade 12. The CBC's approach to broadcasting at the time, somewhat more elitist than the present day, gave me a rounded experience in announcing that ran the gamut from introducing Italian opera and Dixieland to reading blank verse and doing news and sports. I was also a disk jockey for the program *What's New*, a pop music show featuring late record releases we scrounged from new music outlets in Detroit, which was also broadcast over CJBC in Toronto. That station is now a French-language outlet, but at the time it was the key station of the CBC's Dominion network. Its format featured lighter fare, still delivered with quality in the spoken word, as well as newscasts and other material offered up to private stations that wanted it.

By the time my three-month summer relief period had expired, luck struck once again. Just when I was beginning to think about getting back into private broadcasting, one of the other three announcers at the station obliged me by accepting a job at CKEY in the burgeoning commercial market of Toronto. I was offered the position, filled his spot and was confirmed as a full-time CBC announcer.

I could now count as my colleagues—although they were very far up the line at headquarters in Toronto—people like Earl Cameron, Allan McFee, Lamont Tilden, Elwood Glover and John Rae. It was a heady time, and I was determined to work hard and move forward quickly.

It is impossible to exaggerate the importance of the announcer to the CBC in the fifties and early sixties. He stood at the centre of all the network's program activities and represented the very essence of the image the Corporation hoped to display to the public. There were no women on staff—their voices were not considered authoritative enough, according to a CBC policy of the times. The announcer was expected to have a pleasant voice, a sincere manner and sound knowledgeable on a wide variety of subjects. Under the tutelage of Steve Brodie, who would visit us all like a friendly school inspector on a regular basis, we would be put through our paces and expected to keep up to date with foreign pronunciations and changes in national and international affairs. In those years, long before the age of specialization, announcers did virtually all of the on-air work at the CBC. They read all of the news and most of the sports, conducted interviews for various programs and went into the field to do voice reports for the news and live special-events broadcasts such as royal tours.

One of the most famous examples of an announcer pioneering as a radio reporter was J. Frank Willis, who was on the air for hours at the site of the Moose River mine disaster in Nova Scotia in 1936. He held the country and much of the world in thrall for several days with his reports from outside the mine, where three men were trapped during a cave-in and eventually had to be pronounced dead. No one knew or cared whether Willis was identified as an announcer or a reporter.

The people who wrote the news to be delivered from the studios were usually hired from newspapers, or they may have been university graduates with Bachelor of Arts degrees. Certainly, they were not hired to go on the air, and when the CBC eventually signed a union contract that allowed them to deliver their own written reports, often with embarrassing results, the first faint images of the writing on the wall were there for the announcers. This happened even though many of the announcers had considerable experience in the editing and gathering of news material.

I had done several pieces for CBC Radio's *News Roundup* and a nightly show called *Roving Reporter*, whose star contributor was a brash Scotsman who had just immigrated to this country to settle in Vancouver and would go on to become a national celebrity. His name was Jack Webster. But what the announcers had contributed in terms of broadcast journalism mattered little in the long and bitter turf war that developed within the CBC between unions representing the news people on the one side and staff announcers on the other. The battle would take several twists and turns over time, including the ridiculous restriction that announcers were forbidden from writing or editing any of the news material they read on the air.

The CBC's attitude toward the presentation of news was still rooted in the war years and before, when the person reading the news was expected to be merely a "detached voice," intended to ensure that the news would never be stained by charges of bias. Announcers read "news bulletins" from the Canadian Press wire service that were altered very little, if at all. CP was a cooperative newsgathering operation used by newspapers and radio stations to collect stories from across the country, including the nation's capital. If a politician, or anybody else, complained about being misrepresented or treated unfairly, a CBC manager could simply say, "But we got it straight from CP," which was regarded as a model of objectivity and neutrality. With so many newspaper clients of different political stripes, it had to be. While the approach may have served the CBC well during that early period, it became sadly outdated with the arrival of television. TV news was vastly different from radio in that direct visual coverage of events was required. The CBC had to start doing its own newsgathering in a big way, and major stories had to be seen to be covered by a CBC correspondent. Which meant, of course, the Corporation could not claim that anyone but the CBC itself was responsible for what it presented on air. Dramatic expansion within a very short time in the fifties and sixties led to a dividing up of news service functions among a range of unions, as a nervous network and news managers tried to keep up with the new pressures and the unions strove to ensure they all had a piece of the action. The assignment of stories, copywriting and editing, including the selection of stories, the prominence given them and the order in which they were presented, became the responsibility of the Canadian Wire Service Guild. Staff film cameramen, film editors and other production personnel had another union. In still another jurisdiction were the directors, who were concerned with getting the newscast on the air with as crisp an appearance as possible. Foreign correspondents usually had special service contracts. But for the announcers—the people out front and the primary point of contact with the audience—nothing changed. They were held to the old ways. The meek little union to which they belonged tried to insist they still had the right to do reports, but the larger and more powerful Wire Service Guild simply ignored the challenge. The result was that announcers simply read what they were given; any deviation could lead to an immediate uproar and a formal grievance by the Guild, on the grounds that only its members were trained journalists.

There was always a way for announcers to allay frustrations, of course. We used to have fun with the openings of radio newscasts that began: "Here is the CBC News, read by (announcer's name)." Sometimes, in late-night listening periods, "announcer's name" would become Orson Welles, Winston Churchill or Dagwood Drumbeat—read with flat intonation and totally deadpan. We never heard of a manager's complaint.

But the approach of the detached news reader was about to collide with the growing expectations of audiences that the person who delivered the news, and appeared in their living rooms every evening, was presumed to know what he was talking about and be thoroughly acquainted with the material being presented. In this sense, we were influenced by the great broadcasters from the U.S. who beamed into Canada, including Walter Cronkite, Chet Huntley and David Brinkley, each of whom brought their own distinctive styles to news broadcasting. By no means did this mean colouring the news to their own beliefs. It simply meant total involvement in the gathering, preparation and presentation to enhance the credibility of the person delivering it.

It was one of many ways in which early Canadian TV would follow a U.S. lead. American cultural dominance forced Canadian news organizations to compete with our southern neighbour's broadcasters for audience; we had to appear just as polished and professional. In news, we succeeded in that unique Canadian way of adapting some of the U.S. production methods so that our programs looked just as good as theirs, while delivering information with sound editorial content tailored to our homegrown viewership.

My Windsor entry into the CBC world had been relatively calm. But since the last years of high school, I had been plagued by severe, grinding stomach pains. I was suffering from these again now. There were days when the pain was so bad I could barely function and had to fight hard to appear normal while often looking dreadfully pale and tired. A few trips to the doctor revealed the problem to be a duodenal ulcer. One physician was surprised that someone so young should have a condition usually related to the sorts of tensions and pressures that hit people later in life. I came to understand that holding in my worries about life at home, with my mother's mental illness and my father's declining health, had taken its toll on my own well-being. In my view, it was important to appear normal to the outside world and pretend to be leading the kind of stable existence exhibited by my friends and other kids. I had perfected the art of putting up a good front; no one seemed to notice there was anything wrong. For a time, I tried to control the debilitating pain through diet—eating no spicy foods, drinking lots of milk and keeping alcohol consumption to moderate levels. That prescribed regimen, plus over-the-counter antacids, kept the problem controlled to some degree.

But I wasn't ready for what hit me in Windsor. I woke up in the middle of the night at my boarding house feeling worse than I had ever felt in my life. The nausea was extreme, and I was soon vomiting heavily and almost unable to crawl back into bed. By morning, I was ghostly pale and too weak to get up. My kind landlady called her family doctor who decided, very quickly, that I should be hospitalized. It turned out the ulcer had caused a blood vessel to rupture and I was in desperate condition. In fact, if not treated immediately, I could have died. It took several pints of blood and a few days of rest to restore me to health, but that wasn't the end of the problem. There were many more bouts with the same nagging ulcer in years to come, often disrupting my family and professional life. Finally, through modern medication and a more settled lifestyle with Nancy and family, the ulcer healed over and there has been no sign of it for years.

If there was an upside to the hospital experience, it was meeting Molly Maguire. She was a pert and pretty nurse with black curly hair and flashing eyes who helped bring me back to health. We became fast friends and eventually had a short-lived romance. Nancy and I, while remaining enamoured of each other, had gone in different directions and had agreed we should see other people.

In the mid-fifties, television was increasingly making its mark on the broadcast landscape in Canada. CBC stations were opening up across the country and private broadcasters were establishing outlets. We were told to appreciate the vast potential of this new kid on the broadcast block, but few of even the most prescient experts on media grasped the revolutionary role television would play in changing the nature of twentieth-century society. Canadian media guru Marshall McLuhan made the most profound utterance with his famous "The medium is the message"— a phrase that echoed through the lexicon of media babble for years. Some of my more senior radio colleagues believed TV couldn't last. Others predicted the demise of the senior service. That didn't happen either; radio simply changed course, as portables sprouted everywhere, playing music of the nascent rock era to kids at the beach or suburbanites in their cars, as well as bringing the full range of entertainment and information programming to a more mobile audience that television could not easily reach.

While my Windsor experience was proving valuable, I also knew it was to time to move on and get established, if possible, in the new medium, which held out the promise of a challenging future. The Windsor radio outlet, even though it had proven a useful introduction to CBC ways, had limited potential for professional growth. It would never originate major blocks of network programming; that was left to the new broadcast centres being built in the larger cities around the country—Toronto, Montreal, Vancouver and, in a smaller but no less important sense, Winnipeg and Halifax. Jobs were opening up everywhere, and the bulletin boards across the CBC system began overflowing with new positions in television. Two announcer vacancies were posted for Winnipeg. I applied for one of them, while my friend Warren went after a new position in Toronto.

While Toronto was the go-to destination for many announcers within the CBC system, I knew it was too soon for me. But Warren was extremely anxious about it. What a shock to him when word came down that both of us were being sent to Winnipeg. He was so angry he burnt out his car's transmission on a wild drive over rocky Northern Ontario roads as he made his way west. I chose to take the train. My last memory of the lovely Molly was waving goodbye as she stood on the station platform while the train pulled out of the Windsor station on a chilly day in early January of 1956. In a few months, I would write to her that I had become engaged to Nancy and we would be getting married.

In leaving Windsor, I was transforming my life once again, and in a more profound way than I realized at the time. I was deserting the glittering attractions and bigger-money lure of the U.S. (in Detroit), and was about to form a stronger bond with the country of my birth.

5

Testing and Transitions

A S THE CN TRAIN ROLLED NORTH AND WEST THROUGH the winter countryside, the snow got deeper and the nights darker. The days were often bright, with the sun casting luminous reflections off the crystal-white snow, and on the clear, brisk winter nights, the moon provided pools of light through the dark bare forest and across the crusted snow of the open plain. There were quick stops at little places with vaguely familiar names, like Hearst and Cochrane, in Northern Ontario. After three days and three nights, the train began to slow for its arrival in Winnipeg and finally pulled to a stop just after eight in the morning at the railway station at the forks of the Red and Assiniboine rivers.

It was a cold, bright January day and, stepping out onto the platform, wearing a light topcoat, I ran smack into my first experience with the dry but still bone-numbing cold of prairie legend. The cab driver who had been hired to meet me and make sure I got to the CBC building on Portage Avenue chuckled at my outerwear and insisted we stop at the Hudson's Bay store, where I would buy the only kind of coat that made any sense in a Winnipeg winter. It was the designer clothing of choice in the "gateway to the west": a big, fur-trimmed, hooded parka. I wore it with pride as I strode into the tidy-looking three-storey building, underneath a huge transmission tower that housed CBWT, Winnipeg's first TV station. The parka would make them understand that this eastern kid was smart enough to come prepared. I stuffed the light topcoat in my suitcase, and with it any Upper Canadian airs I might have acquired, and got set to be overwhelmed by that famous western hospitality. I wasn't disappointed.

Winnipeg too often gets a bad rap from the rest of the country. Yes, it is isolated and the winters are cold, but it is truly a cultural oasis with thriving theatre, ballet and symphony. It has an NHL team, the Jets, and a lively media presence led by the venerable *Winnipeg Free Press* and at least four television outlets and several radio stations. The city has large clusters of carefully nurtured green space through extensive parkland and, best of all, some of the warmest, friendliest and most caring people I have met across the world. It couldn't have been a better place for an ambitious young broadcaster to launch a television career.

The TV station, CBWT, had been on the air for little more than a year, and those of us who were lucky enough to get in on the ground floor had to learn by doing. With the notable exception of a Ryerson course in Radio Arts in Toronto, there were no college or university courses to teach anything about broadcasting, and certainly none to unravel the intricacies of the new medium, which developed its own codes, language and practices as it grew. While we were young and enthusiastic about trying out our new toy, we also quickly discovered that television was an unforgiving medium. It was unkind to those who didn't look "right" for the unrelenting gaze of the camera or who had unfortunate tics or other habits that the audience found distracting. And there were the distractions within the studio itself: the huge, hulking cameras that were pushed around the floor, the searing intensity of the blindingly bright television lights required in the early days of TV, and crew members who, after spending many hours setting up the studio for broadcast, would nod off to sleep in the middle of your spiel—there was even one who broke into a snore while I struggled to get through a newscast. It took tremendous focus to look into the lens of the inanimate camera and, as Steve Brodie had directed us, speak as though you were addressing just two or three people at a time. If you managed to cope with all of this, you would also have to deal with the heavily applied, runny, tan-coloured makeup, "plastered on with a trowel," as we used to say. We needed it, though; otherwise, the person looking into the lens would appear ghostly under the hot glare of the huge lights set in large, saucepan-like containers called "scoops," usually pulled down from a grid hung from the ceiling. Even the men had to apply a light layer of lipstick so their lips could stand out from the heavy layer of makeup. It brought hoots from the makeup artists to see the guys furiously scrubbing off the lipstick before they ventured onto the street. Yes, breaking into television was a very Darwinian process— there was a thorough weeding out.

The Winnipeg station was part of the budding national CBC television network, but here, on the local level, to my surprise and delight, there was lots to do. Winnipeg was the capital of the "keystone" province of Manitoba and, as noted, it was a lively place with a sense of its own importance as a major transportation hub; there was a newness and an energy that were part of the bubbling and bustling openness that infused the local populace, whatever the weather, and dominated all activities, from curling in the winter to baseball in the summer. The local station tried to reflect it all through coverage of sports events, variety shows and daily news and magazine programs. The mainstay was a nightly show, similar to others of its kind in major broadcast centres, that combined news, interviews, sports and weather with a carefully chosen cast of characters intended to become evening companions for people as they came home from work and settled in for the dinner hour with the family. Winnipeg's version was called *Spotlight* and, among its main personalities was our sportscaster, the late "Cactus" Jack Wells. Jack had worked his way up through local radio, and he was Winnipeg personified: happy, friendly and delighted to take newcomers under his wing and make them feel welcome. Jack never took himself seriously, and would occasionally show up on a Friday night after downing a few pints with buddies at the golf club and amaze the rest of us by breezing flawlessly through his sportscast after weaving toward his chair. Jack was a true legend among broadcasters of the era and was happy to tell stories on himself and hear others tell them about him.

One that constantly made the rounds involved Jack's play-by-play description of two opposing team members who got into an altercation at a Winnipeg Blue Bombers football game. He described them as throwing "epitaphs" at each other. When later corrected and told the word he wanted was *epithets,* Jack replied, "What the hell? If I said they were epitaphs, that's what they were." Even in the drab black-and-white programming of the times, Jack had to be described as colourful.

Many of the stories you've heard about those early times are true. All of what we did was "live"; there were no teleprompters to aid newscasters, so if you lost your place while trying to look up and speak straight into the camera, you simply had to fumble around and find it again. People were constantly forgetting their lines on commercials, and yes, there are those who swear they have seen it: the announcer in the U.S. who actually managed to paint himself into a studio corner while enthusing about a particular brand's colour. The director could only fade to black, and the outraged advertiser would have to be allowed a "make-good." Cue cards held by a stagehand off to the side of the camera could be used, but that made the presenters look shifty-eyed as they moved back and forth between the words on the card and the lens of the camera. Broadcasters who could memorize quickly, or speak extemporaneously when they had to, progressed faster. The medium was brutally harsh to those who hesitated or looked uncomfortable.

On our announce staff in Winnipeg was a retired naval officer who had seen action during World War II, a wonderfully friendly fellow who loved to tell old war stories and was gracious and helpful to newcomers to the city like myself. One night while doing the weather on the big chalkboards used in those days, he suddenly lapsed into talking about winds coming to the port and starboard side, looked out at the camera with a befuddled gaze and paused. The director faded out, and that well-used "Technical Difficulties Are Temporary" graphic appeared on the screen. Our friend was soon back in radio.

My first few months in Winnipeg were marred by an event that had only a marginal relationship to my television work but which disappointed the brass at the station, all of whom liked to believe that their broadcasters were a cut above those who practised their craft in the private sector. As a staff announcer, I was expected to do my share of community appearances, and the regional program director, the tall, lugubrious Don Cameron, whose brother Earl was later to gain great prominence as a

national CBC newscaster out of Toronto, decided I should serve
as a master of ceremonies at a charity concert to be attended by
many of the city's cultural elite.

The concert featured some of the wonderful artists who
sprout with the proliferation of spring flowers in Manitoba.
One of these young, up-and-coming notables was to sing "The
Gordian Knot Untied." I had vaguely heard something about
this story during references to Greek mythology in school, but
the details hadn't stuck with me. The song refers to an intricate
knot tied by King Gordius of Phrygia, in what is now central
Turkey, and cut by Alexander the Great with his sword, upon
hearing from the oracle that whoever loosed it would rule all of
Asia. If I ever knew about the song, I had forgotten as I stepped
onto the stage and blurted out the title as "The Gordian Knot
United." There was barely a ruffle in the oh-so-discreet audience, but the steely glare I endured from Cameron after the
performance told me I hadn't measured up to his expectations. After that, it took a while before I was judged competent
enough to do much more than station breaks and late-night
music shows on radio.

It turned out to be a year of life-changing transition. My father
died in April of '56. I was deeply saddened, but not surprised;
he had been in failing health for some time. The long train ride
home to Stratford suited my reflective mood and the burden of
guilt I carried that I had not been there when he passed. The grey
skies, the patches of melting snow in the barren fields and the
gentle rocking of the railway cars had me in a trancelike state as I
reviewed my young life and appreciated the powerful and positive
influence of my father. George Henderson Robertson had given
me as much as he could: a strong set of core beliefs to live by and

an example of endurance through adversity while always considering others. He was a model of strength, wisdom and generosity of spirit. I hope he would have been proud of me, not for what I've done with a career, necessarily, but for what I became as a man.

One stark moment stands out from the funeral: my mother, in her "marble calm" state after her lobotomy, asked me why I was crying about my father. She would never again connect emotionally. The fact that my early contacts with her were so scrambled and confusing left me to realize, sadly, that I had never experienced the touch, the glow, the magic of a mother that so many of my friends and colleagues discussed with such a deep range of feelings. But, as my father had constantly reminded me, it wasn't her fault and, later in life, I was able to adjust to that reality. She would have given anything to be a better mother to her son, and I felt genuine compassion for a woman who was intellectually bright but trapped in the dark universe of a disturbed mind. What a terrible waste!

As she faded into old age, my half-sister Ethel and I found a comfortable nursing home for her just outside Stratford. Ethel was a twin of Irvin, and she too went the distance to help me, in the same unwavering manner, as though my father had told them both, "Look after that young lad—he won't have much." Through the years, I visited my mother often, and the staff assured me she was comfortable and would ask about me frequently. Lilly Frances Robertson died peacefully at the age of ninety-one, finally at rest.

A few months after my father's funeral, in July of 1956, came the most important event in my life: marriage to my high school sweetheart, Nancy. She was a strikingly beautiful twenty-two-year-old by this time, and with university and teacher's college behind her had joined the staff at Avon Public School in Stratford. Even though we had both gone out with several others following our intense romance after the high school prom five years earlier, we continued to be drawn to each other. There were letters and phone calls back and forth, and our mutual interest never waned. She had become so attractive and accomplished, I couldn't resist her. While she had been waiting for someone else to ask her out at the time of the school dance, there was no hesitation when I asked her to marry me. Nancy decided I had passed all the tests and, this time, would be the chosen one. She admits to having difficulty in those early years breaking through the emotional shield I had constructed to shut out the pain of earlier times. Fortunately, she stuck with me and I am a better person as a result.

It might have happened anyway, but I like to think that marriage suddenly contributed to turning my luck around. I received a call from a producer that had me roaring in disbelief. I had won an audition to host a western music show on television with a prominent Prairie group: Vic Siebert and His Sons of the Saddle. The show, called *Saddle Songs*, ran successfully for a number of years.

Vic was a lanky fellow with jet black hair, an easy smile and a gracious manner. He was a typical "western gentleman" and brought with him a cast of characters who were both good musicians and sometime comedians. As the host, and in the absence of a script writer, I had to weave together the elements and develop my own ideas for continuity. I introduced the songs, always with an eye toward working in a few well-worn corny jokes:

LLOYD: Hey, Vic, what to do you get when you cross a fish with an elephant?

VIC: I dunno, Lloyd . . . what?

LLOYD: Swimming trunks.

AUDIENCE: Oo-ouch!! (Loud country music playout)

In answer to the obvious question, yes, I did sing with them once, but I learned from that experience that my career track was not about to veer into the western music world. While I was to go on from there into much heavier involvement in news and anchoring coverage of special events, it was the *Saddle Songs* job that stuck fast to my career summary through the years. As I moved on to larger broadcasting ponds in Ottawa and Toronto, the picture of me smiling happily, dressed in a western shirt and pants with the kerchief around my neck, continued to hold a place of prominence in the lobby of the broadcast centre at CBC Winnipeg. For years to come it was a great talking point for colleagues and a good laugh for me.

People often ask about my most embarrassing moment on the air. Well, I'm happy to report, there has been more than one. The first happened when I was host of *Spotlight*. The central person on these evening shows was called upon to do nightly interviews with local and visiting artists and celebrities from all walks of life (all the "ham-and-egg acts," as my friend Warren called them), everyone from politicians to symphony conductors to entrants in the Miss Manitoba pageant.

A prominent pop singer of the period, Tommy Edwards, famous for his fifties hit "It's All in the Game," was appearing at a local nightclub. This was long before the word *gay* had been adopted for the lifestyle of homosexuals. Edwards may or may not have been gay, but he appeared to act the part live on air with me. When I asked what had brought him to town, he responded with a toothy grin and a pronounced lisp, saying, "Oh well, Lloyd, I only came to Winnipeg to see you." Every time I tried to ask a question, he dodged the answer and turned it into a swooning compliment to me. Finally, squirming in discomfort, I said, "Thank you Mr. Edwards, good luck with your Winnipeg appearance," and threw a very early handoff to our durable weatherman, Ed Russenholt. In later years, such an incident might go almost unnoticed, but on the Canadian Prairies in the late fifties it was a sensation, and I lived with much teasing about it for weeks and months afterward.

My moment of greatest excitement in those early times on the Prairies came when Nancy and I were able to call home to Stratford and tell the folks to watch TV on Christmas Day in 1956. At the end of my first year in the west, and at the tender age of twenty-two, I had somehow managed to draw a plum assignment: my first national broadcast. What a thrill, but also a scary challenge. The show would be seen right across the country. I'd better not mess this up!

CBC was televising a national show on Christmas morning, and I was chosen to host a six-minute segment from Winnipeg about two youngsters trying out their new skates. The kids with the skates were the son and daughter of a CBC staffer's neighbour. We made a little rink out behind the broadcast centre, and the old, grainy black-and-white TV picture showed host Bill Walker in a Toronto studio introducing me: "And here's Lloyd Robertson in Winnipeg. Tell us about the day where you are, Lloyd." I went on about it being "warm for this time of year,

Bill," and told him, "I'll be back to introduce some special guests later." He said, "Right, Lloyd," and was off to the next stop as he brought in Vancouver. The kids and I were left to wait for another half-hour before Bill called me in again. "All right, Lloyd, tell us what you've got for us." "Right . . . here we come, Bill." The boy and girl skated in my direction to talk about their presents. All went well enough, but by the time the kids and I got to our little interview, our mouths were tight from the cold, and I'm not sure my muffled vowels were very impressive to the bigwigs in the east. When the girl said she liked Elvis Presley, I replied, "Ah yes, whether you're nine or ninety, these days it's all about Elvis." Hardly a banner first outing on the network, but it still brought the customary congratulatory note from the eastern brass. It was understood, though, that you would get one of those notes when you did something special for the network—unless, of course, you really blew it.

It was about this time that the first indication of interest from a U.S. broadcaster came my way. KVOS-TV, a CBS affiliate in Bellingham, Washington, just south of Vancouver, was trying to dent the British Columbia market by hiring Canadian talent.

Cec Montgomery was a local advertising and agent type, and he quietly sounded me out on the idea. My TV career was just getting launched, and I thought jumping forward that soon might be a mistake, so I declined. Also, I really didn't want to leave Canada, which seemed a much bigger move then than it might for young talent now, and my father's Depression-era admonition about getting a good job and sticking with it loomed large in the back of my mind. In quiet moments, I would sometimes ponder what might have happened if I had made the jump, and I've always concluded that, apart from enjoying the much larger salaries, I surely could not have had the great life I've experienced by staying put in Canada and growing up with my country.

Like much of the rest of the Western world, Canada was in the boom of the postwar years of the fifties, with young families sprouting everywhere and consumption of new products like washing machines and TV sets hitting record levels. In Ottawa, the Liberals were coasting along after more than twenty-two continuous years in power with no apparent worthy opponent in sight, and the much beloved Dwight D. Eisenhower, the revered former Second World War general, was in the White House in Washington, allegedly spending more time on the golf course than he did running his nation's affairs.

It was a simpler time. Men went out to work and earned a living to support their families and the women stayed back to run the households and look after the children. Nancy, like so many other smart young women of that era, was caught in this time warp. When our first child was born in 1957, she did what women of the time were expected to do: suspend their work activities to look after the home front while the husband continued to build his career on the outside.

At that time, I was also becoming more and more immersed in the larger story of what is lovingly called our Great White North. The election of 1957 was one of the most dramatic nights of those early days. Since CBC Winnipeg was both a radio and TV operation, the newer, less experienced broadcasters were assigned to radio while the more senior hands took their places in the TV studio. I was assigned to provide returns on radio across the three Prairie provinces of Manitoba, Saskatchewan and Alberta, and it was a great place to be on that night. An electoral firestorm was brewing; it was starting on the Prairies and moving across the country in both directions. The excitement built to a fever pitch when it became clear that the Liberals' long reign in office was being seriously challenged by the Progressive Conservatives, led by the fiery lawyer from Prince Albert, Saskatchewan, John George Diefenbaker. It was a watershed in the politics of the time, and all of us who covered the story were captivated by it.

Louis St. Laurent's government couldn't win enough seats to keep control of the House of Commons, and the Conservatives formed a minority government. The next year, Lester B. Pearson, a Nobel Peace Prize winner and the Liberals' new leader, heeded some terrible advice from his colleagues and called for the country's government to be handed back to the Liberals. It seemed like the most arrogant of ideas, and Dief was in his glory as he ridiculed the Liberals. Nine months after his first minority victory, he swept to power in 1958 with the largest majority government in Canadian history. I was moved to the TV studio for the big broadcast on that night of March 31, and recall riding the wave of this groundbreaking story and understanding that I was cutting my broadcasting teeth in a form of coverage that would have a strong attraction in years to come. Yes, politics and current affairs, including election nights, conventions and other major national events, would help form the core of what I would become known for. It also meant getting to know more about my country and its people, along with their regional differences and idiosyncrasies. I was a willing student, and the work at the CBC provided a wonderful platform for learning with some great teachers, most of whom were highly skilled producers and broadcasters in their own right.

The four and a half years in Winnipeg were among my happiest and most productive. I learned how to do television and adapt my talents, such as they may have been at the time, to conquering the many demands of the new medium. Nancy and I were now parents of our first little girl, and we established lifelong friendships with some of the finest people we've met anywhere.

When the opportunity arose to move to the nation's capital, I knew I had to take it, but it was going to be hard to leave Winnipeg. In 1960, the CBC-owned-and-operated station in Ottawa, always under intense scrutiny from the politicians who controlled CBC budgets as well as the brass of the Corporation's head office, was trying to build a model operation. The task of making it happen fell on the capable shoulders of the young Peter Meggs, the new manager of the Ottawa station, who was given the right to choose his talent in a cross-country search of private stations and other CBC outlets. Meggs decided I would fit well into his plan and offered me a staff-announcer job in Ottawa with a $1,500-a-year boost in salary, up to $6,400. While the Winnipeg management was not happy about one CBC station raiding another, they eventually agreed, and I headed back east.

Perhaps, without knowing it, I had just made an even firmer commitment to staying in Canada.

6

Capital Bonus

W ITH A HEAVY HEART AT LEAVING THE WEST, BUT looking forward to the challenges ahead, Nancy and I set out on the long drive to Ottawa, new offspring in tow. Our British-built Morris Oxford wasn't the most comfortable car for this kind of trek, but with a lot of grumbling and puffing it managed to deliver us straight to Parliament Hill. It was the appropriate first stop in Ottawa for two eager young people from poor families who, both at the age of twenty-six, were getting their initial glimpse of the centre of their country's political life. Even in the pouring rain that day, we were enthralled by the sweeping grandeur of the buildings on the rocky promontory of "the Hill" overlooking the Ottawa River and the cities, rolling hills and farmlands of Quebec, just beyond.

In 1960, it was easy to think of the Ottawa-Hull area as just emerging from its years as a lumber community, a kind of down-at-the-heels afterthought as a choice for a national capital following Queen Victoria's rejection of Kingston, Ontario. In spite of its strikingly attractive physical setting and the glorious Gothic architecture of the Parliament Buildings, the area was a ramshackle collection of old and new, with few indications of a developed plan to suit the needs of the capital of a major nation. Gradually, those refinements began to appear, with the National Arts Centre and the Museum of Civilization, as well as other major efforts and beautification programs that made better use of Ottawa's natural surroundings. However, at the time, its small-town and wannabe-big-city feel made it a great place to live.

My duties in Ottawa were similar to those in Winnipeg, with one notable difference. While I was working for the local station, CBOT, I was able to spend a lot of time getting around "the Hill" and focusing on what would become a central theme of my broadcasting future: the coverage of politics. John Diefenbaker was the prime minister of the day, and the old Chief cut a wide swath in his prime. In my brief encounters with him, he was friendly and garrulous and never held back in telling me what he thought about the current CBC management ("Liberal party hacks," he would say). Diefenbaker would remain a larger-than-life personality on Parliament Hill to the end of his life, adored by many, scorned and ridiculed by others. Whenever I came upon him throughout the years, he had a hearty greeting and a compliment on the progress of my television career. There was always a quip or a story, usually at the expense of his enemies.

He was particularly bitter about Flora MacDonald, who had been his executive assistant and then joined his enemies to help oust him from the leadership. When this charming and much-loved woman ran for the Conservatives under Robert Stanfield and won in the constituency of Kingston and the Islands, the old Chief described her as "the finest woman ever to walk the streets of Kingston."

Nancy's mother, who had come from England and believed Diefenbaker was right in trying to retain firm ties to the U.K., was swept away with him and was thrilled when I was able to produce an autographed photo for her. She was one of millions of Canadians who felt Dief was speaking directly to her and cared about her concerns. Diefenbaker often said to me, "Everybody's against me but the people, you know." By 1960, the long downhill slide was just beginning for him, and the leader of the Opposition, Lester Pearson, a distinguished diplomat, would be head of government within three years as Diefenbakers' enemies, inside and outside the Conservative party, finally did him in. Interestingly, enough members of Dief's "average Canadian" constituency, the people he would celebrate in his long-winded speeches, continued to hold Pearson's Liberals to a minority government until both had departed their leadership positions, something for which the battle-scarred warrior was intensely proud.

While meeting and getting to know some of the big names in Canadian politics was an added bonus of being in Ottawa, my principal field of work continued to be local. From 1960 to '62, I expanded my horizons considerably, hosting a show on all the High Commissioners and ambassadors in Ottawa called *Diplomatic Passport*, an afternoon interview program called *Afternoon Edition* (for lack of a more imaginative title), and a sports show on the Ottawa Rough Riders called *Football Huddle*, as well as the daily supper hour newscast.

I also hosted a couple of eerie documentaries in which I stood in front of grey concrete-block walls while telling people how to build bomb shelters. In black-and-white television, the images of those bare cement walls stocked with canned goods were scary and ominous. I thought I looked ridiculous trying to be pleasant, even friendly, while explaining shelter construction and how much food to store in the event of a nuclear attack. Nancy thought seriously of moving with the children to bunk in with relatives in Northern Ontario until the immediate threat passed. This was leading up to the Cuban missile crisis, the chilliest point in the Cold War, and we all believed the capital of the country would be a potential target if hostilities broke out.

Of all the interesting work in Ottawa, there is one event that stands out, not for what it was but for what it wasn't. From just one night of broadcasting there flowed a stream of recriminations, bad jokes and career rethinks for a number of people.

In the early sixties, the lines of battle grew sharper in the long and exhausting fight within the CBC between the news writers' union, the Canadian Wire Service Guild, and the group representing announcers. Since I was a member of the latter and judged to be competent as a front person on news broadcasts, I was called upon to be the "host," since announcers, according to the rules of their union contract, managed to hold on to the thin thread of jurisdiction that allowed them to perform as "hosts" of news programs. Basically, this meant using your broadcast skills to try to intelligently improvise and handle the traffic flow among reporters and commentators and work with the producer to keep the show on time and moving smartly forward. However, this role could be limited to simply making announcements at the opening and closing of segments if the news people decided it should be that way.

On this occasion, I would have quite a lot of latitude. This night was to be the big test of whether news people—the reporters, writers and editors—really could do it all, to the exclusion (with my lone exception as host) of anyone categorized as an announcer.

The show began ominously. While the opening was unfolding on screen, there was a loud crash and a yell just off set as one of the painters collapsed onto the floor in convulsions. The poor fellow had been working around the clock, and when he was pressured to finish the job at the last minute, it was too much for him. Trying not to appear affected by the chaos around me as people screamed and rushed to him, I breathed deeply and soldiered on: "Good evening, and welcome to this CBC broadcast of the 1960 municipal election." Then came the introductions of our stalwart reporters at their various locations, and what slowly unfolded gave us a foretaste of what was to come over the next few hours. There were several examples of that "deer in the headlights" look as some of our intelligent young worthies froze when cued to start their commentary. One of our more experienced reporters, who was assigned to a campaign headquarters, walked from his desk toward the television cameras, stopped and stared with a blank look—not a word came out of his mouth. Then he turned around and, with his back to the camera, returned to his chair and sat down. Our harried director, the talented Gilles Thibault, could only lapse into his favourite French expression of frustration: "*C'est sacrifice.*" It was to be his mantra through my earpiece, hour after hour, as the painful night wore on. Gilles and I have had many a laugh about those moments since then, but it was anything but funny at the time.

The next day, the local TV critics were justifiably harsh about the broadcast, and while I managed to get a compliment from the *Ottawa Citizen*'s Bob Blackburn for keeping cool under pressure, it was small consolation for the torrent of outrage and insults that poured into our station from the viewing public. The grand

experiment for the news people had been a dismal failure. Some
of us thought this event would change CBC management's mind
about signing away all of the announcers' rights to the news
guild. But nothing changed. In fact, the blinkered decisions of
Corporation managers for years to come only made things worse.

I did well enough that night because I managed to find the
right words for the sometimes raucous and constantly uncomfortable situations in which we found ourselves. If I was to any
degree successful working in the trenches of TV, it wasn't by
chance; much of it was accomplished through hard work and
observation. Like other young broadcasters, I was keeping an eye
on the people who were becoming the established professionals
of early Canadian television.

There was one in particular who seemed to have figured out
how to meld his personality to the new medium. Fred Davis
was cool and elegant and always able to keep control of potentially inflammatory situations that might arise in programs like
Front Page Challenge, when the bumptuous Gordon Sinclair and
the smart and acerbic Pierre Berton were duking it out to try
to identify mystery guests. Davis was always there with just the
right tone for the occasion and, with brevity of speech, he was
gracious and restrained. He was the ideal front man, and I was
fascinated by his performances.

There was a colleague in Ottawa who shared my admiration
of Davis's abilities. David Scrivens was a tall, cool and scholarly announcer with a wry sense of humour who seemed better suited to the university lecture hall or the diplomatic section
of government service, where he eventually ended up, than the
rough and tumble of TV. David and I decided at the same time
that we would need to improve our vocabularies so that the right

word would land on our lips when we had to improvise in chat situations or on special-events broadcasts.

As a result, there is buried among my memorabilia a well-thumbed early notepad, one of many, containing lists of words and their definitions. I grabbed at new words as they came at me. The first in the collection is *inexorable,* defined as something that cannot be influenced by persuasion or entreaty. Next is *perspicacious*—having keen judgment or understanding, applicable to someone who is discerning. Next on the list is *obsequious*—excessively willing to serve and obey, fawning. David and I would greet each other every day and try to stump the other with new words. If I passed him in the hall and told him how perspicacious I thought he had become, he might respond with "Don't be obsequious, Lloyd." Of course, we also had to understand, as drilled into us by Steve Brodie, that we were obliged to use everyday language when appearing on air. Still, it was good to have those triple-barrelled words in reserve. As I leafed through that old notepad recently, it occurred to me why I had kept it as a special treasure. When I turned over a page, there were several purple crayon scrawls through the print; on the next page was red, then yellow. Our little girls had picked the notebook up off a table one day and decided to create their own abstracts. It's been a constant source of amusement through the years.

While it was useful for the broadcasters to have the right word available—and I admit I haven't always managed this—the viewer had to know that you were more than just a reasonably competent talk machine. There had to be substance there as well. I was very conscious of my lack of post-secondary education and tried to make up for it by reading extensively on a wide range of subjects, especially history. Fortunately, I enjoyed books, so spending more time with them was in no way an effort. Also, before the big broadcasts, I burned the midnight oil to be sure that I knew as much as I could about the subject at hand. It's a process that has served me well down through the years. It would come to mean understanding the names and organizational structure of Canada's native groups to prepare for covering a war canoe race at the opening of Expo 86 in British Columbia; knowing the history of the old castle and the surrounding area in Wales where Prince Charles was invested as Prince of Wales in 1969; and, of course, for political coverage, the names of ridings and candidates for federal election broadcasts. Here again, it couldn't be simply a spouting of facts and general information; it meant understanding the context of the separate events and stories and then trying to lay them out for your audience in the most comprehensive way possible.

One of the bonuses of working in Ottawa was the time I spent with Patrick Watson, a brilliant young producer on his way up in the CBC system. Pat is one of the most innovative thinkers ever to grace the Canadian TV scene. He was among the first to understand that a hard-edged editorial approach combined with engaging production values could build an audience for public affairs programming, which had generally been considered a backwater in Canadian broadcasting. Pat would soon be a central member of the on-camera cast and production team on the landmark *This Hour Has Seven Days*. To this day, it's one of the most talked-about shows in Canadian TV history. Alas, it was too much for Pat's bosses. Even though the show was enormously popular, the CBC brass wanted rid of it; *Seven Days* too often brought Monday morning complaints from members of the Liberal government of the day who felt, rightly or wrongly, they had been unfairly treated or represented on the Sunday night blockbuster. Patrick went forward with other pursuits and later, irony of ironies, became chairman of the CBC.

My exit from Ottawa to Toronto in 1962 caused nary a blip on the TV radar screen compared to Patrick's successful move. The call that answered my long quest for a job at the centre of broadcasting in English Canada came just after the spring election that saw the Diefenbaker government fall back into a minority. I had been host that night of the regional coverage that dealt with all the Ottawa-area ridings.

My star was soaring at the time in news and current affairs broadcasting, but it was about to crash back to earth quickly. In fact, I was being reminded, "Not so fast, kid." I was, after all, still cast in the classic role of the CBC announcer—"all things to all people all the time on both TV and radio," from children's shows to dance remotes and classical music programs, all the while trying to keep my hand in news. As it happened, I was part of the last group of new hires in Toronto lucky enough to be a part of the golden age of CBC announcing.

The bosses in Toronto also made it clear I was extremely fortunate to even be considered for a position in the "Big Apple" of Canadian broadcasting. Therefore, the transfer would have to be lateral, meaning no increase in pay. Nancy and I were now the parents of two girls, and while my salary had crept up over the two years in Ottawa to about $8,000 a year, that wasn't going to get us much in the way of accommodation in Toronto. Not surprisingly, we found ourselves less than totally enthusiastic that my race to the top in broadcasting had finally been realized and we would have to leave Ottawa.

7

The Cronkite Effect

TORONTO PROVED TO BE AS DAUNTING AS EXPECTED. I was one of more than thirty staff announcers and, as the new kid on the block, was given my share of the late-night and weekend booth shifts. These were the long tours of duty in both radio or television when an announcer was required to sit in a small, enclosed, soundproof booth and, on every hour or half-hour, say, "This is the CBC," or some other network or station identification. While these breaks all had to sound good, it was understood to be the bottom rung of the announcing ladder, and many used the time to catch up on correspondence, do crossword puzzles or doze off. The more adventurous of us might dash across the road for a beer. Occasionally, there would be a breaking news bulletin to read—otherwise, it was mind-numbing boredom. This is one example where the age of automation helped wipe out dull work. All of the station breaks and network identifications we hear so frequently now are recorded in advance and played back at the appropriate times.

For CBC announcers of the era, though, there was no way to avoid the stultifying monotony of booth work unless you were working on a program. In that respect, I got lucky in my first few months at the centre of broadcasting in English Canada.

Out of the blue, there was a request to be a part of a summertime kid's show. Titled *Vacationtime*, it was to be an ad hoc mix of gently funny skits and short video inserts intended to be educational ("Now watch how the nice lady makes hemp in India"). The show's budget allowed me to suit up in a cheap-looking short-sleeved sports shirt, the kind with a checkered brown pattern, another with wide black and white stripes, and a pair of jeans. While two shirts could be purchased, only one set of jeans was allowed, and they had to be worn five days a week. I was nervous about this, my first major assignment in what was regarded as the "big time," but staffers were expected to take on a wide range of chores, and there was also an agreement between the announcers' union and the CBC that producers were to do their level best to use announcers on their programs. In the end, I swallowed my hesitation and jumped in.

I recall being pretty brutal during this first exposure in a regular series on the full CBC network, but I was lucky to have two skilled and empathetic sidekicks in actors Tom Kneebone and Toby Tarnow, who were tolerant of my lack of experience and helped pull me through.

Only real professionals could rescue a greenhorn with material like this:

> *Lloyd and Tom standing on either side of a large box carved in the shape of a casket and topped with an Egyptian logo*
> LLOYD: "And just what is this—and don't tell me it's a mummy case."
> TOM: "Well, it certainly isn't a daddy case."

It was undoubtedly helpful that *Vacationtime* was only a three-month effort that ended in September and was quickly forgotten.

Back to reality. I was sitting in the CBC canteen, gabbing with friends on a November afternoon in 1963 when one of the duty managers came running to look for me. I was about to take over afternoon booth duty on radio, with its usual run of station breaks and short newscasts—but there was to be nothing usual about this day. The news wires had begun moving a story about President Kennedy being shot in Dallas. After racing into the booth, I read an update with more detail on the location of the shooting (Dealey Plaza), but with no new information on Kennedy's actual condition. After an agonizing wait that seemed interminable came the stunning and horrifying news. I opened the microphone and read, as calmly and deliberately as I could, the text of the message that millions around the world were reading or hearing at the same time: "John Fitzgerald Kennedy, the thirty-fifth president of the United States, is dead. He was killed by an assassin's bullet at 12:30 p.m. Dallas time while riding through the city in a motorcade."

We immediately joined U.S. network coverage on both radio and TV, and the whole world was instantly transformed; everyone stopped what they were doing in shops and offices and went to their radios or TV sets. The next three days were probably a blur to the many of us who lived through them, but, inside the broadcast industry, there was a realization that we had marked the dawning of a new era. The TV age had truly been launched.

Up to that time, television had been a questionable and not very reliable partner to radio and newspapers when it came to disseminating information. Littered with cheap quiz shows and old movie reruns, TV was being called a "vast wasteland" by those empowered to regulate the industry. While there were stalwart attempts to cover the news by the main networks, the sheer gathering of the information proved so expensive and cumbersome that network bosses wrote off news departments, if they bothered with them at all, as loss leaders and chased after the cheap and profitable. The Kennedy assassination coverage changed the game. The dramatic black-and-white pictures of Jacqueline Kennedy in her bloodstained dress, the live on-air shooting of Lee Harvey Oswald by Jack Ruby, and those heartrending glimpses of the Kennedy children at their mother's side during the funeral procession with little John Junior saluting the gun carriage, left lifetime imprints on the minds of millions the world over. TV was set to become the natural gathering place when big events dominated the public agenda, the place where people would congregate to watch election night results, the landing of men on the moon or their favourite sports events. Yes, the full potential of a remarkable and ultimately very powerful medium was finally being realized.

The Kennedy assassination also brought an important change to the way the public began to regard newscasters. Walter Cronkite's presentation of the Kennedy death announcement, with his voice quavering followed by his endless hours of calm, thoughtful and thoroughly engaged commentary through several days, vaulted him into a new category of TV persona. This became known as an "anchor," intended, according to *60 Minutes* producer Don Hewitt, who coined the term, to mean the person others handed off to and who would clarify, elaborate and put the subject into current or historical perspective for the viewer at home. The anchors became the viewer's guides and friends, and while it was not possible for them to be fully knowledgeable and briefed on everything, they had to know how to distill, edit, lead and add context where possible. This added a huge dimension to the newscaster's role, and not everyone was able to do it. Some fell by the wayside; others, who were considered good announcers with a following but not capable of the larger role, were kept in their chairs and producers simply worked around them.

This is not to denigrate the role of the announcer. In the CBC especially, announcing was a highly developed art form, and many today lament its passing. There were rules to be followed on pronunciation and grammar, and a Supervisor of Broadcast Language made sure they were enforced. In the seventies and eighties, those rules began to break down under the pressure of calls for a more informal, "less stuffy" approach. But there are certain fundamentals that cannot be denied even today. Reading news takes skill, and it's a bedrock principle that, if you can't read with clarity and understanding, you won't be an anchor either.

During that period in the early sixties, in the centre of the English Canadian TV universe, my career began to edge forward. I was delighted to be chosen as prime-time host for the Tokyo Olympics in 1964, an assignment that brought me into contact with a brash, talented, cigar-chomping executive producer and director named Don MacPherson. He had cleverly blended some experienced hands, like sportscasters Ted Reynolds and Ward Cornell, with younger types like Alan Hamel and me.

It was my first trip outside of Canada. I had always thought my initial foreign journey would be to Britain or the European continent, but it was to Asia and the exotic wonders of Japan. When we emerged from our long flight, some of my colleagues wanted to take in the sights right away. A few were eager to sample the massage parlours or seek the company of the geisha girls they had heard so much about, but before the conversation went any further, I felt a tap on my shoulder. Ward Cornell, who was my roommate and something of a mentor to me on the trip, intervened: "Lloyd, remember you're our host—the front face of the broadcast. If there's a police raid on any these questionable places, you can be sure the news will eventually find its way back to Canada. Not a good idea, especially for you." Ward was from London, Ontario, and was the erudite host of *Hockey Night in Canada* in the 1960s. He was quiet and scholarly, but with a mischievous twinkle in his eye much of the time. He was said to be the only sportscaster with a copy of the literary magazine *Saturday Review* on his coffee table when you went to visit. We kept contact through the years, and I always appreciated his wise counsel in helping me understand the pitfalls and responsibilities of having your face on national TV.

We made history as the first Olympics to be broadcast via satellite. At the opening ceremony, Ted Reynolds and I looked across the stadium to see, in person, the emperor and empress of Japan. Just nineteen years earlier, Emperor Hirohito had read a message of surrender to his people and the world, ending the Second World War. It was a humiliating and desperate moment for a proud nation that had seen two of its major cities reduced to ashes, with thousands of deaths, in the atomic attacks on Hiroshima and Nagasaki. The harsh militaristic regime that ruled Japan had suffered ignominious defeat and was driven from office. The emperor, who was revered as a god by his people, was chosen by the allies to remain as head of state and provide continuity while the victors, led by the U.S., laid the groundwork for a new nation. This was Japan's coming-out party to announce to the world that a new and modern country had emerged from the ashes with a new look and attitude and was taking its place among the advanced nations of the world.

It was my first contact with Olympic coverage, and I was awed by the standard of performance of the young athletes and the noble ideals, expressed through the Olympic movement, of bringing together the youth of the world in friendly competition to build character and broaden understanding. Even though those ideals have been frequently tarnished over the years by the actions of officials, governments and sometimes the athletes themselves, they continue to stand as the ultimate goal of one of the few world institutions that can pull people together in a community of shared interest with millions of viewers around the globe.

Four years later, I found myself in Mexico for that country's splash on the world stage. Politics pervaded the 1968 games as some big-name American athletes displayed the Black Power salute and Mexican authorities disgraced themselves by the rough handling of student demonstrators just before the events got underway. The country was trying to throw off its leisurely and carefree *mañana* image and present itself as a modern player in the international community. Here again, there were opportunities to stray. Two policemen, obviously on the take from the big city's fleshpots, showed up one night at the bar and restaurant of our hotel and began quietly approaching us individually with the line, "Hey, there—want to go see the girls for a good time?" Along with most others, I turned away these shady and thoroughly corrupt pleasure ambassadors.

Ted Reynolds and I once more provided commentary for the opening ceremony and, after the experience, were given to wonder whether Mexico's hope of being seen as a new and modern nation could be fulfilled. We were set to go, microphones in place, but on the usual facilities checks that preceded the broadcast we became aware that the satellite downlink in Canada wasn't receiving any sound. With about two minutes to go before the ceremonies unfolded on the field and we would be expected to start talking, a smiling young man entered our booth at Aztec Stadium and pointed to two wires hanging loose outside a wall that appeared not to be plugged into anything. He shrugged his shoulders, gave us a broad grin and left. We were to discover that Canadians saw some beautiful pictures of singers and dancers for the first thirty minutes of our broadcast but heard nothing from their Canadian commentators. It took another visit from our friendly technician, and some heated exchanges in Spanish outside our door, before we learned that all was well and commentary and stadium sound were reaching Canada. In the end, it was precisely the casual *mañana* image that made the games a success, with the cheery Mexicans serenading their visitors and providing a blanket of warm hospitality throughout the full two weeks that the spotlight rested on their country.

The Olympics are a dream come true for most broadcasters because the stories are so dramatic and personal, and I was fortunate to be on the scene for several more Olympic games, winter and summer, in the years to come.

At the dawn of Canadian television, the CBC led the way in news and, as a publicly funded broadcaster, it was able to devote more time and money to its gathering and presentation. For many years, it was the only game in town, but by the early sixties, in time for the dreadful news of the Kennedy assassination, there was a new kid on the block.

The country's recently licensed private network was on the air and servicing commercial stations established in major cities across Canada. It was called the Canadian Television Network (ultimately, simply CTV), and it began exchanging and producing programs and building a competitive news service. My late friend and colleague Peter Jennings was lured from the CBC, where his father was a vice-president, to become an anchor of their nightly news. Peter was young, restless, girl-magnet handsome and very talented. He was also determined to be fully involved in his broadcast. Peter headed for Dallas and sent back reports on the Kennedy tragedy by whatever means he could, sometimes just over the phone. He set the pattern for Canada that was already well established in the U.S. of anchors being involved in the editorial decisions that go into structuring a newscast. The CBC's tangled bureaucracy, with its overlapping union jurisdictions, didn't seem to understand this new concept and remained aloof to the changes. The old system of the detached reader reigned, and the Corp. was supreme—so why rock the boat?

The CTV people knew exactly what they were doing. It was mainly due to the wisdom of two CBC veterans, Ernie Bushnell and Stuart Griffiths, who established a newscast for the private network that originated from CJOH, the affiliate station they owned and operated in Ottawa. They could see that the old inflexibility could not continue and ditched what they regarded as the stodgy and outdated Canadian broadcast news model to produce a breezier, more viewer-friendly presentation. While they didn't have the budgets to compete with the CBC, they believed the audience would watch news not just out of a sense of civic duty, but because they liked the personalities and appreciated a more personal, but still credible, style. Their front people, including Peter, laboured under no restrictions, aside from the laws of libel and standard journalistic practices of fairness and balance. Since they were based in Ottawa, all were accredited to the Parliamentary press gallery, and all were reporters as well as anchors. When the main newscast moved to Toronto a few years later, the same practices continued.

Rolling through the sixties with Mother Corporation, I was lucky to be brought in touch with one of the icons of Canadian literature and broadcasting. Harry J. Boyle was a communications genius who came out of the farm country around Wingham, Ontario, and never forgot his roots. He was well known for his program *Assignment*, a daily radio show of short features about life in Canada that helped develop a number of broadcasting careers. Could Harry transfer what he had accomplished in radio and turn around some of the problems of early CBC television, which he felt had become too sophomoric, with a lot of insider humour that wasn't touching Canadians at their roots?

He asked me to be his host in the second year of the show, called *The Observer*, which was to establish its presence in Toronto, Ottawa and Montreal, with designs on becoming a national coast-to-coast supper-hour newsmagazine program. I would be following my colleague Al Hamel, who had moved on to other activities. Don MacPherson was given the job of producer-director, and Harry proceeded to assemble a collection of young, smart and headstrong people who would move forward to establish themselves as leaders in media and related fields in the years ahead—among them, editor and researcher Patrick Gossage, who would become Pierre Trudeau's communications adviser and then run his own successful media relations company; Tim Kotcheff, a talented and fun-loving writer and editor; and the brilliant and beautiful Starr Cote, a pro-gram producer who broke a thousand hearts before settling in Toronto with her writer husband.

The Observer was infused with a youthful spirit. Most of us were in the formative years of our careers, and this often led to hijinks that weren't always appropriate to the occasion. For exam-ple, Starr had produced a serious piece regarding the abuse of prisoners at the former Mercer Institute for Women in Toronto. Tim had conducted all the research, so he was best briefed to come into the studio and sit beside me to outline the story for viewers. But he had never done on-camera work and was terri-fied at the possibility of going live into the show. He lit a ciga-rette—a very common sight on television in the sixties—hoping the smoke would spiral to cover the horror that he felt must have been apparent on his face. By then, Tim and I had established a relationship in which we played tricks on each other relentlessly. Unfortunately, I chose this moment to be the clown. It was no excuse that I was goaded on by other members of the team. As the countdown began for Tim's appearance, he heard me say, "Tim, buddy, I hope you're ready for this. A million people are out there, and you're likely going to screw up." His eyes began to shift as he furiously puffed away, creating an ever-larger cloud above his head. I kept at it, repeating the countdown as it came to me: "Six . . . five . . . four—don't screw up, Tim, or it's the end—two . . . one."

We were up, and as I asked Tim to give us the details of the story, it sank in that he was overwrought—the TV makeup and cigarette smoke couldn't hide his ashen features or the look of sheer terror on his face as he sat in stony silence. It hit me that I'd taken the joke over the top in a thoughtless way and at a very inappropriate time. My friend was about to start hyperventilating, so I worked to change the dynamic to a friendly and more soothing tone and prompted him to begin: "Tim, we're told there are some grim examples of abuse at the Institute. Tell us about them." He began haltingly, but became more sure-footed as he continued. When it was over, he said with perfectly good humour, "Don't worry, I'll get you for this." "Sorry pal," I apologized, "that was totally wrong, especially on such a serious story—really stupid of me." I felt bad, but it didn't dent our friendship. We were still kids, after all. We grew up and, yes, Tim did get his own back.

Harry Boyle's first major challenge for me as a host-reporter on his broadcast was to find out whether James R. Mutchmor, then the moderator of the United Church of Canada, had a side to him other than the stern, hectoring pastor who was a regular fixture in the newspapers and on the television screens of the period. Mutchmor was a tall man with granite features and thin grey hair combed flat over his head. At every opportunity, he pronounced on the evils of booze and pornography until the writers and commentators of the "swinging sixties" began to paint him as a boring old moralizer who should shut up and go away. In my interview with him, he was gracious and charming, and while he didn't hold back on his views about drinking, he revealed a softer side that spoke to his humanity and compassion on such matters as the treatment of prisoners and the abuse of women. He called to tell me afterward that he was astonished at the positive reaction he had received from people both inside and outside the church. It seems there was a sudden recognition that he was more than a narrow-minded old bore. Harry was delighted with the piece, not because it made Mutchmor look better, but because it opened people's eyes beyond stereotyped images. He pronounced me a "young fella with potential," quite ready to take on a variety of assignments for him while he turned his show into a prominent cross-country vehicle.

When Winnipeg came on stream and *The Observer* morphed into *Across Canada*, our bright young correspondent from the Prairies was Craig Oliver, and there began between the two of us a lengthy friendship based on our similar poor-boy backgrounds. As Craig says of his early years in his book, *Oliver's Twist*, "My father was a bootlegger and for a time, a jailbird. My mother ran a successful taxi business, also for a short time. Both were alcoholics." As in my own case, his parents weren't capable of raising him and, like me, he displayed a driving urgency to get out into the world and prove himself.

Harry Boyle was doing what he felt the CBC was mandated to do: show the country to itself in interesting and colourful ways every day of the week. The program was certainly judged a success by Canadian audiences, but because Harry had a drinking problem that would too often take him out of action while he went on benders, and because he tended to openly bad-mouth the CBC's top brass, whom he regarded as faceless and soulless bureaucrats, he had few friends within the upper echelon. When the hammer came down on all current-affairs programming in 1966, he was not spared.

CBC management, having decided that the highly successful—but, for them, troublesome—*Seven Days* had to go, swept away a whole raft of programs in its wake as it changed the direction of its news and information programming. We were caught in that downdraft, and try as we might to persuade the managers that our show was answering the needs of viewers by making local matters relevant to a national audience while also fulfilling the CBC mandate, the mighty machine of bureaucracy had started rolling and there was no stopping it. Local news programs showed up on Corporation stations across the country. Knowlton Nash, Washington correspondent for CBC News, took control of the huge news and current-affairs empire in both radio and television under the rubric of CBC Information Programming, and *The Observer* became a museum piece to be memorialized by those of us who cared about it. Ironically, the local news shows never drew much audience and were eventually cancelled, only to be brought back once again as Mother Corporation, in yet another makeover, tried to lure local audiences away from private stations. Harry faded away for a while, but came back strongly a few years later as chairman of the Canadian Radio-television and Telecommunications Commission (CRTC), which licenses and regulates broadcasting in Canada. He had conquered his problems with the bottle and told me proudly during that time that he would never drink again. To the end of his life, the commitment held.

I look back on *The Observer* and my time with Harry Boyle and his talented team as the period that added much more depth and dimension to my profile as a broadcaster and provided critical personal growth as well.

Years later, when I was receiving an award from the Canadian Association of Broadcasters, Harry wrote a letter to the organization speaking of his influence on me: "I have a particular interest in Lloyd in that I propelled him into TV current-affairs programming when, believe it or not, the conventional opinion of other producers was he was too 'pretty'—or not rugged-looking enough. I also pushed him to do his own research and handle interviews." Indeed, he did. Harry will always have a prime place in my personal hall of honour.

8

Rising to the Occasion

AS IT TURNED OUT, THE DEMISE OF *THE OBSERVER* DIDN'T hurt me much. I was immediately signed up for a training program to prepare a team of commentators and producers for the celebrations of Canada's Centennial year in 1967. This is the kind of thing the CBC did well, and I am forever grateful for what I learned at the knees of some of the best in the business, and in all regions of the country, during that intense period. The team leaders were the legendary CBC broadcaster Byng Whitteker and the prominent commercial announcer and CBC classical music broadcaster John Rae. As Craig Oliver notes, "We joked about our classes in Hushed Voices 101."

Rae put us through our paces with regular lessons on protocol when dealing with the Royal Family (she may be referred to as "Her Majesty," but not "the Queen," and certainly never "she"). Nothing less than strict adherence to the rulebook would be tolerated. We had to be ready to identify the stripes and insignia on all the uniforms parading in front of us, and know by heart the names of the Canadian regiments of which Her Majesty was colonel-in-chief. It seemed to me there were often more rules about what we *couldn't* say than what we could. As might be expected, the strict parameters made for a stuffy, too formal style of broadcasting not suited to the changing times. Even as we were in training, we knew the rules being prescribed were under attack. Royal visit coverage would soon be transformed.

I was out of the country at the Tokyo Olympics as the old approach began to collapse in 1964, when the cameras of the CBC Outside Broadcast unit were deliberately turned away from anti-monarchy demonstrations in Quebec. The commentators, under tight control, knew their audiences could hear the shouts of the protesters but were not allowed to identify their origins or explain what was going on. The broadcast's director shouted to the cameramen to "stay with the shot" of Her Majesty quietly smiling and making her way through a small but friendly crowd. It was left to a CBC *Newsmagazine* program to tell the whole story later.

After that very public debacle, the old rules began to change. They had been put in place by people who had come through the war years and saw information media, especially when managed by a government Crown corporation, as a propaganda machine to promote the values the government of the day espoused. By the Centennial year, a more relaxed and newsy approach was being encouraged. That effort was led by Wilf Fielding, an intense and highly experienced producer who had spent much time in early TV in Britain and was brought back home to inject new life into royal coverage. He succeeded by leaning on his commentators, including me, to understand and feel the flavour of events and become more intimate with the audience rather than simply standing back as detached observers. I was fortunate to be teamed frequently with the talented Barbara Frum of CBC Radio's *As It Happens*. She struck just the right note in moving royal commentary into the modern era by emphasizing the Queen's role as a woman on the world stage and how she was brilliantly establishing a place for a twentieth-century monarchy that worked.

Byng Whitteker was a big man with bigger appetites and, as part of the training plan, he devised a radio program for us called *Stranger at Home.* The idea was for young announcers to be sent to an area of the country they had never seen before and record a thirty-minute broadcast from there. He chose me to go to what is now called Iqaluit, then known as Frobisher Bay, in the eastern Arctic, a long plane ride north from Montreal. I was well into the taping of the first show and had already outlined in detail the stark landscape of the tundra through the eyes of a novice visitor when Whitteker called from Toronto. "Now, see here, Robertson!" he exclaimed. (That generation loved naval terminology, addressing others by surname only.) "You're costing too much and you'll have to figure out a way of doing a second broadcast." I was appalled. How was I supposed to do a second thirty-minute show when there was barely enough material available for one? Fortunately, a contact put me in touch with an Anglican priest who had been in the region for ten years, and I put together a full half-hour on the wonderful stories this man told about how the North, with its bare, scenic grandeur and its warm, innocent and vulnerable people, had captured his soul and how he had committed himself to staying there to help them. I learned a lesson about the irresistible call of the North. In spite of its harsh environment, the region appeals to the hardy and innovative survival spirit of so many Canadians who choose its freedom from the norms and its wide-open spaces, and who make their homes in a place where they can live much closer to the rawness and reality of nature and with a camaraderie seldom seen elsewhere.

Whitteker was pleased that I returned south with another broadcast, and it's likely that this effort alone assured me a place on the commentary team for Centennial year.

During this same period, I was called upon by Byng to work with him on a major royal broadcast of the Queen Mother presenting new colours to the Black Watch regiment, of which she was colonel-in-chief, at Molson Stadium in Montreal. The day of the broadcast began with a breakfast meeting in Byng's suite at the Queen Elizabeth Hotel in Montreal. On the table, beside the orange juice for producer Henri Parizeau, Byng and me, was a triple shot of expensive Scotch. While I enjoyed a drink occasionally, I had never taken to drinking until late in the day and certainly never at breakfast. Byng stared at me with an amused grin and said, "Drink up, young man." I was stewing inside about what to do. Then, during the complex discussions about camera positions and other production matters, I began to notice Henri occasionally slipping into the bathroom with his glass in hand, and his drink looked considerably watered down when he returned. He had obviously dumped much of it down the sink and replaced it with water; he had to be surreptitious with this manoeuvre so as not to be caught by Byng. I followed suit, and from what I could see, Byng was none the wiser. For a long time afterward, of course, I lamented the waste of good Scotch.

On the broadcast that afternoon, Byng became so annoyed with Henri's nonstop babbling of instructions that he threw his headset against the wall, shattering it to pieces, and bowed with a grand gesture for me to take over completely. I'm sure the

Mother Lilly.
Trapped in the
dark universe of
a troubled mind.

Father George. Strength, wisdom
and generosity of spirit.

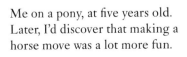

Me on a pony, at five years old.
Later, I'd discover that making a
horse move was a lot more fun.

On set with Knowlton Nash—friend, occasional adversary and competitor—and singer Julie Amato, from the long-forgotten and unlamented *CBC Weekend*, 1969. CBC STILL PHOTO COLLECTION

The young anchorman and his family (along with Friendly the dog) pose for a magazine story in their suburban backyard, 1975.

A fleet of CBC anchors from 1952 to 1978 (from left): Larry Henderson, Earl Cameron, Stanley Burke, me and my successor, Peter Kent. CBC Still Photo Collection

On CBC Radio's *As It Happens* after my departure from *The National*, laughing it up over who should succeed me, with Barbara Frum, Alan Maitland and Alan McFee. CBC Still Photo Collection

Getting ready for coverage o
the *Apollo 11* mission, which cu
minated in the first moon land
ing, in 1969. I had to pinch my
self to believe I was part of i
CBC ARCHIVE SALES

Bundled up for the CBC's first
live satellite TV coverage from
Canada's Far North in 1973.
CBC ARCHIVE SALES

Suiting up for Maritime weather.
A gift of rain gear at the opening
of the Saint John, New Brunswick,
press club in 1975.

booze had caused this normally cool professional to completely lose it. I was left with no choice; somehow, I soldiered on and later won kudos from Byng and others for having the stuff to fly alone—and by the seat of my pants—while quaking inside at the same time.

Sadly, my last memory of Byng comes from a New Year's Eve gathering at our home in 1969 that included Wilf Fielding, Byng and his partner of the time, former broadcaster June Dennis. Byng was having health problems—swelling in his legs, which made standing and walking awkward and painful for him. When he tried to stand up from a comfortable leather chair where he'd been ensconced for the evening, several of us had to help him to navigate his considerable girth out the front door, where he went down on his knees on the cold pavement. We couldn't budge him. An ambulance had to be summoned to transport him home, where he died a few weeks later. Our neighbours, two of whom strolled past the house during the midnight drama, had lots to talk about regarding the goings-on at the Robertsons' that New Year's Eve.

While Byng's assignment had provided me with my first look at Canada's North, it was on a later royal tour, in Churchill, Manitoba, that I was to meet and introduce a young man who was making his first appearances on the full CBC Radio network. He was tall and impressive-looking and possessed a voice that, like my own, had turned a lot of attention his way through the years. It was Peter Mansbridge, and I recall thinking that this lad was not destined to live out his broadcast career in Churchill, as exotic and hauntingly beautiful as the place can be. It wasn't long before Peter became a regular reporter contributor on *The National,* when I took over the role of front person in 1970.

The time I was able to spend back in radio was thoroughly enjoyable. I found myself doing the announcements on legendary programs like *CBC Stage*, a weekly series of live dramas featuring some of the greatest Canadian actors of our times— Bruno Gerussi, my pal Gordon Pinsent, Martha Henry, Frances Hyland and crusty Ed MacNamara, with Christopher Plummer, William Shatner and Don Harron occasionally dropping by. Just to be in the same studio with these people was an inspiration. Gerussi and I became buddies. He had an impish wit and could contort his face into various disguises that would break me up just looking at him. His favourite trick was to start mumbling variations on "Lloyd doesn't know what the hell he's saying" or "You're blowing it, Robertson, you're blowing it" in a low growl very close to me, but always just off mike, while I was trying to do the opening for the drama of the week. I can remember my stomach aching more than once as I tried to hold back the laughter. Much as I begged him to stop, he kept it up more every time he appeared on the show.

In spite of Bruno's shenanigans, I was able to learn a lot about pacing for dramatic effect and reading for colour and emphasis. The *Stage* series was produced and directed by Esse W. Ljungh, probably the last of the great Canadian radio drama directors. He would also direct his announcers, cueing them line for line and indicating what was expected, as we read a short set-up for each play to explain what it was about. While TV news people don't always like to admit that there is any performance dimension in presenting their material, all of us know otherwise. Thousands of dollars have been spent by news departments over the years to bring newscasters and reporters up to speed with what are described as "presentation skills." They are all about being connected to what you're reading and looking comfortable to the viewer. It took a long time for some print people and academics to admit it, but there is a right way and a wrong way of delivering information, and while it doesn't have to be style over content, there is an industry standard and it's understood that if the style isn't right, the content won't have an impact.

This is not to say that a broadcaster delivering the news should think of himself or herself as an actor. It's a matter of applying techniques that work for the individual and, as I've always said to young people breaking into the business, you've got to be the best at what you are when you're on the air. You can't be anybody else! In news, you grow and you learn, and then you grow and you learn some more until the full range of experience begins to show in your work.

While I was busy doing a lot more radio and occasionally popping in for a newscast on television, we all noted the big changes rocking the news division. Bill Cunningham, a scrappy and innovative young producer bubbling with ideas, had taken over as head of the division under Knowlton Nash and was signalling that anchors on the national news would now be expected to be more than readers and would have to play a role in the preparation as well as the presentation of the broadcast. The CBC was finally relenting to the pressures from other broadcast organizations, in particular CTV, and realized they had to move to the more modern model. It mattered not to Cunningham that union rules prevented such an arrangement; he was determined to work around them. The first casualty of the new plan was the iconic Earl Cameron. Earl had been doing the national news for seven years, and while he never pretended nor desired to be anything more than an announcer, the audience had grown accustomed to his uncle-like, straight-ahead presentation of the stories of the day. He was unceremoniously dumped, to be consigned to the announcing pool, handling station breaks and general duties, and replaced by Stanley Burke, who had to sign on as a CBC announcer in order to become the chief newsreader.

The move, a little too clever by half, pleased neither the news writers' guild nor the announcers' union. The announcers felt that many of their worthies, like the estimable George McLean, were being overlooked, while the writers were distressed that the Corporation was invoking a new policy over their heads. The fact that Stanley was an established journalist whose credentials couldn't be challenged on that front didn't make any difference to the leadership of the news union. He would still be called an "announcer" for job-description purposes, and they were not prepared to buy into what they regarded as bureaucratic trickery.

Also, the treatment of Earl Cameron provided an object lesson for many of us. We became aware that if the benevolent Mother Corporation decided to change direction, it didn't matter which one of us was standing in the way—we'd be gone. That fact was certainly in my mind ten years later, when I was going through the agonizing decision whether to cut the apron strings from the CBC.

As for Stanley Burke, he was a charming and engaging man—a ruggedly handsome raconteur who had been the network's United Nations correspondent. Unfortunately, he was also well remembered for an episode of on-air cussing that stands as one of the great examples of how not to behave when rattled. He was cued too early during a news special originating from the UN that also had inserts from Toronto and Ottawa. When the director, who was in Toronto, cut quickly to New York and then broke into Stanley's earpiece at the UN and told him to "start talking," viewers saw Burke pawing through his script trying to find his place—whereupon he snarled, "Jesus Christ, don't cue me now." He had every reason to be exasperated, but knew he should have also kept his cool. In spite of that incident, Stanley had an impressive track record and had spent several years in the news service reporting from various parts of the world. He certainly had the credentials Cunningham was looking for in his lead anchor. To back him up on weekends and holidays, Cunningham chose people he felt had shown news acumen over time, and I was judged to be acceptable based on my work on radio and in television specials.

As the main weekday anchor on *The National*, Stanley found the union restrictions on what he could do frustrating, but he managed to make an arrangement that he could write at least the opening page of the broadcast, and he seemed content with that for a time. He left after a few years to pursue his passion for an African cause, creating a gaping hole in the Corp.'s plan to present its main anchor as a Cronkite-style personality who would lead the news division's total broadcast effort. Bill Cunningham also moved off shortly afterward, and the department was plunged into chaos once again.

In spite of the never-ending tumult that engulfed the news division in those years, we managed to have some fun and a few laughs, often at one another's expense and, in this case, my own. I was pinch hitting for Stanley one night in the spring of 1968 when Lyndon Baines Johnson was making his big announcement that he would not run for re-election.

In the course of the statement, Johnson made a "plea for peace." In reading the copy on air, I left out the critical letter *l*;

the studio crew was immediately in stitches, but I knew I dare not go back to try to correct the flub because it would only have drawn more attention to it. When I resurfaced in the newsroom about half an hour afterward, the writers were holding up a sign that read, "Robertson's Pee-In for Peace." It was one of the most memorable gaffes of my years in front of cameras and microphones.

Before and during my time as Stanley's backup, I was thoroughly enjoying a developing role as an all-around broadcaster—just what CBC announcers were expected to be.

Among other assignments, I hosted a Saturday afternoon sports show called *Kaleidosport,* a mix of live and taped items that covered everything from tennis at Wimbledon to motorcycle racing on ice in Quebec. Our producer was the charming, easy-going Donald E. Browne. He made life interesting as a guy who loved getting to the airport just as the wheels of the aircraft were close to lifting off. He was also well known for agreeing to join you for dinner and then sticking to his steady daily diet of potato chips and Coca-Cola while you ordered a real meal. It was my time with "Brownie" that brought me closest to a spectacular accident on live coast-to-coast TV. During one of the telecasts of motorcycle racing on ice, Brownie had been assured by the event organizers that they would hold off dropping the flag to start the vehicles around the track until two minutes after we had signed on. This would allow me time to do a brief set-up on the other side of the track and then get out of the way. I had just begun to speak when I heard the engines start to roar and realized they were coming straight at me. The TV audience watched as I gestured behind, saying "And here they come" while I dashed for the sideboards, leaping over them into the stands. As far as we could tell afterward, no one thought anything was amiss.

Centennial year was a high point. I was pegged for the opening day broadcast of Expo 67 and had the thrill of seeing a clip from that show appear on the *CBS Evening News* with Walter Cronkite. When he introduced me by name, I gulped and watched in frozen silence. A few days later, on one of the weekly shows from the Expo site in Montreal, I was preparing nervously for an interview with Lester B. Pearson, the prime minister of the day, when he walked in early and totally disarmed me. I had never met Pearson, who had been in power for four years following John Diefenbaker, and I didn't know what to expect. He and his Liberals had a lukewarm relationship with Canadians and, in spite of the considerable and generally positive change they had brought forward, never managed to achieve majority support.

We shook hands, and the first words out of his mouth were: "Hi, Lloyd, how's your rotten management?" He said it with a mischievous grin and a chuckle, and I realized he was referring to a statement made a few weeks earlier by cabinet minister Judy LaMarsh, who had blasted the "rotten" CBC brass for what she regarded as their inept handling of the crisis over *Seven Days*. Pearson certainly broke the ice, and I found him utterly charming and cooperative in the interview. He was open, didn't shy away from difficult questions, and seemed to possess a kind of worldly wisdom that went beyond the too-frequent partisan pettiness of everyday politics.

I have long thought of Pearson as the best of a generation. He prodded the people around him to begin to deal with the difficult issue of Quebec's place in Canada. Pearson recognized that Quebec nationalism could become a potent force when it turned into the quest for a separate state, and he did what he could to stem the tide. He recruited a group of Quebec stars, dubbed "The Three Wise Men," in the persons of Gérard Pelletier, Jean Marchand and—the one who would make the biggest mark—Pierre Trudeau. On other important fronts, he began the process of building up the country's healthcare system which, while far from perfect, does the job of covering Canadians in time of need, and his government also gave us a distinctly Canadian flag, now recognized everywhere as a refreshing symbol of a young and vibrant country.

On the eve of Canada's one-hundredth birthday, I was pegged to host a show leading up to the midnight countdown on the Peace Tower clock. What a moment to be on the air to the nation! As the last bong sounded, I shouted the greeting "Happy Birthday, Canada!" over the whoops of the crowd on the Hill and watched as the fireworks ushered in a second century for a place I had come to truly love and admire.

On the afternoon of July 1, 1967, I shared a broadcast with a strikingly beautiful young Chinese-Canadian from Hong Kong who was just then beginning to soar as a rising star at the CBC. Adrienne Clarkson would go on to become governor general twenty-five years later, but that day she and I had to clamber our way up a set of rickety stairs leading to our broadcast platform on Parliament Hill. It was ladies first, of course, as I steadied the ladder and moved up behind. Just as she was about halfway up, a gust of wind on that warm summer afternoon lifted her beautiful sheer white skirt and exposed a considerable length of the future GG's shapely thigh. I assured Adrienne I had averted my eyes. "Oh sure, Lloyd," she said with a smile and a twinkle, and we went on with our broadcast of the afternoon's festivities. Adrienne and I have had many a laugh over the incident since.

The late Pierre Berton described Canada in 1967 as a "nation in love with itself," basking in the warm glow of international applause brought on by the unexpected success of Expo 67 and pumped up by a year-long birthday party that had us all singing Bobby Gimby's "Ca-na-da," led by groups of prancing youngsters all across the land. When Lester Pearson stepped down at the end of the year, the country was ready for exciting and dramatic change. It came like a meteorite crashing onto the Canadian landscape in the form of Trudeaumania in 1968.

Pierre Trudeau had already attained heroic status among many Canadians when, as Pearson's minister of justice, he changed laws governing marriage breakdown with the rationale "The state has no place in the bedrooms of the nation." The charismatic Quebecer knocked off several high-profile establishment candidates within Liberal ranks to become Pearson's successor and went on to sweep the country in the federal election of June 1968.

I worked in the same studio as the legendary CBC correspondent Norman DePoe that election night and learned some invaluable lessons. Norman was arguably the most skilled TV newsman the country had ever produced. He knew the candidates and the ridings like the back of his hand and, with style, enthusiasm and humour, he led the audience through all the drama of a country going through a sea change as Pierre Trudeau began his long reign as a major force in Canadian politics. While I had been involved in many election broadcasts over the years, Norman's mastery of the detail and understanding of the scope of the big story were awe-inspiring. I knew that to get to his level I had to step it up a notch by knowing as much as I could about the ridings, the candidates and the regional issues all across the country for my first big anchor job on a major national election, which would come four years later. By then, Norman's health problems, to some extent caused by years of living the high life, were pushing him to the sidelines. It was so sad to have to stand by helplessly and watch the withering of a great talent, even as my own career was beginning to soar ever higher.

In July of 1969, as the decade headed to a close and my star kept rising, I was placed alongside newsman Gordon Donaldson to co-anchor the network's coverage of the Apollo moon shot. Gordon, a smart and playful Scot, was a great reporter and writer, but his television skills were underdeveloped for the long hours of coverage and the extensive cueing and trafficking to remotes required in live television. I can still recall taking a break on the night of July 21 and walking out to the parking lot to look up at the moon in a beautifully clear sky. Neil Armstrong had already uttered his famous line about the "small step for man, giant leap for mankind," and I had to pinch myself to be sure that I was really living through this momentous time: the first landing of men on the moon. While we relied on Walter Cronkite's CBS coverage for main moments, the CBC created hours of its own, and it certainly helped my profile with the audience to be seen on such a broadcast over a three-day period.

The same year, I made my first trip to the United Kingdom for CBC coverage of the investiture of Prince Charles as Prince of Wales. It's an ancient rite in which the British monarch honours the Welsh by giving the first-born son, at the age of twenty-one, a personal designation for them and a special place at court. The old castle at Carnarvon echoed with the glorious sounds of the Welsh massed choirs, and since colour television was making more inroads in Canadian homes, the rich red and purple robes of the participants made for a colourful spectacle. My co-anchor was the Corporation's London correspondent of the time, David Halton, one of the finest men and best reporters I have come to know.

When we first arrived in Wales, we checked into a motel in an idyllic valley surrounded by high hills swarmed with hundreds of grazing mountain goats, about an hour outside Carnarvon. U.S. broadcaster Barbara Walters was at the same location, and we had a pleasant exchange with Barbara and her researcher that evening in the little motel's spartan dining room. After getting to bed late and falling into a deep sleep, I was startled in the middle of the night by the ringing of the phone on the bedside table. The researcher, whose name I recall as Margaret, had a question: "Sorry to bother you, Lloyd," she chirped, "but what the hell is a Knight Pursuivant of the Garter? Barbara wants to know." In my fogbound state, I did my best to explain my limited understanding of the arcane mysteries of knighthoods and heraldry and fell back to sleep. When I asked later whether any of the information had been useful, Margaret said, "Nah, Barbara realized Americans wouldn't give a damn about that stuff."

On the morning of the investiture, David and I were on the air to Canada with a preview of the day from the castle. I was in the courtyard, standing next to the scarlet throne chair, explaining its significance and briefing viewers on the ceremony to follow. David was outside, describing the history of the castle and surrounding area and talking with the crowds that were gathering in the streets. We put together a snappy and thorough presentation before going inside to continue our commentary—voice-over pictures. Barbara Walters, who had been watching us just off camera with NBC London correspondent Ray Shearer, said to me, "Hey, you Canucks are pretty damn good. We'd better pick up our game." David and I were amused that the Americans should seem surprised that we Canadians might meet their professional expectations. We thanked Barbara and moved on.

Back home, on a weekend current-affairs show, I met and interviewed the iconic Beatle John Lennon. The Vietnam War was still raging, and he had just completed his famous bed-in for peace in Montreal.

John was thoroughly charming—very friendly, but a little vague about it all. Yoko sat beside him and said little, but was a prompt for him.

> LLOYD: Why was the bed-in held in Montreal?
> JOHN: I don't really know. It was really a mistake, we just sorted of ended up there.
> YOKO: It was meant to be.
> LLOYD: Canada is known for promoting peace. Could that be a reason?
> YOKO: Mmmm.
> JOHN: Canada is the first country that wanted to help and didn't want something from us—the first place where the media treated us respectfully.

I came away from the interview liking John enormously, but a little wary of Yoko. She was there to protect and pounce when necessary—clearly, the power in the pair.

The sixties had also been productive on the personal side. Nancy and I were now parents of four—all girls, including a set of delightful twins.

Nanci Lee was born in Winnipeg, Susan arrived in Ottawa, and now the twins burst into the world in Toronto.

In those times, fathers were not allowed into the delivery room, so I dropped Nancy at the hospital and went to work while anxiously awaiting the call. In our last phone conversation through the waiting hours, Nancy told me she didn't think she wanted go through with the scheduled arrival of the matched set. I responded that we didn't have the option of a rain check. Eventually, Lisa and Lynda timed their arrival for the precise moment I was on the air doing a show called *The Umbrella*, hosted by Canadian artist William Ronald. I was Bill's sidekick and enjoyed his wild and unpredictable ways. He was disappointed that I hadn't told him about the twins' impending arrival, so the next week he presented me with one of his abstract paintings while announcing their birth to the nation. Bill's painting soared in value over the years, and while it's probably worth a lot, its value is negligible compared to the joy the twins have brought over the years.

Yes, kids can be tiresome and troublesome when you're an upwardly mobile father with a busy career, but I have concluded what many other distracted fathers learn in maturity: there is nothing to match the unconditional love your children can have for you, and you for them. My relationship with our daughters has grown ever stronger over the years, and I appreciate them more and more.

Nancy was increasingly concerned that I was becoming a workaholic. But as Craig Oliver said, "Hell, we were all workaholics, the challenge in those days was not to become an alcoholic as well." I loved broadcasting and was able to justify my work hours to Nancy by telling her that, as a father of four, on a not very princely CBC announcer's salary, I had to keep my nose to the grindstone.

9

Breaking Through the Barriers

STANLEY BURKE'S DEPARTURE FROM *CBC NATIONAL NEWS* (now dubbed *The National*) in 1969 caused a stir in the media as well as large segments of the public who were just getting used to Stanley and his idiosyncratic but charming presentation. It also created a stark dilemma for news division managers. Could they suffer the embarrassment of going back to straight announcers, or "readers," to front the news, having disparaged that approach so thoroughly when they hired Stanley, or was there a middle way that could point to some progress on the union jurisdiction front, when, in fact, there had been none?

They decided on the latter and invited my old friend Warren Davis to take the helm. At the same time, some people in both unions and management began to talk up the idea of broadcast journalists, a new category that would have to be accepted by both union groups, and give anchors an editorial role in newsrooms with the chance to both write and report. I was among a group that included people such as Warren; Bruce Rogers, a talented writer and broadcaster with extensive news experience; and George Finstad, a promising newcomer from the west with a news background. At first, there seemed reason to hope that a way might be found through the thicket of clashing jurisdictions, but as Warren began his brief stint on *The National* and tried to be more involved in the process of putting the program together, he was sharply rebuffed by militant newsroom-union types. Warren was well known for his hair-trigger temper, and it wasn't long before ugly arguments were breaking out on a nightly basis between him and members of the news guild.

The atmosphere became so poisonous that Warren abandoned the position after just nine months, and one of the smartest and most talented of the CBC's stable of broadcasters suffered a severe dent to his career. He also became an asterisk in the lineup of people who presented the CBC's main newscast over the years. Most remember Earl Cameron and Stanley Burke, but "Warren who?" is the response from players of Canadian trivia games when they're reminded that he was the anchor from 1969 into 1970.

For the second time in four years, the CBC found itself in a crisis over its anchor, the most consistently visible element of its news operation. And the Corp. was also trying to figure out how to confront something new: a direct bid for its news audience from a serious competitor that had formerly been regarded as a mere upstart. The CTV network had moved its news up to eleven o'clock, the same time as the CBC in those days, and had begun broadcasting in colour ahead of its public-corporation rival. Equally as important, a popular and steady anchorman had settled in for them in the person of the avuncular Harvey Kirck. Harvey had been a radio reporter and newscaster with CHUM, the popular Top Forty radio station in Toronto, before moving to CTV affiliate CFTO in Toronto, where he was soon catapulted to news director and a few years later was drafted as principal anchor of the private network's flagship newscast, first from Ottawa and then back in Toronto. Here was someone who brought news credentials to the chair, and the CBC would have to move fast to stem a developing perception of drift and decline in its prized news service.

On the anchor front, speculation began to move in my direction since my work on the weekend show and previous stints on specials like the Apollo moon landing and political programs proved to managers that I had news acumen and knew how to handle live TV. Oh, there were a few who judged me as barely passable, but I was comforted in the understanding that no one was ever perfect at the CBC in those days. While *The National* presented the top prestige vehicle for announcers, we were all aware it had been badly tarnished, so some, including myself, looked warily at a position that had snuffed out or severely diminished the careers of three formidable talents—Cameron, Burke and Davis—in less than five years.

When Knowlton Nash called me to his home to talk about the job, I was well aware that a stint in the main anchor chair could give me a high profile with the Canadian audience for life, but there were still serious pitfalls. I told him I would prefer to eventually be posted to London as a correspondent. I had visions of following in the footsteps of the great war correspondents, American Edward R. Murrow and Canadian Matthew Halton. He said that would be impractical and impossible for some time because too many union journalists with experience would be lining up for that job. Then, to my surprise, he committed himself and his department to solving the union jurisdictional mess once and for all and said I could count on the day when I would be thoroughly involved in the editorial, reporting and assignment decisions of CBC News. He said that the "broadcast journalist" idea of a separate group, including people from both the announcer and news unions, free to perform all newsroom functions, including writing, editing, reporting and anchoring, would win the day and the problems would be solved. Such a plan, he added, would be a win for both groups, and patience was all we needed.

At the same time, Knowlton guaranteed, I would also be anchoring specials, as Stanley had done, and could continue work in the features and special events department on key projects like royal tours. He effectively handed me a Walter Cronkite role, but without the authority to write or tinker with copy on the newscast or report into the program from the field on occasion, both rights held by the person who would become my opposition, Harvey Kirck. However, there was enough on the table for me to accept, and I decided not to press the point about the writing authority, thinking it could be worked out gradually with the folks in the newsroom. Knowlton then told me that if I rejected the job, he would be offering it to Peter Trueman, a longtime print journalist who was learning the ropes of television at the CBC and would eventually go on to become the highly successful anchor of the Global regional network centred in Ontario. His mention of Trueman as potential anchor confirmed that, despite the obstacles, Knowlton and the Corporation were definitely moving toward the more modern system of anchors being involved editorially.

I decided to take the leap. There was a minor pay adjustment, taking my salary into the $45,000 territory, and on October 1, 1970, I launched a lifestyle that would dominate my existence for the next forty-one years.

For some, working evenings sounds like heaven, mainly because you can sleep late every morning. The biggest challenge, though, is being wide awake to perform at your very best at the end of what are often long and extremely busy days that start around three o'clock in the afternoon. At home, there are countless adjustments to be made. Nancy had to get used to my absence five nights a week, while my daughters had to learn to chill in the mornings and not have bathroom fights because Dad would be trying to sleep.

Nancy became an expert at managing all of this and running her own teaching career at the same time. She and a partner were now busy operating a successful pre-school, and she juggled our daughters' schedules, making sure they were occupied with lots of activities outside of school in the hope of keeping them out of the kind of trouble in which teenage girls can become enmeshed. I found myself becoming more deeply involved in work and was too often distracted on the home front. My time with family was not always of the quality I would have preferred, and my relationship with my daughters was too often peripheral at best. Fortunately, I was able to remedy this later in life, as my confidence grew and I learned to better handle the tensions and pressures of the job.

I had no idea the nightly news gig would last so long. In fact, given the experience of my immediate predecessors, it could have been quite short-lived. In any case, I set out to make it work by starting with a question for a longtime colleague about my approach in going up against the stolid but solid Harvey Kirck every night at eleven.

Don Cumming had worked with me as producer on the CBC *Weekend* show and had been instrumental in the earlier struc-

turing and success of the *CTV National News.* He was one of
the best TV writer-editors in the business and always seemed
to be a fount of collected wisdom, even as young man. Don had
an intimate knowledge of both private and public broadcast
systems, as well as the styles and ranges of both Harvey and
me as anchors. His view was that Harvey had a very deliberate,
slower and somewhat stylized delivery, and that I should do what
I did best naturally—a higher-energy, more involved presentation—and not be afraid of showing a lighter and more viewer-
friendly side when the occasion warranted. I worked for a blend
of energy and authority; soon, I wasn't worrying about the read
and was able to concentrate more thoroughly on the nature of
the stories and how they should be interpreted for the audience,
with the usual combination of fairness and balance.

I also strove to cool the temperature in the newsroom and
try to develop a better relationship with writers and editors.
Very helpful to me in that respect was *The National*'s evening
producer, the smart and affable Don Hearn. He took it upon
himself to make my entry into the CBC anchor position as
smooth and trouble-free as possible by keeping news guild
union militants under control and out of my face. He dubbed
me "golden," supposedly for the tones that radiated from my
voice box each night, and for five of my six years on the CBC's
The National we delivered solid programming that the audience
responded to positively.

Even though I was judged to be doing reasonably well,
there were constant rumblings and grumblings that drifted
down to me through the Byzantine bureaucratic structure of
the CBC. The top brass, it was said, would really prefer someone else. People like Peter Jennings and Robert MacNeil, both

Canadians working in American TV, could bring more heft to
the broadcast, it was said. But, oh well, they would stick with
what they had for now.

Since Stanley Burke's time, the central anchor of the newscast was also expected to be able to pop into the chair and, with
the editors passing skimpy wire copy to him, ad lib around it
fluently and calmly in crisis situations. In these circumstances,
even the most militant of news guild union members knew it
was impractical to demand that the announcers only read copy.
Major breaking news could be swirling around them, and there
wouldn't be time to wait for someone to write the story and hand
it to the anchor. An example of that came quite early.

My first month in the chair brought my baptism by fire. I was
thrust into the middle of one of the most dramatic and dangerous periods in Canadian history just three weeks after assuming
the anchor role. The FLQ crisis burst into the open in Quebec
when separatist militants captured British trade commissioner
James Cross and provincial cabinet minister Pierre Laporte,
whose body was later found in the trunk of a car. The news
broke near the end of the week, and I was called back into the
newsroom for an all-night shift late Saturday after my colleague
George Finstad, who had been chosen as my weekend backup,
had performed the grim task of announcing Laporte's death.

George was shaken. We discussed how horrible it was that
this should be happening in Canada and how it represented a
new and sad coming of age for us. All through that long night,
we were hoping not to have to announce the news of the death
of James Cross, already hinted at in an earlier, erroneous report.
While Cross was being held, I spent most of my days and nights
near the newsroom. In the middle of one of those long nights,

we had to jump on the air quickly to announce that the government had just implemented the War Measures Act, giving police in Quebec the right to round up and hold people on suspicion without laying charges.

Canadians were generally supportive of the action, believing Prime Minister Trudeau's message that we were in the throes of an insurrection in Quebec and that harsh measures were required to stomp it out. After years of reflection, there is now general agreement that the legislation was a heavy-handed overreaction to a small band of would-be terrorists and troublemakers who could have been dealt with through normal police actions. With the courage of his convictions in place, the NDP's Tommy Douglas was the only party leader to speak up against the civil rights abuses. Other parliamentarians of the day, including Conservative leader Robert Stanfield, came to publicly recant their support of the strong actions, but Trudeau never indicated regrets and seemed oblivious to the charge that he took the tough measures to get even with many of his old separatist enemies in Quebec.

Trudeau was always unfailingly polite whenever I met him, but I was also aware, along with all other media people of that era, that this brilliant intellectual had the capacity to cut to the quick if he regarded questions as silly or irrelevant. I observed it many times in news conferences, where Trudeau seemed to be saying to himself, "Why am I wasting my time with these guys?" *Vancouver Sun* correspondent Patrick Nagle told me his knees would shake every time he stood to ask a question. He was sure that Trudeau sensed this discomfort and always paused before starting to answer while poor Pat twisted in the wind, wondering whether he would be submitted to one of the PM's legendary putdowns or, as happened to others, have the question thrown back in the form of "Well, what would *you* do?"

We tend to forget that Trudeau's long run was very nearly blunted after the first four years. Given his tendency to be dismissive of the political pros around him at the beginning, he went his own way and, in 1972, presented Canadians with the bland campaign slogan of "The Land Is Strong," which had no resonance across the country and, when combined with his lacklustre campaign, brought his government to the brink of defeat.

I remember the night of the '72 election for its excitement on a few fronts: the closeness of the vote, with the Liberals ultimately ending up with only two more seats than the Conservatives, and my first federal election in the principal anchor chair. We called the outcome of the election correctly with the help of our spanking new, but still cumbersome, computer system and were spurred on in the knowledge that CTV's computers had crashed that night, leaving Harvey and his colleagues blathering on aimlessly with no numbers to talk about until they were finally reduced to listening to us on a headset and vamping as best they could. Craig Oliver, who by then had made his move to the private side and was working on CTV coverage, continues to crow to me that, even using our figures, they still called the election outcome first.

There is always a lot tension in control rooms on election nights, as staff work feverishly to try to determine who's winning. The first network to call the outcome of the election likes to brag about it the next day, but I've always contended that, while it's great to be first, you'd also better be right. The fallout from the embarrassment of a wrong call is something no one wants to live with. After the election, I felt more certain of myself in the

daily news anchor chair and was now convinced that news was
the natural place for me to be.

During a trip to New York for American political coverage, I met Walter Cronkite, by then the master of the TV news
universe. He was friendly and helpful and introduced me to
CBS veteran Douglas Edwards, who was doing a daily midday
newscast at the time. As we compared notes about our respective systems, Edwards was puzzled by the restrictions placed on
anchors in the CBC newsroom. I tried to explain that the differences had to do with overlapping union jurisdictions between
the announcers' group and the news service employees. While
they both understood, Cronkite finally said, "Well, you've got to
get that changed," and Edwards added, "Audiences now expect
the person telling them the news to be a news person first." He
spoke from a position of authority, because he had come from a
purely broadcast background; Cronkite had spent the war years
as a wire-service correspondent for the United Press, with stints
in radio before being recruited for early television. They both
agreed that I should be in the news service and a member of
the news division. That brief but memorable meeting further
sparked my determination to break down the barriers.

Much later, after I had moved to CTV and had been accorded
all of the anchor rights that are now accepted as a matter of
course, I met Walter Cronkite once again. It was at a reception
and dinner at the Canadian consulate in New York in 2003. While
we talked, I thanked him for inspiring me, and he proceeded to
tell me about his love for Canada and Canadians. It was just
after George W. Bush had launched the invasion of Iraq. Jean
Chrétien's government had decided not to participate, although
this country had supported an earlier operation against Saddam

Hussein in the Persian Gulf War of 1991. Cronkite said to me, "You must be happy and proud to be a Canadian right now." He thought the Bush incursion into Iraq was a disastrous move and Americans would have trouble extricating themselves. He was right about that, just as he had been right decades earlier when, breaking from his unstinting objectivity, he called for American troops to leave Vietnam. Despite his important role in the public eye over the years, Walter Cronkite never pretended to be anyone special and declared himself to be "a reluctant big shot." He affirmed that news people weren't natural stars but became celebrities only because they were on television.

While I was able to provide stability in the CBC anchor chair through the early to mid-seventies, there was one period when I learned that the highest-profile job on the announce staff also made you a marked man. The Corporation suffered through one of the ugliest strikes in its history in the spring of 1972. All of the technicians were out across the country, and there was pressure on members of other unions not to cross picket lines. The announce staff in Toronto, the largest and most influential in the country, would give the cue to the other regions on how to behave in such sticky circumstances. The technicians were important to us as colleagues; they handled all of the equipment, including the microphones and cameras we used every day. We valued their services, and many of us had developed friendships with them through the years. The Toronto announce staff was badly split on what to do, even though our own union said we were expected to fulfill our contractual obligations, and indeed by law could suffer the consequences if we didn't. Many of the senior members of our staff were adamantly opposed to taking any action, while some of the younger ones, and those with long-standing grievances, also wanted to poke a stick in the CBC's eye. Whether I would cross the line to do *The National* became the key question, and others looked to me for guidance.

It was important for the announcers to show a united front in this stormy situation, and many colleagues began to press me to take on a leadership role. Since this would have to supplement my already busy work day, I agreed only reluctantly. When militants from various Corporation unions joined the picket lines, the atmosphere turned poisonous: angry taunts were shouted at those who dared to cross, tires were slashed in the parking lot and cars with passengers in them were violently rocked back and forth as the anger that had built up against the CBC from so many of its employees burst into the open.

Since the RCMP and the government would have been interested in identifying agitators inside a Crown corporation, we were certain our phones were tapped. We had no hard evidence, but there were constant clicks on the lines, and my pal Tim Kotcheff once joked that there were so many people listening in on our conversations we couldn't hear ourselves speaking.

Ultimately, there wasn't much to joke about. The announcers finally agreed to stay out for one full day in support of our technician colleagues, and I made sure we informed management of our intentions since, again, by law, we could all have been dismissed.

That sincere gesture toward our colleagues wasn't enough for the union hardliners on the announce staff, and the phone calls and meetings at all hours continued. My role expanded to try to organize more days in support of the technicians. Being the man in the middle was no fun. I was considered "not a good union man" by the militants, and the rest of the announce group, by far the majority, were either simmering with anger at the hardliners or desperately worried about losing their jobs. I was frustrated and angry that all sides had adopted such rigid positions, and began to boil with resentment at both the CBC and its hodge-podge of union regulations and jurisdictions. Finally, something inside me snapped. The result was scary for Nancy. She became deeply concerned one night when I woke up and began walking the floor and hallucinating, spouting gibberish. When she was unable to contact our family doctor, I was shunted off to a CBC physician, who quickly concluded that I had to be hospitalized.

It was all conducted under the strictest secrecy. While there was no doubt genuine concern for my well-being, CBC managers were panicked that the Corporation's main anchor, who had to be seen as a pillar of strength and reliability at all times, was collapsing under strain. I was dispatched to Homewood, a mental health and addiction facility in Guelph, where a number of well-known CBC alcoholics had spent time over the years.

It was a frightening episode. I recall losing touch with reality, fighting for control of my own thoughts, while seeming to be pulled down into a dark abyss by my aching and exhausted body. When I arrived at Homewood, I told the admitting psychiatrist that I was too tired to sit up and proceeded to lie down on the floor; oddly enough, I don't recall him offering a couch. He determined that I was suffering nervous exhaustion and should spend a few days at the facility. Shortly afterward, the staff ushered me into a sparse but pleasant room with twin beds.

A few hours later, I acquired a roommate: a tall, thin, ramrod-straight young man with dark hair and a thin moustache. As we slowly struck up a conversation, I noticed how interested he was in gathering information from me while he refused to give me anything other than sketchy and irrelevant details about himself. I quickly became suspicious—was he from the RCMP, perhaps, or from CBC management? I will never know, but my reaction spoke to the atmosphere within the CBC at the time. It was driven by fear, anger and suspicion.

The mystery man was gone the next morning, and I had just enjoyed my first sound sleep in weeks and was feeling much better. The staff told me that my condition was nothing unusual for people who had been working hard under pressure and not getting enough sleep. The doctors advised me to stay with them a few days longer, but I had to get out, get my life back under control and be back at work as soon as possible. Nancy came to pick me up, and we went off on a brief vacation. I was still shaky for weeks after the event, but what drove me was the fear that some of my mother's genes were fighting for dominance within my system, and I was determined not to let them get control of my mind. My earlier ability to continue with daily life as though nothing was amiss kicked in again, and no one seemed to notice I was having problems. After several weeks, and with only a minimum of medication, the fog lifted and a sense of normalcy returned. It's hard to avoid pressure situations in television, but I eventually learned to pace myself and not be pulled into quagmires by other people. Most important, as some of my early peers would say, using an old war quotation, "*Illegitimi non carborundum.*" Don't let the bastards grind you down.

The bitterness of the strike also left its mark on a shaken CBC management. There seemed to be general agreement within the upper reaches of the CBC bureaucracy that more professional management techniques had to be employed and, in the news division in particular, control had to be wrested from the wild-eyed union militants who were constantly bullying and browbeating their more mild-mannered colleagues into actions that were hindering the smooth running of the news service.

Knowlton Nash proved to be an effective department head, but the newsroom was only one of his overall responsibilities and it seemed impossible to keep a chief news editor, the newsroom boss, in the chair for more than a few years at a time. It was a next-to-impossible job, with managers pounding on your head from above and unions beating on you from below.

After a long search, Knowlton and his group found just the right person. Denny Harvey arrived at the Corporation from the managing editor's position at the Montreal *Gazette*. He was tough, smart, spirited and eminently fair—and, just as important to me, shared the vision of how the news department should move forward, with anchors following the Cronkite model. With his ruddy complexion and often pugnacious style, he was a physical force to be reckoned with in the newsroom and brooked no nonsense from those who didn't want to pull their weight by invoking obscure clauses from the union contract. As the late Ottawa correspondent Charles Lynch said of him, "This was a guy who spit bullets when he talked." Some complained that he had very limited TV experience, and that was a problem a few times, but Denny compensated with his willingness to listen and to admit he wasn't afraid to make mistakes—highly unusual for a CBC bureaucrat. The newsroom began to settle down under this new leadership—at least for a while.

I was on board and in the anchor chair for the next federal election, which saw Pierre Trudeau's Liberals return to majority government in July of 1974. My colleague at the main desk that night was David Halton, and we watched in fascination as our former colleague Ron Collister went down to defeat as a Conservative candidate in the Toronto area. Collister had come from a distinguished career at the CBC parliamentary bureau, and although regulations had allowed him to return to the Corp. after running for elected office, he was dispatched to Washington, since it was felt there would be a high level of discomfort should he continue in Ottawa, given some of his anti-Trudeau rhetoric during the campaign. In one bizarre assignment, I was sent to Washington to sit by his side during live coverage of a Trudeau visit to the American capital. My only role was to keep a tight rein on Ron and make sure he didn't lapse back into campaign mode.

Trudeau had previously caused the American administration to squirm with his crack about "Pentagon pipsqueaks" when answering a question about U.S. defence policy, and reporters, including Ron, were on careful watch for any indications of strained relations with our most important foreign partner. While Trudeau and Richard Nixon were publicly polite to each other, the truth about Nixon's feelings came out later when he referred to the prime minister as an "a-hole." Trudeau cracked in response, "I've been called worse by better people."

As for Ron, he was perfectly professional, as I knew he would be. Eventually, this highly qualified and capable man, who had to assume he was no longer wanted by his employer, chose to leave the CBC and pursue journalism elsewhere—in the newspapers, and as a hot-line radio host in Edmonton.

Pierre Trudeau's legacy with Canadians remains secure. He came onto the scene at a time when we were ready to be challenged to be bigger than ourselves, to open our hearts and minds and accept the simple fact that the French helped establish this country, even though they were defeated by the British on the

Plains of Abraham, and deserved to play a more prominent role in its future. We became officially bilingual, and we were encouraged to be multicultural as well. While Trudeau's economic leadership is still regarded as haphazard and uncertain, he never failed to reach out and touch people on an emotional level. When he was lying in state before his funeral in the autumn of 2000, long lines of Canadians waited for hours to pay respects, and so many in those lines on that day told me that they owed him a lot. He had opened up this country for them and had made a difference in their lives.

Denny Harvey's reign in the newsroom had its share of bumps along the way, especially when he took leadership of the idea to remove "Mister" from in front of family names for men mentioned in the broadcast. The point he made in defence of the move, which several of us were uncomfortable with, was that convicted felons who were in the news almost daily had no right to such a title. What about the prime minister and others who were not about to go to jail and were in the news almost daily? The complaints were heard, but ignored. Denny prevailed and pushed it through in spite of the resignation of one of his key local news directors, Ken Brown, in Ottawa. Brown said he could never work for an organization that would invoke such a policy and that everyone, regardless of status, deserved to be treated with respect. The argument over this seemingly innocuous matter rages from time to time, and you will have noticed that while *The Globe and Mail* and *The New York Times* still use "Mr.," the *Toronto Star* and many other dailies have ditched it, and all TV and radio news outlets simply use the last name without the title most of the time.

After a few years in the chair, I became accustomed to the range of compliments, complaints and questions an anchor can receive from the general public. Some letters were gushingly over the top, while others spewed vitriol about everything from my alleged support of some political party or cause to the colour of my shirt or tie. The funny ones were always the most pleasant to read, and there is one that stands out from my early anchor days. A woman in British Columbia wrote to tell me that she was constantly warning her husband about trimming his toenails while he watched the news. She was certain I could see him, and she thought it very impolite. I wrote back to tell her that while she and her man could see me, the technology had not yet been developed to allow for two-way viewing. I went on to say that should the day ever come when that was possible, it would still be okay with me if he trimmed his nails while watching the news.

Change is the one constant we could always count on in the CBC news division during the turbulent and increasingly competitive years of the early seventies. Denny, who had brought some order and discipline to the news service and whose decisive leadership style was appreciated by his more timid masters, soon found himself elevated to an executive position with the entire CBC English TV network. He immediately brought in his protégé, Michael Daigneault, also from the Montreal *Gazette*, to fill the position he was leaving as chief news editor in charge of the daily news programs.

Daigneault was a thin, unassuming-looking man with a will of iron who seemed almost eager to take on the roughest union of them all, the Canadian Wire Service Guild, in the newsroom. And I was to figure prominently in his plans. It was the spring of 1975, and events were set in motion—with me in the middle of them—that would slowly begin to spin out of control. I had been anchor of *The National* for five years and had grown into the job; audience reaction was largely positive, and the feeling from the supervisors around Knowlton Nash, who was still head of all news and current-affairs programs, was that I seemed to be holding my own. Working the news specials had helped build my credibility with the national audience, but when I walked into the newsroom to anchor our nightly broadcasts, there was to be no writing of copy, no editing, no real input into the editorial decisions, even though by this time I'd accumulated much more experience in news than several of the people working on the desk. My main competitor over at CTV, Harvey Kirck, could brag that he was the real news guy; he could perform all of these functions with no restraints.

While I had maintained a good relationship with the news guild and didn't want to rock that boat, both Mike Daigneault and I agreed that something had to be done to bring the CBC's main newscast into the modern age, with the anchor as a main participant in the editorial structuring of the broadcast. Mike was adamant that we had a perfect right to push forward by having me report into *The National*, in the face of sharp resistance from the news guild union. He almost revelled in confrontation as a way to clear the air in difficult circumstances, and an opportunity soon presented itself.

I was set to travel to Moscow in June of 1975 for an hour-long program produced by the current-affairs division on the Apollo–Soyuz space shot, the first joint venture between the U.S. and Soviet space programs. Since I had accumulated some expertise in space matters, the guild did something quite unusual: it granted a waiver and agreed I could also file a report for the *The*

National. This would be a first for me, and was a major concession on their part. Then Mike pushed harder. He ordered that, on the way over, I should also do a report for *The National* on the vote on Britain's entry into the European Common Market, scheduled to take place just before the Moscow trip. My friend David Halton, the regular London correspondent, would be away at the time, and it was felt that an item had to be filed on such a big story. Giving the assignment to me meant raising the stakes considerably. It was a highly provocative move that the news union hadn't approved, and it opened the way for the hardliners to get control of the situation, which they orchestrated in spectacular fashion.

The entire news service walked out in protest for twenty-four hours. There were no reports into any of the CBC newscasts from across the country or around the world, and the main newsroom in Toronto, the only one in operation, was staffed by management types who were former news department employees. Announcer Jan Tennant had to read copy, written by the substitutes, about the high-profile dust-up. As you would expect from Jan, she was perfectly professional but, as one of my announcer colleagues, she must have been steaming inside at having to present a story about the entire CBC news staff, national and local, being absent for a whole day and then having to explain my role in the affair before she went on to introduce the report I'd put together on the EU referendum.

As if to place emphasis on the crazy times, it was one week later that *The National* ran the item on the Apollo–Soyuz space link-up without incident, and I had some memorable moments on my first visit to Moscow. After a forty-five-minute lecture on the glories of the Soviet space program by the president of the Soviet Academy of Sciences, the assembled press corps, under tight control, was ushered into a mockup of the simulators in which the cosmonauts, called astronauts in the U.S., conducted their practice runs. Compared to the American facilities, they were pretty basic. Those of us who had requested interviews with Soviet cosmonaut Yuri Gagarin, the first human being in outer space, were ushered into his presence and allowed to ask our pre-set questions. Gagarin was affable and kept repeating, no matter what the question, "Everybody want [sic] peace." He was charming and laughed a lot and was no more or less threatening than his U.S. counterparts. As I would discover time after time while covering politics, people everywhere have the same basic desires: peace, a decent standard of living and the wish to be left alone to raise their families free of the constraints imposed on them by their various governments.

When I returned from the trip to London and Moscow, there was a new mood in the newsroom. Some friends told me that there had been grumbling among union members that Daigneault was using me as a club to beat them. While shrugging outwardly, I was uncomfortably aware that to continue the pursuit of greater editorial involvement would risk damaging my relations with some of the news guild membership. I made the naive assumption that the goodwill expressed by a clear majority of them would carry the day. What a mistake!

Mike Daigneault's next chapter in his plan to push through his policy was to assign me to the Habitat conference in Vancouver in the spring of 1976. If there was a beginning to the end in the Robertson departure story from the public broadcaster, this was the moment. I was very reluctant about the assignment, but eventually agreed, in the knowledge that I was now too far into a high-stakes game to back away. It was one of the great ironies of the period that, as news union members in Toronto succeeded in blocking my reports out of the conference, an item I had done on Imelda Marcos, wife of the president of the Philippines, the generally despised strongman Ferdinand Marcos, found its way onto an American network. Friends informed me it had been seen on some CBS network affiliates south of the border, and a copy of it lives in the CBC archives to this day marked "Amnets," meaning it had been brought in from a U.S. network. It never made it to air on the CBC.

The long-running dispute had taken on a new dimension. I was the meat in the sandwich between union and management, and it was getting uglier. Would I be the fourth helmsman of the CBC's main newscast in ten years to bite the dust over this crazy dispute? I would, but not in any way like my predecessors.

10

The Phone Call That Changed a Life

THE MONTREAL OLYMPICS BURST ONTO THE CANADIAN scene in July of 1976 and I was honoured to be asked to host a portion of the daily broadcast every evening. It was not an assignment Knowlton Nash was happy about, as he noted in his book *Prime Time at Ten*. Knowlton believed the news should take precedence over any sports event, and while I agreed with him, these were the first Olympics to be held on Canadian soil, after all, and as someone who had the highest-profile anchoring job at the network, as well experience covering the Olympics, I was anxious to participate. His superiors, including Denny Harvey and Don MacPherson, who was now vice-president of English TV services, agreed, and I was off to Montreal. In spite of the grim financial legacy the Olympics left for Montreal residents, the Games were a big hit at the time. The Queen added lustre to the opening ceremony, and a petite Romanian gymnast, Nadia Comaneci, rocketed to international stardom as she performed elegantly perfect routines every time out.

Halfway through the coverage, I received a call from a long-time acquaintance, Don Cameron, director of news for the CTV network. He congratulated me on my work in Montreal and asked to have lunch as soon as the Games were over. While I was aware of some interest from CTV in my services over the years for shows like *Canada AM* and *W5*, I had no idea what was really coming down the track.

Cameron was one of those high-living, hard-drinking TV characters of the era, and he had an unerring instinct for the big story. He also had an uncanny sense of people's strengths and vulnerabilities and, as a former CBC type, had been following with interest my problems at Mother Corp. He would have been aware of my frustrations, and felt the time was right for a serious approach about a job. When he took that idea to his vice-president, Tom Gould, and network head Murray Chercover, they concurred and gave the green light.

The day after I said yes to a meeting, Don suggested we meet at Tom Gould's townhouse in downtown Toronto rather than a restaurant convenient to both of us. With the ground rules suddenly changing from a casual chat between two old colleagues to something more serious, my curiousity was piqued about what they might have to say. And there was a reason I was so ready to listen.

On returning to the newsroom after the Olympics, there was a notice of a grievance against my assignment in Vancouver posted on the bulletin board. A full discussion of the "Robertson affair" was being called for. It was not a happy homecoming. A letter to the editor from a guild member in Edmonton showed up, castigating me for wanting to take on newsman credentials without having served proper time in the trenches as a reporter. I knew this was becoming a widespread sentiment. I tried to counter it by pointing to my reporting work before unions arrived at the CBC, and all the editorial judgments I had made on news specials over the years, often on the fly. I noted that I had been judged competent enough to remain in those jobs. But nobody was listening. The subject had become highly politicized and the union had drawn its line in the sand and set out the talking points for its members.

After the high of the Olympics, the future for me in the news service looked bleak. I was reflecting on all of this as I sat on Tom Gould's balcony overlooking his beautiful Japanese garden and listened to him and Don talk about a job they were offering at CTV. When they started mentioning the anchor position, I said, "Whoa! You already have an anchor in Harvey Kirck." They allowed that Harvey had some problems. What I didn't know at the time was that the network had managed to squelch negative publicity from his first drunk-driving charge and they were clearly worried about his future with them.

I had come to like Harvey, and firmly rejected any idea that I should replace him. I was also aware that it would be a public relations disaster for me with Harvey's fans, still in considerable numbers, yelling epithets at me through their TV sets and perhaps even turning away from the *CTV National News.* Apart from concern over Harvey's vulnerabilities, what was driving the CTV brass to make such a radical move was the realization that ratings for the CBC's newscast had been on a steady upward curve for more than a few years. *The National* was drawing about 1.6 million viewers to CTV's 948,000 in the month they approached me.

We discussed sharing the newscast over seven nights, with Harvey doing weekends while I did Monday to Thursday. Harvey would have been humiliated by this, so we moved on to another interesting possibility. It was an era of news anchor teams in TV, with Barbara Walters moving from NBC to ABC to link up on the anchor desk with Harry Reasoner. NBC had moved through various combinations of two-man teams—including John Chancellor and Tom Brokaw—to succeed the duo of Chet Huntley and David Brinkley. So, what about a two-man anchor team for Canada? The idea appealed to me only if I could grow as a broadcast journalist, and that would mean the freedom to write and edit scripts and go into the field on occasion to report into the newscast. CTV agreed to all of this and threw in the sweetener that I would become their prime anchor for news specials. CTV could make these wide-ranging proposals because, while the network had unions in its technical and production divisions, there was none in the news service.

Also, it was understood that I would not be displacing any news writers or editors; I would simply have free rein to change copy as I saw fit, in appreciation of my experience, and to facilitate a better read. CTV also added the plum of continuing work on Olympic coverage. Through the negotiating skills of the irrepressible Johnny Esaw, the network's vice-president of sports, CTV had acquired rights to the Winter Olympics for several years, and I would be welcome to continue hosting. Then, in closing, Cameron and Gould made a gesture that proved how much they wanted me to join their team. They offered a five-year contract, starting at $85,000 per annum. They said they would send me an offer of intent in a few weeks.

As I left the meeting and got behind the wheel of my car, my head was spinning. They were offering almost twice what I was making at the CBC, where the extra money for *The National* could be lifted and I could be removed from the news at any time on an executive whim. Still, the CBC's basic salary, with its defined-benefit pension, would be with me no matter what happened. As a child of Depression-era parents, that security mattered a lot. What would become a bigger issue as the story unfolded was the right to what I had been wanting for several years: editorial input into the newscast. Here was my chance.

But there was a big problem. In my head and in my heart, I really didn't want to leave the CBC! I believed in its national mandate and had been weaned on its mission to tell the country about itself. Being sought after was flattering, and there was certainly an impulse inside me to kick over the traces and go for it, but there was also a gnawing feeling of disloyalty at the simple thought of leaving. However, as the CTV executives pointed out, joining them would still mean broadcasting to the nation, and the private network, which had nurtured the likes of Peter Jennings, was by this time a major player on the same Canadian stage. I couldn't dispute that, but I was far from ready to change the channel.

By now, we were late into the month of August of 1976. The CBC's annual presentation to the national press announcing its lineup for the new season was scheduled for mid-September. If CTV was going to drop a formal offer, it had to happen soon. A part of me was hoping they would forget about it, while another part was eager to see what the offer would contain. All things considered, I just couldn't imagine myself walking away from the CBC and, for that reason, decided to stay mum about my conversations with the CTV executives. What if they were just sounding me out, after all? Perhaps no offer would materialize.

The daily drumbeat of news continued. With the Liberals still holding a comfortable majority in Ottawa under Pierre Trudeau, attention shifted to U.S. politics. Jimmy Carter was selected as the Democratic Party's presidential nominee to challenge Gerald Ford, the Republican incumbent who had taken over two years earlier from the disgraced Richard Nixon. While I had decided not to murmur a word about my lunch with Tom Gould and Don Cameron until there was a formal offer, I noticed a peculiar increase in interest in my activities from CBC executives.

Mike Daigneault accompanied me on a trip to the U.S. for the convention coverage, and while he was very friendly, he seemed to be listening and watching rather than engaging me in any conversations about my future. I was shocked to learn much later from reliable sources within the Corporation that they knew about CTV's interest in me quite early and could have headed it off right then but, for reasons that are still inexplicable, decided not to act. That inaction led to seven days that changed my life.

11

The Big Leap

O N A TUESDAY MORNING IN EARLY SEPTEMBER OF 1976, I received a call from CTV informing me that an important document was on its way to my home. The offer of intent outlined what had been discussed at the luncheon meeting with Tom Gould and Don Cameron and set a seven-day deadline that would expire at midnight the following Tuesday. Perhaps not coincidentally, the CBC national press "meet and greet" was set for the following Wednesday morning. This annual event brings in TV critics from across the country and they, along with advertisers and departmental executives, are presented with a preview of the fall and winter season. Would CTV steal a march on the public network by scooping up its anchorman and gaining a headline when Mother Corporation was trying to promote her own shows? It was the worst possible time for the CBC to have to cope with such news, and I was troubled by the thought it could happen, but also realized there wasn't much I could do about it. With the offer now formalized, I immediately called the CBC to inform the various interested parties of what was happening. An appointment was set up that very day for a meeting with Knowlton Nash.

Knowlton had been the majordomo of all information pro-gramming—news, current affairs, even children's shows—for over ten years. He was unfailingly pleasant to staff and spouses, and he had kept up his public profile from his on-camera days with his writings and speeches on behalf of the CBC across the country. The reputation he had brought with him from his days as Washington correspondent was that of a solid and dependable colleague, unless the occasion arose when you found yourself offside of him. He was a cool customer and had an effective way of dealing with people that left no tracks returning to him. I was determined to bring him completely into the picture so that he would have a full understanding of my motives and intentions.

With clear nervousness and somewhat haltingly, I outlined the entire offer, from the money to the unimpeded access to a wide range of editorial functions including reporting, writing, editing and anchoring news specials as well as the nightly newscasts. I also made it clear that CTV had approached me, and this could be confirmed—I had not been out shopping for offers—and that while I had no desire to leave the CBC, the scope of the proposed deal was such that I felt there was no choice but to have a look at it. Knowlton was clearly startled by the money being offered and assured me once again that the Walter Cronkite style of involved anchor, which was now being pursued with greater vigour, but unfortunately at my expense, would one day be in place. It had been six years, and I wondered how much longer it would take—and how much strain we would all have to endure to make the change happen.

Knowlton acknowledged that the offer was a good one and that, yes, I should look at it. It was a very civilized conversa-tion between two professionals, with no rancour on either side. I wondered later about his relaxed attitude, but I came away with the clear understanding that the stakes were much higher for me than for the CBC—probably the exact message a good corporate officer would wish to convey.

I had now taken the step. There was no turning back from at least looking hard at the private network's offer, but I was terribly conflicted and wasn't sure where to turn. I had to be very careful with whom I shared the information; otherwise, the whole affair would be leaked to the press, causing unforeseen complications and potential damage to all parties involved. I desperately needed independent legal advice and turned first to an old broadcast industry friend.

Over the fourteen years we'd lived in Toronto, Nancy and I had developed a friendship with CBC broadcaster Bill McNeil and his lively and charming wife, Eileen. Bill was the familiar voice on CBC Radio's popular *Assignment*, another Harry Boyle creation. He had also worked with me on Harry's TV show. Both Bill and Eileen were from Cape Breton and had a down-home Maritime honesty; you could share your secrets with them and you could be sure they'd carry them to the grave if necessary. Through Bill and Eileen, I was introduced to an excellent legal team that would help me navigate the complexities of the next seven days that would rock my world. John Scandiffio was a bright, fastidious young lawyer with a passion for the law and legal history. He also happened to be a fan of the CBC who fully appreciated my commitment to the Corporation and understood why I would hope to remain in its employ. His more senior partner, Leo Adler, was cool, deliberate, and had an unerring instinct for striking to the core of any argument. John was the detail guy, while Leo stood back and assessed the bigger picture.

I had not previously entertained the idea of using lawyers, but realized that my life was at such a crossroads I needed objective advice from people who had no real reason to support one side or the other. These two were my principal guides through the uncharted waters of a hectic week. All bases would be covered but, in the end, the decision was up to me.

Managers at the CBC were dragging their feet getting back to us. The Corporation had never encountered anything quite like this. I sensed some people were seething inside that this upstart announcer was putting them through such nonsense. Program talent was simply bothersome, after all. In fact, my former executive producer from *The Observer* days, Don MacPherson, who had now been catapulted to the top job as vice-president of the English network, snidely remarked over a dinner, "Lloyd, you're not my only problem." Nancy, who was present at the time, was furious that a man who was supposed to be a friend could be so crudely insensitive at such an important time in our lives. My friend, John Rae, who by then had the title of Supervisor of Broadcast Language, a kind of emperor of the spoken word on the CBC, quietly told me that he saw the announcer's role in the Corporation as being at the beginning of a sharp decline and that I should judge accordingly.

CTV, in the meantime, and with no prompting from me, became even more aggressive, taking the $85,000-a-year offer and pushing it up by $5,000 each succeeding year to a maximum of $100,000 by the end of the fourth year. Then, in an unprecedented move for a Canadian network, they provided me with a one-way option for another five years. They were committing to a ten-year deal, but I could get out after five if I wanted. They attempted to allay any fears I might have had about the two-man anchor desk by saying I would often be in the field and would be principal anchor on all news specials. I was invited to see it as a growth opportunity, to hone my journalism skills on the writing and reporting side while enjoying the comfort zone of doing what I was familiar with on the anchoring and presentation front.

And so I was faced with one network pulling out all the stops to lure me on board and the other, my current employer, showing no inclination that it was important or urgent for them to keep me.

Knowlton seemed to be doing his best, and I gave him the benefit of the doubt as he explained on the weekend before the Tuesday deadline that the president, Al Johnson, would have to give his final approval for any counteroffer, and that was a problem because he was out of town. Days and hours ticked by until the Corporation finally turned up with a response on Monday night—after six days, and slightly more than twenty-four hours before the deadline on the CTV offer. The CBC's counterproposal came in about $20,000 a year less than CTV and offered only five years on the news. That was the only moment in the week-long exercise when I felt the sting of anger rising in my chest. CTV was prepared to offer a ten-year term, while the company to which I had dedicated twenty-two years of my working life would offer only five. Knowlton said he couldn't go further. I would later learn the roadblock was Knowlton's superior, my old friend MacPherson again, who shot off a line to a reporter that he wouldn't "offer the Queen a ten-year deal." Nash tried to reassure me, saying there would always be a place for me at the CBC, and that I could go into management down the road. That idea held no attraction. I had already seen some of my former colleagues, who were good broadcasters, vanish into the management maze and live to regret their decision.

The lawyers, and an accountant they had brought along for the meeting with Knowlton, judged the offer inadequate and even insulting, and when we convened back at their office that night, I was gloomy and confused. I had been so sure that the CBC offer would be good enough to accept that I had bought a bottle of high-quality Scotch to mark the occasion. It remained unopened.

John Scandiffio was soothing. He knew that I wanted to stay where I was, and although he was disturbed at what was lacking in the response coming from the Corporation, he felt a few tweaks to the CBC offer could make it more acceptable and would prevent me from having to eat too much crow. Then Leo Adler uncoiled with a few well-chosen lines that changed the dynamic and moved the discussions to another level. He reminded me of my long commitment to broadcast journalism under the Cronkite model, which meant editorial involvement in the newscast. "Lloyd, you really have to think about this: sitting in front of you is what you've always said you wanted. If you're true to yourself and honest with Canadians, you have to be serious here." What more could I ask— an excellent long-term contract, freedom to write and edit news copy and to report, and continued growth as a journalist with a major Canadian broadcaster. He was right, and if I stayed with the CBC and the details of the CTV offer leaked out, as would surely happen, I could be seen as someone who was not prepared to stand by what he had long said was important to him—not a good position for a newsman. Indeed, I felt my own credibility was now on the line, and unless the CBC could come up with a quick idea to break the impasse between announcers and news people, I might have only one way to jump.

Suddenly, for me, the issue that had dogged the CBC and its anchors for so long took on a new urgency. I had to be sure the door to greater editorial involvement in the daily newscast was really closed. Oh, CBC management would say all the right things about pushing the effort, but what did the union think? I asked for a meeting with the executive of the Canadian Wire Service Guild for the next day. They immediately agreed to see me. We had found ourselves on opposite sides many times over the previous few years, and many hurtful things had been said, but the union executive must have sensed, as I certainly did, that we were approaching a watershed moment, a time when something had to give in what was now a ten-year battle over jurisdiction.

As I got into the car on the morning of "decision day," I asked Nancy which way she thought I should jump. Without hesitation, she responded, "CTV." More than anyone, she was aware of the long struggle over editorial restrictions imposed unfairly on announcers who had news experience and was obviously still ticked over the Corporation's apparent arrogance and indifference toward me during this tense negotiation period.

As I stopped for a traffic light on the way downtown from our suburban Toronto home, a line from Shakespeare's *Julius Caesar* flashed through my mind: "There is a tide in the affairs of men which taken at the flood leads on to fortune." Fortune, in this case, applies not just to money but to the whole resolution of one's life. I was living in that moment.

Now, with less than twelve hours to the deadline, I met two guild union executives, Doug Fraser and Rick Wellbourn, at Bassel's restaurant-bar at Yonge and Gerrard streets. It was a favourite watering hole of the time, one of those dark places where plots and deals were hatched in corners. To the tinkling of glasses and low murmurs about business deals and office politics in the background, I told them this was a secret and urgent mission to find out whether the broadcast journalist category, which would offer new opportunities for members of their union as well as the announcers' group, had a chance to work from their perspective. I asked for confidentiality. It was granted, and I only hoped they would keep their word. While they must have figured out that something was happening in my world, they showed no inkling of knowing anything. It was time to pop the question: Could they see a time when members of the announce staff—including myself, of course—would be able to share jurisdiction with the Guild and allow the front person on newscasts to be more than a reader?

Their response was categorical. Almost in unison, they said, "No way," that they would fight that idea to the finish. While both took pains to point out that it was nothing personal against me, they felt I was being used as a "battering ram" to break through their jurisdiction and, if I were allowed to succeed, it would be a significant defeat for them. While accepting that they meant nothing personal, I was left to ponder the blinkered attitude that only outright victory for their side was acceptable and there was to be no acknowledgement that a compromise might be good for them as well as helping move the CBC forward into a new era and give it more equality with its ever-increasing competition. I also saw their dilemma. These well-meaning men would have had scorn heaped upon them by their own members if they had done anything else. The membership was clearly not ready for the kind of change being proposed. I chose not to argue; I was only collecting information, after all.

Back out in the bright September sunshine, the path ahead became much clearer. If I were to stay at the CBC, it would be a long and maybe even uglier fight with no sure victory at the end. Why not achieve what I wanted by moving across the street? Knowlton would later write that the guild had "frightened" me into leaving. Nonsense! What would be the wisdom in staying around for a fight I had little, if any, chance of winning? In my mind, the momentum was clearly shifting to CTV.

Going into our second and last meeting with CBC management just hours before the deadline, I had a bad case of nerves. The weight of the decision to leave my broadcast home after all those years, leaving an institution I was so strongly attached to and saying goodbye to friends and acquaintances seemed an overwhelming proposition. I realized that my own insecurities about my background were surfacing. Here was this uppity kid from Stratford with nothing more than a high school education preparing to spit in the face of the company that had broadened his horizons, taught him so much about his country and allowed him to grow into a major Canadian TV presence.

Competing with that understanding was the certain knowledge that my current position had to change or, at the age of forty-two, my career development would be stunted. I could probably hang on to *The National* for a while, but the changes sweeping the industry that saw generalists like myself and other announcers fading, and specialists in news, sports and other areas coming to the fore, could only mean that the CBC would be under pressure to have a fully involved journalist as its headliner, and I was not yet at that point. It was a classic head-and-heart battle and a watershed for me, as it turned out to be for the CBC in terms of dealing with on-air talent.

My stomach was in knots on that mid-September evening as I tried to eat a roast beef sandwich and a glass of milk just before entering Knowlton's office at CBC headquarters. Inside, and with news boss Michael Daigneault present, I made the point that because the CBC benefits package and its pension guarantees were so solid, the financial offer could probably be accepted with a few adjustments. The real obstacle, I said, centred on the nagging restrictions on the editorial side, and it was clear that the current approach of throwing me into the fray to try to break through these limitations was not working. Knowlton was shocked that I had talked to the union, but I could see no passion rising from behind the lenses of the Coke-bottle glasses he was famous for wearing in those days. In his book, he wrote that he knew "the cause was nearly lost" after I explained the negative outcome of my talks with the guild representatives. He and Mike had nothing new to offer and were clearly unprepared to deal on short notice with a problem that had taken up years of everyone's time and left so many walking wounded in its wake.

We shook hands with CBC brass one last time, and when I returned to the lawyers' office I was satisfied that we had studied everything and exhausted all options. I sat quietly stewing in an adjoining office for a long time while the lawyers waited for an answer. I paced back and forth as my stomach, weakened from the old ulcer complaints, began grinding in pain. Leaving would be a terrible wrench and extremely difficult but, after all that had gone down with the CBC, I felt my choice was clear.

Finally, and with little more than a hour to go before CTV's midnight deadline, I walked into the lawyers' room and mumbled, "Okay, let's do it. It's CTV." I contacted the CBC through Mike Daigneault first, as promised, giving two weeks' notice of my departure, all my agreement with the Corporation called for. He said he was sorry and made one last feeble stab at accommodation.

He offered to pick up my legal fees if I decided to stay. That was appreciated, but it was just too little and far too late. We wished each other luck and hung up. The next call, forty-five minutes before the deadline, was to CTV News vice-president Tom Gould. When Tom answered, I proclaimed, "Bulletin: Lloyd Robertson has just agreed to move to CTV." He responded, "Lloyd, you won't regret this and you'll come to appreciate what you've done." We met again at Tom Gould's townhouse, where, with Don Cameron, we toasted the new CTV News team of Lloyd Robertson and Harvey Kirck—or, if you prefer, every second week it would be Harvey Kirck and Lloyd Robertson. Tom proclaimed, "I know I've assured the survival of *CTV National News* for another ten years." (As it turned out, he was only out by twenty-five years. I remained in the anchor chair for thirty-five.) I also persuaded Gould and Cameron to hire Tim Kotcheff from the CBC to begin to further bolster the news service. There were certain admitted weaknesses that only a dynamo like Kotcheff could fix. It was one of the smartest moves I've made over the years.

Don Cameron reassured me that Harvey was ready to go and that there was a news conference being set up for noon the next day. The CTV anchor had been sent off to the affiliates for a week-long tour of the regions, obviously designed to keep him away from home base while the future of his newscast was in play. Over at the CBC the next morning, stagehands who were setting up for the Corporation's fall launch presentation were told to remove my pictures from the walls. They were astonished and questioned the action. "Down they come," they were told.

At the CTV news conference, where I sat beside a rumpled and tired Harvey Kirck, who had just flown in from Regina, I quipped that I'd negotiated him a pretty good contract. I had insisted that our pay be equal, taking away a potentially contentious issue between us. Harvey later said publicly that he was doing even better because he had asked for and received a thousand dollars more for every year he'd been at CTV, taking him to $12,000 more per annum than I was making. I never questioned or disputed the story. What did it matter at that point? Harvey admitted he had agreed to the team concept because he knew the CTV brass was insistent on change. We showed a comfortable togetherness, with Harvey saying, "I have great respect for Lloyd, despite his youthful appearance." I was determined not to show any anger or bitterness toward the CBC. I simply tried to explain that the long battle over union jurisdiction had been the prime reason for the move and did not criticize the CBC directly.

The friendly relations were not reciprocated. I was immediately yanked from the CBC's national newscast. No warm goodbyes for me—nothing like the on-set party NBC had thrown at about the same time to wish Barbara Walters well when she jumped from the network's *Today* show to become the first female co-anchor of an evening national newscast with Harry Reasoner at ABC, a match that proved not to be made in heaven. I was immediately marked as an outcast and spent the last two weeks cooling my heels and gathering mementos together. It seems incredible in the highly charged and competitive climate of TV that I could simply slip away on such short notice but, as a CBC staff announcer with no contractual language holding me back, two weeks' notice were all that was required. The departure, and my arrival at CTV, became an overnight media sensation, all played out on the public stage and punctuated with parting shots from the CBC.

The CBC's public relations managers kicked their well-oiled machine into high gear to make me look like a money-hungry mercenary. Mike Daigneault claimed that, as a Crown corporation, the CBC couldn't guarantee money over a period of time the way CTV, as a private company, could. This claim went unchallenged by the print press, even though the CBC had consistently guaranteed long-term contracts for Olympics and other events.

At least one politician had to try to make yards with the situation. Ed Broadbent, then leader of the New Democratic Party—while being interviewed, ironically, on a CTV public affairs show—described my reported $100,000-a-year salary as "scandalous" and said it meant I would be making more than the prime minister, with much less responsibility. He was promoting the idea of a fair-income policy in which governments would try to freeze everybody's pay at certain predetermined levels. I had met and interviewed Broadbent before, so I called to complain and remind him that I remained a member of ACTRA, the Canadian radio and TV artists union. He cheerily replied, "Nothing personal, Lloyd." To me, it was most certainly personal and seemed to reveal a mentality that sneered at people who aspired to advance themselves. None of the leader's rant affected my editorial approach to the NDP, and I bent over backwards to be sure that any coverage with which I was associated involving his party was completely fair and balanced. A few years afterward, I was happy to be pictured with the legendary Tommy Douglas, the former Saskatchewan CCF premier who had gone on to become the first leader of the new NDP and was widely regarded as the father of Canadian medicare. To me, he was never one to concern himself with abstract theory. He went into politics to do his best to help the less fortunate, and he never veered from that path.

While my fellow staff announcers at the CBC appeared universally enthusiastic about my move and sent warm congratulations, I was acutely aware of a lot of negative attitude flowing in my direction at the same time. It was akin to what the Australians call the tall poppy syndrome, whereby those who are seen to have become "too big for their britches" are targets of resentment and are "cut down." Was this some kind of colonial hangover that made those us who were born and grew up in the far reaches of the fading British Empire lesser mortals than our old-country counterparts? Perhaps so, but there could also have been a uniquely Canadian dimension to the phenomenon. American journalist Andrew Malcolm, who was the *New York Times* Canadian correspondent, wrote in the 1980s that when a Canadian wants to show how successful one of his compatriots is, he will say the person turned down offers from the United States. "Oh, he must be good then! The American offers confirm his quality. If the success is attained only at home, it can make friends and associates 'maliciously envious.'"

I like to think this country has matured since 1976. At the time of my move, most people in the employ of big companies, with perceived jobs for life, stayed put. It was considered foolhardy, even dangerous, to do otherwise. Since then, the average working Canadian can look forward to being with two, four, or more companies and even completely change career paths two or three times in a lifetime.

It took a while to get the message through that my jump to CTV was about a lot more than just money. Eventually, the early cheap shots about the "turncoat" and the burst of publicity over "the million-dollar baby in the five- and ten-cent store" (Knowlton's line for the times) began to wane, and a few newspaper columnists acknowledged that the real reason for the move was editorial involvement in the newscast. The most prominent among these was Scott Young, a senior writer and journalist of the time who was also musician Neil Young's father. In his column in *The Globe and Mail,* he slammed the CBC and Knowlton Nash for being "uncharacteristically simple-minded" in presenting my move as being all about money, and went on: "The interference of the Canadian Wire Service Guild with what Lloyd Robertson had a perfect right to think was his natural function—to go out and do some reporting from time to time—was intolerable and nobody with any guts would take it for long. After a certain stage money means little or nothing, but career fulfillment means more and more as a person gets older." Also, and to my great surprise, Bill Johnson, one of the most hard-boiled of the CBC newsroom militants, came over to me in the parking lot before I left to say "Congratulations, chum. That took guts."

The newspapers had a field day with the story for weeks afterward, and some of it was funny. Gary Lautens, a clever humourist with the *Toronto Star,* calculated that I had to be making about $400 for five minutes, or about $80 a minute. He said he didn't think the news he was hearing was worth that much and called for more stories about a kind of event he had witnessed where a motorcyclist in downtown Toronto was cruising along with a fully grown dog on his lap. "Now that's a lead story for a highly paid anchorman," he proclaimed. *The Globe and Mail* ran a story on potential replacements for me that included a picture of Raquel Welch, a sex symbol of the era. The CBC's *As It Happens,* with my friend Barbara Frum, did a series of mock on-air tryouts for the job, with politicians reading the opening lines of a fake newscast while I was called upon to judge them on their potential for anchoring *The National*.

But some of the joking had an edge and a purpose. For several weeks, the *Toronto Star*'s TV magazine ran a comic strip–style Lloyd lookalike contest. In one case, the winner was a fire hydrant at an intersection in downtown Toronto. Several of my colleagues were angry about *Star Week*'s approach and felt it was designed to cheapen me and take a shot at CTV for not being a serious contender for the public's attention where national news was concerned. That's exactly what was intended, of course, and it must have been complaints from their own readership that forced the *Star* to back off at the end of the year. They suddenly presented a form of apology, acknowledging that I had taken all of this abuse and never complained. They then wished me and my family a Merry Christmas.

The general public had a mixed reaction. Some were congratulatory, others chose to believe the welter of CBC publicity about my grabbing for riches, and still others, like the devoted CBC fan I met outside a general store in Temagami, Ontario, expressed puzzlement. She was a pleasant woman, possibly in her late forties, who just couldn't comprehend why anyone would leave the CBC. It was the national broadcaster, after all. It was "The Word" in Canada. In a gentle tone, she chided me: "Lloyd, I always liked you, but I won't be seeing you anymore. I just can't desert the CBC."

Such was the state of public consciousness; the CBC's grip on Canadians may have been waning, but it retained a powerful hold on their affections as the source that best expressed their identity and was still a treasured companion in their homes.

My longtime pal Craig Oliver, who had left the CBC for CTV

five years earlier, was stunned by my move. He had been called by Don Cameron a few weeks before it happened—woken up in the middle of the night, in fact. "Craig, I'm going to hire Lloyd away from the CBC, and maybe Kotcheff too." Craig thought Don had been drinking, didn't believe what he was hearing, and told him to go back to bed. I wouldn't have dared tell Craig anything about my plans—he might have let them slip out—but afterward, and with his typical flair for the cogent line, he summed up my feelings perfectly. "I know," he told me, "it's like being excommunicated from the Vatican."

Exactly! I was out of the comfortable cocoon of a Crown corporation with many of those who were still on the inside whispering that I'd regret my wayward actions and soon be crawling back. I had to admit to fighting a feeling of emptiness and a sense of loss while trying to savour my new status and look forward to the challenges.

While I had made my exit from Mother Corporation, I had yet to cut the umbilical cord. That shock was still to come a few months after the move.

12

Life with Harvey

ON OCTOBER 18, 1976, "THE HARVEY AND LLOYD" NEWSCAST was launched, and we would become the most enduring national anchor team in Canadian television history. Introducing me, Harvey said, "Lloyd Robertson joins us tonight for CTV News . . . and he couldn't have come on a busier news day." I opened with announcements of defeats for the Liberals in several by-elections held across the country that day. It seemed a turning point for me was also a crossroads for Pierre Trudeau's government. The country was tiring of the leader and the party, but it would still be two years before a general election in which Canadians would switch, and then only tentatively and briefly, to the newly crowned Progressive Conservative leader Joe Clark.

After the opening report, it was on to other news, and then we shared the camera for a segment of short feature stories that would become a popular item in the newscast. One of the oddest to capture our imagination on that night was that British Labour Party leader Michael Foot had a case of the shingles. At the end, having overcome a significant case of the butterflies at the top of the broadcast, I said, "We made it, Harvey," and we both spoke our goodnights. There were high-fives all around afterward, and the reviews the next day were quite favourable, with most saying that the new look, with its fresh set and double-anchor format, promised to give the CBC and its newly minted anchor, reporter Peter Kent, a run for it. Peter was a friend, and I was happy for him even though Knowlton Nash felt it necessary to make the point that he would earn "nowhere near" what I was collecting from CTV. In choosing Peter, a highly qualified journalist, and passing over my long-standing backup George Finstad, the CBC was signalling the dawn of a new era. George was an excellent announcer who also had reporting experience to his credit, but it didn't matter; we were in a watershed moment, and in spite of telling the public the job was open to all comers and categories, the CBC had decided to make a statement with its choice. George was an announcer, and I would be the last one from that group to sit in the main anchor chair at the network.

All went smoothly for me the first month or two at CTV. I was especially enjoying the chance to get more involved in my own copy and to occasionally go on the road to report back into the newscast with no hassles or restrictions. It was almost as though I was now a grown-up and had graduated from high school. While my reception from management and staff alike at CTV had been overwhelmingly positive, I was aware of certain pockets of discontent and resentment. The news division had been turned upside down, after all; not only had I come crashing into their lives, but I had brought with me the feisty Tim Kotcheff, with his piercing eyes surveying all before him as he prepared to make hard judgments on how to make their newscast better. Quite naturally, they felt they were doing just fine and that a little tweaking here or there was all that was needed—not the view of CTV management. Kotcheff, with his mandate for change in hand, made some immediate, positive moves that would nevertheless upset some of the newsroom veterans. He demanded crisper reports with more emphasis on clips from real people who would explain how the stories being reported had affected them, and he wanted room in the program for Harvey and me to be able to relate to one another rather than just presenting individual stories or doing voice-overs on edited film packages.

Tim was a true television animal who understood the medium and its power to reflect our lives and times in an interesting and compelling manner. While my move may have made a difference in public perception for CTV, Tim's crossing over achieved his bosses' goal of pumping up the organization behind the scenes.

For me, it wasn't a cakewalk, and I shouldn't have expected it would be. I had some proving to do, after all. My writing needed upgrading to the crisper, more direct style needed in a daily news program, where a lot of territory was being covered in a short time. I didn't miss the head-shaking and eyeball-rolling when my copy passed over the night producer's desk. There were also rumbles from those who felt they had been passed over when corporate bosses decided to go outside to boost the network's anchor presence, and from others who felt my hiring would encroach upon their territory.

Don Newman, CTV's Washington bureau chief, jumped to the CBC shortly after my arrival and became a featured and durable anchor on the public network's fledgling all-news channel, Newsworld. Although some contended that my arrival had thwarted his anchor ambitions, I understood it was nothing personal. Don and I got along beautifully, and I completely accepted that his move was simply to take advantage of a new opportunity. He and I continued a warm and friendly relationship for years afterward. CTV's Ottawa bureau chief, Bruce Phillips, a renowned veteran journalist, posed a different problem. He was outraged that I was being allowed to crowd into his territory on news specials. To him, I was a wet-behind-the-ears CBC announcer pulled in by panicked executives and allowed to be slotted near the top in a craft he had spent years honing to a fine art. Phillips was a tall, saturnine fellow who was given to dark moods and fell distinctly into the category of "dour Scot," among those still fighting the Battle of Culloden from 1745 that brought eventual union with the English. He told colleagues that if I could suddenly become a journalist just because I wanted to be, he could immediately become a brain surgeon if *he* wanted to be. Nevertheless, looking beyond his bitterness, I recognized Bruce was a formidable journalistic talent, both as a writer and an on-air presence. I could understand his objections and was appropriately solicitous of him whenever we were thrown together on a broadcast. It took three years, but after he worked beside me all evening on election night in 1979, when Joe Clark's Conservatives won a minority government, Bruce finally acknowledged that CTV management had made the right move in recruiting me from the CBC.

When people ask me about the differences between the CBC and CTV, I frequently point to one of my first specials for the private network. I was dispatched to Montreal for one of the momentous events of the period: the election of René Lévesque and his separatist Parti Québécois. Tim Kotcheff was the commander on the bridge in the control room when we decided we had to seize the whole network, once it became clear that the Liberals under Robert Bourassa were going down to defeat. This would be a historic night; we would see the election of the first government in Quebec officially dedicated to taking the province out of Confederation, albeit under the euphemistic term sovereignty-association. During my excited, rapid-fire introduction to the dramatic events unfolding, I began to hear Kotcheff in my earpiece saying, "Lloyd . . . cut . . . hold it!" Assuming we were still on air, I galloped on and then heard loudly, "Lloyd! Stop! We're not going anywhere." Indeed, we weren't yet patched into the network, which at CTV was always a more complicated and contentious procedure than at Mother Corp. Even after I started all over again, the British Columbia affiliate decided it would not pick up the network feed, believing that its audience couldn't care less about separatists being elected in Quebec. Too much attention was already being paid to the complaints of spoiled Quebecers, in their view.

I was learning that the CTV network, which was contracted to provide its affiliates across the country with forty hours of programming each week, was very effectively managed. But the members of the highly experienced television team, including president Murray Chercover, the dapper entertainment VP Arthur Weinthal and the effervescent director of programming Philip "Pip" Wedge, were often treated like second-class citizens by the very people they sought to serve so well. In many ways, though, it was a more accurate representation of the country, with its regional differences and spats between federal and provincial levels of authority.

On the news side, if the CBC was the giant ocean liner sailing comfortably along with more than adequate resources, CTV was the tugboat trying to occasionally ram the liner from the side, and often enough making an embarrassing dent. There was an immediate ratings surge as a result of the huge publicity leading up to the Harvey–Lloyd launch. Some were tuning in to assess whether this unusual pairing was really going to work. The numbers then settled in above where they had been before the two-man team made its debut, sometimes about even or a little above the CBC. News, which is a daily television staple, has to be measured in the long run. If the ratings are trending downward over a period of several months, you know there is a problem, but if they are maintaining the perceived average range and soaring during high-interest, heavy news periods, you can breathe easier.

As the weeks rolled by in the fall of '76, right across the country most agreed that Harvey and I were clicking well together—perhaps because, as he explained in his book *Nobody Calls Me Mr. Kirck*, we presented such different images for the viewer. "There was an interesting contrast between us. . . . Lloyd, neat and trim, rather serious, and perfectly poised behind the desk; me, the rumpled one, slouching, sartorially less than elegant." As we warmed to each other in those early times, we even managed to turn what could have been a nasty episode into a mock-serious little play.

With Harvey standing over six feet tall and me at about five foot seven, Tim Kotcheff had ordered our floor director to crank up my chair each night so I would appear to be sitting even with Harvey instead of having him tower over me. Each night, my chair would be heightened, and Harvey, who instantly noticed what was going on, would come in and raise his even higher. The first night it happened, I looked askance, but then I began laughing about it, as did the crew and eventually everybody on the show, including the two principals. We had fun letting the story seep out and get to the gossipy CBC insiders, who would be anxious to speculate that Harvey and Lloyd weren't getting along and would cite this as an example of the beginning of dissension that would soon get out of control and cause CTV's pet two-anchor project to collapse in ruins. Ultimately, Kotcheff, with his innate inventiveness, let Harvey crank his chair to the top, and then he put a platform under me that would solve the problem and have us sitting evenly. Harvey and I had many a laugh as we told this story to friends over the years.

Harvey could sometimes be stubborn and difficult, but he had what could be described as a "good soul." He had a hearty laugh and was great fun to relax with, although he admitted he had too much of an acquired taste for alcohol, which would eventually threaten his career and reputation. While we enjoyed a celebratory drink after our first month together, we had no idea that thunderbolts were heading for us from two different directions.

Harvey was about to undergo a public humiliation. First, though, it was my turn. In early December, I received what seemed an innocuous call from an old CBC pal that was to lead into a nightmare, straining my relationship with CTV and prompting me to offer my resignation to the network after less than three months on the job.

Cliff Lonsdale was the executive producer of *The National* at the CBC. He was a tall, thin, talented man, always bursting with energy, and was one of the best TV news writers the country had ever seen. Cliff wanted to let me know that the news union had withdrawn its grievance against my Vancouver activities and that, had I still been working at the CBC, the way would have been clear for me to do all the things I had wanted. Instead of simply thanking him and leaving it at that, I foolishly engaged him in a fantasy of what might have been. Even though the verdict was handed down "without prejudice" and could be challenged in law, I was curious about this strange action and called a few other people at the CBC, including chief news editor Mike Daigneault, to confirm what was happening and to clarify its meaning. Somewhere, in an unguarded moment during those conversations, I may have left the impression of wanting to return to the Corporation. I knew, of course, that this was impossible and could never happen without severe damage to myself and CTV.

About two days after these conversations, *Globe and Mail* reporter Barbara Yaffe was investigating the rumour that was floating around about my return to the public network. I was alerted to this by CTV public relations people and delayed talking to Yaffe while I tried to figure out what was going on. Without my knowledge, she managed to get Nancy on the phone and, with clever coaxing, gathered just enough information to begin piecing together what the *Globe* seemed to think was a major story. At this point, I called Yaffe and tried to explain that, while I had had a few informal phone chats with CBC people, I had no intention of returning. That didn't stop the *Globe* from blasting a headline on its front page saying, "CTV's got him, but Lloyd longs for CBC," with a huge accompanying photo from the CBC archives in which I am striking a faintly sad pose. The editors jumped on every thread they could find to support their apparent conclusion that I was going back to the CBC in spite of my claims to the contrary. Nancy was quoted as saying, "After twenty-two years, he still hasn't lost his love for the CBC." Daigneault told Yaffe that if assertions that I would remain with CTV were printed, "the story won't be accurate." Clearly, the *Globe* chose to believe him rather than the central subject of the story—me.

The moment the first edition of the paper hit the stands on a Friday night in early December, the *Toronto Star* called me, and I immediately denied I would be returning to the Corporation, saying I was "happy with CTV." The *Star* ran the story on an inside page and showed me smiling out at the camera, along with the quote, "Why would I want to return to an organization that put me through considerable agony when they should have moved to fix a thorny problem regarding union jurisdiction years ago?" I had a short, sharp conversation with Knowlton Nash early on Saturday morning in which I accused his organization of trying to destroy me. He denied leaking the information to the *Globe*, saying he knew such a move would end any chance of getting me back, and suggested the union or perhaps even CTV may have been responsible. While I believed Knowlton when he said he was not the leaker, the possibility that CTV had leaked the news was ridiculous. The network had had no knowledge of the conversations until they had heard the same rumours as everyone else, and when this happened they had contacted me immediately.

The *Star*'s story was enough to quiet the turmoil I'd set off in the CTV executive suite, but it would be some time before there was a return to normalcy. President Murray Chercover was kind and considerate during these troubles and refused absolutely to even consider my resignation. Indeed, he seemed to understand that, while I had moved to his network for all the right reasons on paper, a piece of my heart still resided at the CBC.

The actions of the Corporation in this bizarre affair served to root out any residual feelings of the pain of departure I might have had, and for sometime afterward I was in a blind fury at the CBC.

The late Blaik Kirby, television columnist for the *Globe,* told me that the leak of my conversations had indeed come from inside the CBC and did not originate with the honourable Cliff Lonsdale. I could only surmise that others had decided it was a way to get even with Robertson for jumping ship. By giving the information about my conversations to someone on the inside whose interests would be affected by my return, they could get the story planted with the *Globe* and either get me back inside and neutralize me in a lesser position, like doing the overnight news on radio, or cause a major embarrassment for CTV and its spanking new anchor team.

A few days after that dreadful weekend, I found myself inter-viewing Richard Hatfield, the former Progressive Conservative premier of New Brunswick, who had gone through many ups and downs with the press. He noted wryly, "So now you know what it's like." Indeed, I did know what it was like to be caught in the middle of a media firestorm. It was a true learning experience to be on the other side and witness how a few inconclusive phone conversa-tions could be taken and spun into front-page news.

As it turned out, the affair had a salutary effect on both me and the private network. It spurred me to work even harder to prove my worth as a broadcast journalist. While the distressing incident, totally played out on the public stage, made for one of the worst weekends of my life, my father's words of wisdom from a Bible passage—"This too shall pass"—sustained me in the dark times.

For several weeks afterward, there were constant rumblings that I would be heading back to the CBC, tail between my legs. Nothing could have been further from the truth. When a stranger stopped me in a Toronto airport to ask about that possibility, I turned to the man with a look of mock horror and a thinly veiled smile, telling him I would rather go to a 100-watt station north of the Arctic Circle than return to the everlasting shenanigans of the vicious, manipulative bureaucracy that so dominated the public network.

I still have a farewell letter from the CBC president of the time, Al Johnson, who graciously thanked me for my contribution during twenty-two years at his network. He complimented me on my "professionalism and dedication" and wished me "continued success." Johnson, of course, was the same person who couldn't be reached, allegedly until the last minute, when I was trying to make a decision about whether to stay or jump to CTV. As far as I was concerned, he had made no valiant effort to keep me there beyond what his managers were offering, yet many years later I was to hear something different.

At an event in Toronto to honour South African president Nelson Mandela, Nancy and I found ourselves at the same table as Al Johnson and his wife. During a pleasant conversation, the former CBC head proclaimed, "If it had been up to me, I would have broken both your legs to keep you at the Corporation." I almost choked on my soup, but stayed composed. Nancy had to turn away to stop from bursting into laughter. Actually, I appreciated his intention in voicing the sentiment and thanked him for it—no harm done twenty years and three CBC anchors later, but it was totally unrelated to what had transpired.

In retrospect, and I'm happy about this, the move brought positive results for all my successors in the anchor chair of *The National*. Peter Kent, Knowlton Nash and Peter Mansbridge would enjoy much more editorial freedom, their salaries would certainly move higher, and the CBC would be less inclined to take those on the front lines of its network for granted.

Knowlton moved into the CBC anchor chair in 1978 amid accusations that he had given himself the job. Our friendship had been badly ruptured during the period of my departure and just afterward, but we struck up a renewed relationship as on-air talent, exchanging anecdotes and industry gossip, and have remained friends and kept contact ever since. In spite of the complaints against him, Knowlton looked to be the perfect fit for the anchor position. He had the news and presentation credentials the Corporation desperately needed after my replacement, the charming and amiable Peter Kent, left suddenly after only two years in the chair. Peter continued a successful broadcasting career before ending up in the political world, which seemed, for him, a natural place to land. Knowlton stepped down in 1988 after ten years as anchor to make way for the durable Peter Mansbridge.

As to the scars and bitterness accumulated through those bruising encounters with unions and the CBC, I have always believed it is better to try to shed old hurts and bad feelings and move on to enjoy and appreciate the banquet of life. Taking the high road, seeing life in its larger dimensions, is always better and is, after all, what a seasoned observer of life, like an experienced news person, is supposed to be able to do.

As I came to enjoy the lively spirit and cut and thrust of the private network, I began to feel a new energy, a sense of freedom and rebirth. There seemed a more freewheeling attitude in the CTV newsroom; all that mattered was getting to the story first and getting it right. Dark hints from some columnists that we were controlled by our advertisers turned out not to be true, from what I could see. In fact, we were never even aware which companies or organizations bought time in the broadcast—during commercial breaks, our studio monitors were in black. The private network was well aware that any apparent interference from advertisers would quickly diminish the credibility of its news service. That is not to say some enterprises hadn't tried to influence the network, and the news division in particular, in the past, but they were shut down by network employees who knew the poison that could be spread by the suggestion that any portion of our program content was controlled by outside interests. Historically, attempts through the years by advertisers to influence content on private networks pales when compared to the attempts of governments of various political stripes to put pressure on the CBC.

I also came to realize that my jump to the private sector had been a humiliating blow for homebodies at the CBC. Here was the person who represented the face of their news service, and he had walked across the street to work for people who, in their minds, weren't in broadcasting for any high-minded purpose of public service but were simply there to make money. The privates were obligated under the terms of their licences to do news programs, but those within the CBC regarded private-sector TV news as dumbed-down travesties of what real journalism should be about—"cookie-cutter news," as one of them described it. This was blatant, self-serving drivel, and that old arrogant attitude was an insult to many of the fine journalists who had moved to CTV from the CBC for many different reasons, or who had come in from other journalistic organizations to be part of the effort of building private TV in Canada. These journalists became too numerous to mention after a while, but they included Bill Cunningham, Michael Maclear and Craig Oliver, to name only a few.

Since my move, the CBC has mellowed in its attitude to the private sector. There is finally an acknowledgement that it's here to stay, so the folks on the inside should just get on with their business and decide how to position themselves in the challenging multichannel universe.

Through all the fuss emanating from the TV side in those years, my old stomping ground of CBC Radio quietly, and with impressive sure-footedness, found a place for itself in the vast spectrum of media, and remains highly regarded and treasured as an indispensable source of information and original Canadian entertainment. The same path should be available to CBC Television. I don't pretend to have an answer to its ills; many good people much better equipped than I have tried to fix it. Given its government funding and the new demands for accountability, it desperately needs a clear purpose and direction. For too long, CBC Television has swayed back and forth between whether it should look like its brothers and sisters on the commercial side, with occasional breaks for programs like *The Nature of Things,* or be more clearly defined as a public broadcaster. It has dallied too long to find a middle ground between these two extremes. It comes as no surprise that calls for it to be "distinctive" are more urgent than ever. Let's be clear: Canada will always need a prominent national public broadcaster. To try to kill off the CBC would be ludicrous. It is a national institution many still cherish, and at its best it has faithfully reflected the Canadian experience through several generations. The CBC is woven into our historical fabric; its problems are surely fixable if its leadership, with sincere support from various levels of government and Canadian society, can find the right vision and then pull behind it.

For my part, I was happy to have spent my early growth years at the CBC. I'll always be grateful for the grounding in the history and idiosyncrasies of my country, and for the way in which the career path I had chosen as a youngster began to take shape.

It took me a while to regain my sea legs after the potentially career-ending debacle over the leak from the CBC, but just as Harvey and I were beginning to sail again, Harvey's drinking problems hit the headlines. He had been charged a second time with impaired driving, and on this occasion there would be no mercy. Newspapers and other media ran the story prominently, and it was noted that he would have to serve time. I pleaded with him not to appeal the conviction, fearing that a loss would prompt another round of sharply negative publicity as the media, fed all the juicy details by Crown lawyers, seemed determined to make him the poster boy of the ever-escalating campaign against drunk driving. He honestly felt the appeal should go ahead, and his lawyer had him convinced there was a good chance to clear his name because of alleged irregularities surrounding his arrest. But the judge concluded that Harvey should not have been behind the wheel in his condition and, sure enough, the appeal was rejected. I vividly recall the headlines in the newspapers and blaring from radio and TV while Harvey and I entered a reception for advertisers where the fall season's programs were being presented.

There were awkward moments all around, but as Harvey tells us in his book, the network's wonderful head of public relations, Marge Anthony, saved the day by grabbing him by the arm and leading him, chin up and head first, into the fray, facing down with a ferocious glare anyone who would dare come near to challenge.

CTV management was understandably furious with Harvey and insisted that his name be taken off the credits at the top of the newscast, allowing his future at the network to become shrouded in doubt. I made the point to them that, as far as I was

concerned, his personal problems would not affect our relationship in any way, and if his name was being removed from the
visual credits at the top of the news, my own should disappear
as well. They concurred, and all that appeared for several weeks
was onscreen signage for *CTV National News.* In the newsroom,
we joked about our "no-name newscast." While the viewers may
not have noticed much about that, they were certainly aware of
Harvey's difficulties, and he wisely chose to stay off the news
for an entire summer, spending the time on his boat cruising the
shining lakes, bays and inlets of central Ontario around Georgian
Bay. While uncertainty hung over his return, a meeting of the
CTV board settled the matter in dramatic fashion.

According to sources close to the gathering, John Bassett,
owner of Toronto's CFTO and a big, gruff and dominating presence in any setting, challenged the other owners to state whether
they had never done anything wrong, never made a mistake or
done something they would live to regret at some point in their
lives. There were no takers for the challenge. It was enough to
assure Harvey's return to the anchor desk as we put the personal
dramas behind us and turned our full attention to the work of
building *CTV National News.* All told, we spent seven and a half
years together.

Life with Harvey was sometimes tumultuous, occasionally
precarious, but never dull. We succeeded in extending our strong
professional relationship into a deep personal bond. Nancy and I
were often guests while he and his delightful, diminutive dynamo
of a wife, Brenda, took us cruising around Georgian Bay, where
we were invited to meet their friends in the boating fraternity.

Viewers asked how we accounted for our success together in
the hurly-burly of TV, with its tender egos and highly charged

atmosphere. Well, first we came to like and trust each other; Harvey appreciated that I had stuck by him during his tough times and, to me, our friendship and the history of our times together meant more than trying to seize advantage and push him out of the way. It was tough for Harvey to have to share the anchor duties after so many years on his own, but, like me, he was practical and knew we had to make it work or we could bring grievous harm to ourselves, certainly on a professional level and personally as well. Canadian TV plays on a relatively small stage; most of the participants know each other at one time or another, and disputes between personalities, while inevitable, are remembered for the wounds they leave.

After a few years, in March of 1984, with his image polished up and having achieved twenty years on *CTV National News,* Harvey decided it was time to step down. He wouldn't be out of sight, but would be giving up the onerous duties of five nights a week. I would be flying solo again. Harvey moved on to create special segments for *Canada AM* and eventually took on the role of lovable curmudgeon on *W5,* a role similar to that of Andy Rooney on the CBS current-affairs magazine show *60 Minutes.*

Harvey's final exit from the network was a sad travesty. He had to read in the newspapers that his contract was not being renewed. He was the victim of one of the many cutbacks CTV was making. Harvey never forgave his former bosses or the network that had made him a household name.

Fortunately, he and I remained friends, and I always treasured his gruff honesty and continued loyalty to me. He suffered heart trouble for several years before his death of congestive heart failure in 2002 at the age of seventy-three. He was the gentle giant that everyone thought him to be.

13

The Mantle of Leadership

IN 1984, WHEN CTV RETURNED TO THE SINGLE-ANCHOR format, Don Cameron decided it was time to elevate my status to chief anchor, senior editor. In his usual understated fashion, Cameron said, "I guess you've earned this." The senior editor title was not handed out lightly. It meant that my role would now be elevated to carry more clout in the daily ritual of putting the news program together.

Don was also sending a signal to the news community that Robertson had attained the full status of a journalist and, given the old warrior's impeccable credentials, most wouldn't argue. I had matured, or so I believed, from the early days before my stint on the CBC's *The National* when Peter Trueman described me to Knowlton Nash as "plastic and shallow" while objecting to my appointment as anchor. At the time, Peter was in CBC news management and would be my first supervisor upon taking the anchor chair. To his credit, Peter never displayed anything other than total support for my efforts. Shortly afterward he accepted a reporting role on the CBC local news side and was later chosen as the principal news anchor for Global, which fulfilled his apparent ambition to be a front man. I had great respect and affection for Peter, but understood that he was one of those former print reporters who believed that unless you were an ink-stained wretch from the newspaper side of the business, you were just one of those "plastic" TV people who could be good performers but were inadequately equipped for the rigours of the craft of journalism.

Obviously, there were some CBC announcers who were either not interested in pursuing a journalistic role or were not suited to the task. Don Cameron knew better than anyone that my attempt to move from announcer to full-fledged news person would present challenges and foster resentments, regardless of the experience I had gathered in news and broadcasting. He and the CTV management group, headed by Murray Chercover, never faltered in their unwavering support and encouragement. Cameron knew that I would have to perform with flair as an anchor of the newscast and news specials, as well as in any field reports, and dare not stumble under the hard-eyed gaze of TV critics, competitors or members of the journalistic community who were perched to pounce on the slightest indication that I was not up to the job.

Don also advised that I take the responsibility of senior editor seriously, but not the rights—which meant not to start throwing my weight around too much in the newsroom. It made sense to me. I had been around long enough to know that while television needed inspiring leadership, it also had to be a team game. The title of senior editor, by the way, doesn't necessarily refer to age. In TV it can mean whatever management decides, and in this case, it gave me the right to prepare and edit all of the news copy I would be reading on air as well as play a leading role with the producers in determining which stories would be a part of the nightly broadcast. I never pressed for final say because, ultimately, in serious matters, that has to rest with the president of the news department. In latter years, after I had gained so much experience covering various stories, editors and producers would just naturally turn to me for guidance anyway.

The eighties brought the age of the "anchor gorilla" in network news. It was a time when considerable power began to flow to the person out front. Dan Rather was the poster boy for this approach. When he took over upon Walter Cronkite's retirement from CBS in 1981, he held to the view that if he was to be successful, he would have to exercise broad powers through the entire system. To him, that meant he had to have his hands in every corner of CBS News, from the hiring and firing of on-air reporters to the comings and goings of all the editorial and production staff. This approach quite naturally spread through the industry and contributed to the blooming, beyond all logical proportion, of various anchor egos. *The Mary Tyler Moore Show*'s pompous and puffed-up Ted Baxter of the 1970s reflected, in hilarious extremes, the dim-witted dandies who allegedly occupied some of the anchor chairs in local U.S. markets. When Mary asked Ted about a certain story he had read on the news one night, he replied, "I don't know. I wasn't listening."

In Dan Rather's case, he was a great newsman but not a comfortable communicator, and when NBC and ABC moved in Tom Brokaw and Peter Jennings for their solo front men, Rather began a slide from which he never recovered. The great *CBS Evening News*, which had sailed like a golden galleon in the sixties and seventies during Walter Cronkite's era, was destined to languish in third place in the ratings for a long time.

Although I regarded the trend of the all-powerful anchor

as excessive and silly, some felt it was fair. Anchor positions are pressure-cooker jobs, and the success of the entire news division often revolves around that one person. The anchor also becomes a talisman for the network itself; he or she is expected to be behave as though the network's call letters were inscribed on their forehead, and there is always the concern that a wrong move, like a drunk-driving charge, can plunge not just the news division, but the good name of the network, into a swirl of bad publicity. It is a high-stakes game; ratings matter. A well-liked and respected anchor can develop a strong bond with viewers that is akin to making that personality a part of the family on a daily basis. Trust is key, and a good anchor connects in a tangible way through his or her own personality so that the audience feels comfortable following them through the often-confusing diet of daily news and wants to be with them for live coverage of major national and international events: elections, moons shots, the outbreak of war or federal budgets.

While a good anchor can't guarantee the success of a news program—the skills of the reporting staff and the quality of the production matter enormously—a poor communicator is sure to have a negative impact. And it is a complicated and subtle matter. For example, Katie Couric was already established as a good communicator when she was hired as anchor to replace Dan Rather at CBS. But the way she addressed the camera during the newscast and her work on news specials often seemed tentative and lacking in strength and gravitas when required. She couldn't nudge CBS out of the basement in the network dinner-hour news ratings. In fact, the broadcast sank further into the dumpster, and after five years Couric moved to ABC and back into a magazine/interview format, the kind of programming that had brought her to prominence on the *Today* show at NBC. Since Couric had been the first woman to become the solo lead anchor on a major U.S. network, some critics were quick to pounce on her. This proved, some dared to whisper, that a woman would not be taken seriously as a network anchor. Nonsense! Being a good anchor has nothing to do with gender. Only an individual's suitability for the job matters. For example, take Diane Sawyer, who assumed the anchor chair at ABC and proceeded to prove to the world that she had the stuff to do it all. Sawyer is powerful in every respect: she gets right inside a story when she is doing a special from the studio or a newscast in the field, and when she's at the desk introducing other reporters' pieces, she gives a sense of knowing what the story is about, and her copy conforms to her smooth, reserved and appealing style. And when she does brief interviews at the desk, you know from her speech and body language that's she is involved and she cares. Her political background as a young aide to Richard Nixon in the seventies gave her an early window into the workings of Washington. She speaks with authority when covering politics. Yes, she is the perfect female anchorperson. Our own Lisa LaFlamme has many of the same attributes and has more field-reporting experience than Sawyer. Destiny is on her side.

News departments, if run seriously, are often expensive operations. It takes a lot of money to cover stories properly, and while corporate bosses understand the importance of news divisions to the credibility of their organizations, they also prefer to find positive balance sheets from newsrooms at the end of the fiscal year. In private TV, good ratings can help boost advertising, and many sponsors like to be associated with a popular news program that they believe enhances the credibility of their own product. At the CBC, ratings have to be reasonably good or the brass worry about rumblings from Parliament that too many tax dollars are being spent on an institution not enough Canadians care to watch. The heat is always on the anchor to ensure that potential viewers are not turned away by his or her idiosyncrasies or the inadequacy of the final presentation.

While the title of senior editor accorded me the same rights as anchors on other networks who may have been called managing editors or chief correspondents, I decided it was better to ease into the role—to constantly consult, and try to spot good people who could help to continue the building of a successful and credible broadcast. To me, this was the grown-up approach to the job. Walter Cronkite had said some years earlier that "no one should be sitting in the anchor chair before the age of fifty." He felt that, especially in national and international news, the anchor had to have a breadth of experience and hopefully have amassed some collected wisdom that could be brought to the table to help audiences understand events unfolding in front of them and place them in context. Most of all, in my view, a good front person understands that TV news is really a team game. As former PBS anchor Jim Lehrer put it, "When I look in the mirror in the morning, I am saying this day is not all about me." Exactly!

While CTV didn't have the resources or the number of people to throw into the field that our CBC friends did, the network had already become expert at targeting the stories that mattered to people, getting to them quickly and, often enough, leaving our opposition in the dust. When it worked, it was an exhilarating feeling: "Yea team!" was a common call in the newsroom.

My opposition at the CBC when I flew solo again was Knowlton Nash. He had been in the chair over five years by this time and was judged to be doing reasonably well as he became accustomed to the unrelenting gaze fixed upon an anchor. He had to endure countless spoofs on his manner of saying "good night." It was the kind of send-off a grandmother might yell from her front porch to a grandchild as the little one was departing; something like "Good-nighhh-t." It provided fodder for comedy shows month after month. Knowlton might have taken comfort in the old saying that the only thing worse than bad publicity is no publicity. Anyway, it's fun to be spoofed unless it cuts a little too close to the bone, as that joke may well have done.

Knowlton was also learning that life on the nightly front line was much more exposed than even the highest-profile bureau-crat's position. In his second week on the job, in 1978, an enter-tainment weekly published the ratings showing that the numbers for *The National* were dropping, trailing those of *CTV National News* by about 25,000 viewers. Much was made of it at the time, but the two news programs had traditionally been running close in the ratings and CTV's time of permanent ratings dominance was still ahead of us.

In January of 1982, the CBC moved its news out of the eleven-o'clock time slot and, combined with the current-affairs show *The Journal*, occupied the hour from ten to eleven. It turned out to be a winner for them and, oddly enough, helped CTV, prob-ably because there were enough Canadians who simply didn't want to abandon the eleven-o'clock habit and came over to us. For news junkies in this period before the rise of all-news chan-nels, it was a bonanza. They got to watch both national newscasts at different times.

A few years later, it was decided to add the chief anchor to the annual *Conversation with the Prime Minister,* a CTV staple that had started in 1966 when the ubiquitous Charles Templeton, the former evangelist who, in one of his many career incarnations, was head of CTV News, sat down to talk with Prime Minister Lester B. Pearson. It eventually became a full hour during Pierre Trudeau's time in office, when Bruce Phillips led the year-end conversations, before giving way to Pamela Wallin when he accepted an appointment to Washington from the incoming government of Brian Mulroney. Now my pal Craig Oliver was returning from his stint in Washington to resume his duties as Ottawa bureau chief, and we began a long run, paired up on these interviews, that took us through the terms of three prime ministers.

It cemented still further a long-term friendship that started originally because we were both small-town boys from poor families with no post-secondary education who happened to find themselves working together in the early years of the exciting new medium of television. Our friendship endured the turbulence all too common in the incestuous high-stakes world of TV news.

Craig and I shared many similarities: we were shunted around as youngsters when our parents, for various reasons, couldn't look after us; we started in small radio stations, where we did everything, including sweep the floor; we had never worked at newspapers; we shared a passion for the broadcast industry as well as for history and the beauty of the English language. We had both had to become self-reliant at an early age, and this had made us more collaborative because we knew that, in most cases, we had to go along to get along.

We came to watch each other's backs and share secrets, but Craig was adamant about one thing: he insisted I never tell him when I was stepping away from the news, because he knew he couldn't keep that secret to himself for long. Craig could quote long passages of poetry and late into the night, after a few drinks, could be called upon to give us a complete word-for-word recitation of "The Shooting of Dan McGrew."

Craig was the smarter of the two of us, but he could be more impetuous, and while he was right far more often than he was wrong, I could bring a measured balance to the table when he was about to rush forward on a story by saying, "Hang on, pal. Have we really thought this one through?" Our frequent debriefs on the *CTV National News,* and Craig's clipped but friendly "Goodnight, Lloyd" sign-offs delighted audiences and became a popular staple of our nightly broadcasts.

The CTV *Conversations* with the various prime ministers took us through fifteen years at the peaks of our respective careers. First up for the two of us together was Brian Mulroney. We agreed that I would take a softer approach while Craig could home in with the tougher questions on the more controversial subjects of the year. The idea was that I could stabilize the atmosphere should the talk become too heated. There were always serious matters to discuss, and with Mulroney's activist agendas on free trade and the Constitution, there was always plenty to feast on.

There is a still a picture of the two of us interviewing Mulroney, with the PM and me decked out in jackets and ties and Craig looking uncomfortable in a turtleneck sweater. It was supposed to be a relaxed and informal setting at Meech Lake in the Gatineau Hills, where the critical conferences on Quebec and the constitution took place, but the rules were changed at the last minute and Craig wasn't prepared. Fortunately, I had brought along a shirt and tie. Craig was left to fidget uncomfortably during the whole interview while the cameras recorded him for posterity as dressed down for the occasion.

In person, Mulroney was gregarious, affable and very human. He always asked about family and colleagues and was filled with charm and good humour. In the eighties, he and his wife, Mila, invited several journalists and their families for social occasions at 24 Sussex Drive. Mila and Brian together were the impeccable host and hostess. She was always radiant and beautiful, and he took charge and escorted the wives through the house. Nancy remembers being shown the space Margaret Trudeau had used as a study and hobby room and, like all the other women in the group, was bowled over by the prime minister's warmth and charm. Some journalism purists argued at the time that news people compromised themselves by attending these functions. But I would contend that it helps to see the prime minister and his family in these kinds of situations; to have informal chats about incidental matters and learn more about what motivates the person who heads our government; to hear about his or her passions and interests and whether these will have an impact on the ways in which the prime minister shapes the nation's policies.

Brian Mulroney was always a fascinating challenge for those assigned to interview him. Before sitting down to get serious, he was the master of bonhomie: cracking jokes, telling tales and often ranting about his opponents in language that could turn the air blue. When the cameras rolled, the persona was transformed into someone who was immediately identified as pompous and self-serving. Occasionally, we might get him to relax, but it was rare.

He could be a formidable force when cornered or agitated, as I was to discover during a taping of his personal story. The former prime minister had written a book about his life and times, and CTV had acquired the television rights with me as interviewer

throughout. The incident happened off camera. Mulroney had
learned that his very capable and trusted aide, Luc Lavoie, had
agreed—in keeping with standard practice—that there would be
no limitations on the questions to be asked. It was the summer
of 2007 and there was an uncorroborated story floating about
that, after he left office, Mulroney had accepted cash payments
from German-Canadian businessman Karlheinz Schreiber. At
the time, Mulroney seemed to be on the brink of putting the
matter to rest; the revelations about where the cash was allegedly
given, how much, and under what conditions would come later
from Schreiber on the CBC's current-affairs program *The Fifth
Estate*. Mulroney hit the roof when Luc told him we might ask
about the alleged cash payments. He stormed toward producer
Anton Koschany and me and let loose, insisting this wasn't part
of the deal, it wasn't in his book and we had no right to ask him
questions about Schreiber. We took the position that our interpretation of Luc's conversations gave us the right to broach the
subject. Besides, Luc was a former newsman for the TVA network in Quebec and knew that we would have looked foolish if
we hadn't, at the very least, asked about the building controversy.
So there was the former prime minister, toe to toe with producer
and anchor, fulminating at full force that there was "no [expletive
deleted] way" we were going to ask him anything about Schreiber
and the money. The storm passed as quickly as it had erupted as
we held our ground and Mulroney had more consultations with
Luc. On the final day of our tapings, I asked on camera about the
reports of cash payments. Mulroney dismissed the subject, saying, "I have won every battle in the courts to this time and will
continue to win."

A few months later, after Schreiber came forward, Mulroney

admitted to accepting $225,000 for work he claimed to have done for the businessman. It was sad to see his reputation stained but, in the end, the image of a former prime minister accepting envelopes of cash had given his legion of ardent detractors all the ammunition they needed.

In spite of these personal failings, Brian Mulroney still gets high marks for his accomplishments as prime minister on free trade and the environment, and his noble effort to get Quebec's signature on the Canadian constitution through the Meech Lake Accord. I talked with other journalists who, like myself, had fought hard to be fair to Mulroney, often over loud guffaws from colleagues, and were prepared to give him the benefit of the doubt. We will always wonder, "What was he thinking?" None of this changes the warm personal feelings the man can evoke through his charm, his loyalty to good friends, and his unmistakable passion for a better Canada.

Craig and I had developed a deep love of Canada during our years covering the country from all corners, and we approached the 1995 referendum vote on sovereignty-association with great trepidation. I recall vividly his remark to me as we tested our broadcast facilities on that historic evening in late October: "I'm scared as hell, Lloyd." Indeed, as we launched our show, it began to look as though the Yes side, in support of loosening and ultimately breaking ties with the rest of Canada, was on its way to winning. We had read the polls and watched the frantic final few days of the federal government's campaign to try to stem the tide of Quebecers' apparent desire to break away.

The studio, which belonged to our Montreal affiliate CFCF, was tense as I helmed our broadcast team, which included former Saskatchewan premier Roy Romanow. He was a model of moderation as we all tried to keep our cool in the face of impending disaster for the country.

Finally, after what seemed like an interminable first hour and a half, it became clear that the No side was going to win, but just barely. The separatist leaders immediately displayed their frustrations at the outcome. Gilles Duceppe of the Bloc Québécois skulked away from our set without goodbyes to anyone, and Jacques Parizeau uttered his famous line that they had lost because of "big money and the ethnic vote." I ended the night by looking into the camera and saying: "Whew. We made it ... and Canada is still in one piece." We looked over the precipice that night, and what we saw was a country squabbling for years over Quebec's departure while the dollar sank and our economy collapsed. Fortunately, we were able to step back from the brink.

Two months later, Craig and I found ourselves sitting down for the year-end conversation with Prime Minister Jean Chrétien. Like most of the others, the talk was conducted at the guest house on the grounds of Rideau Hall, the governor general's residence just across the road from the prime minister's Ottawa home. Chrétien ended up calling us both "friends." I think he appreciated our approach, which was to be tough but fair, with Craig again taking the harder line while I was more circumspect. During these year-end conversations, when Chrétien occasionally got angry with Craig over some perceived slight in his coverage of a story over the previous twelve months, we always seemed to be able to restore the balance at the end, with the PM often inviting us for a drink at 24 Sussex. The interviews took place in a festive atmosphere just a few days before Christmas, with a lot of off-camera bantering. Only once do I remember tensions getting the better of the event, and that was just after the near-death experience of the referendum. On this occasion, Chrétien was on the defensive throughout a series of tense exchanges on how he could have let it happen. I found myself participating more aggressively than usual in questions to the prime minister.

In retrospect, I remember feeling that Chrétien should be held to account for what seemed like blundering inaction and a lack of understanding of the gravity of what was happening in Quebec in the period leading up to the referendum. At the end of the year, Chrétien was still reeling from the close call and was almost snarling at us in his responses. Craig was greatly amused when I received some letters and phone messages from loyal Chrétien followers complaining about my approach. Those kinds of responses were usually reserved for him.

During one of our informal post-Christmas interview sessions at 24 Sussex, Chrétien jokingly asked Craig and me, "Would you guys like to buy the CBC? I'll sell it to you for a dollar." He and the people around him had been outraged when they believed they had been blindsided at one of the network's Town Halls during an election campaign. They contended that the room had been stacked with NDP supporters and the prime minister had been treated unfairly. We responded with a "Thanks for the offer, sir," but told Chrétien we'd probably end up having to fire too many people we knew. While it was understood to be a light moment, it proved once again that no one political party has a corner on hating the CBC from time to time.

Chrétien and I had a long-running gag about retirement, which started during my first interview with him during the election campaign of 1993 against Kim Campbell's Conservatives. He was being referred to as "yesterday's man" because he had

seen long service in the Liberal governments of both Pierre
Trudeau and John Turner before leaving Turner's caucus to
return to practise law. I asked whether he thought he had it in
him to serve a full term if he won a majority and then stand for
re-election when he was close to being a senior citizen. Showing
his natural combativeness, Chrétien asked my age, which, as it
turned out, was the same as his—we were born a week apart in
January of 1934. He declared, "If you stay around, Lloyd, I'll
stay around," and told me that I'd be expected to step down when
he did. The little quip developed a life of its own, especially
after Chrétien gave up the leadership of the Liberals in 2003
at the age of sixty-nine. He and others never missed a chance
to remind me of our alleged deal. To me, the former PM was
hardly retired; he continued to blaze a trail around the world as
a goodwill ambassador and also to practise law.

One of the first to wish me well when I announced I was stepping aside from the news in 2011 was Jean Chrétien. His wonderful wife, Aline, told me he was still going strong because he
preferred to "wear out rather than rust out." We had another chat
on my last day in the anchor chair, and he said, "You'll have to get
out of the house every day, Lloyd. Your wife is not going to want
you around all the time." I like to think Chrétien and I clicked
originally because he could always count on our broadcasts to
cover him fairly, and because I was also a poor boy from a small
town, just like "the Little Guy from Shawinigan."

I came to regard Chrétien as one of our better prime ministers because of the Clarity Act, brought forward after the 1995
referendum, which clearly sets out the conditions Canada would
impose on any attempt by a future Quebec government to break
up the country and separate from Confederation. The Act calls

for a clear majority, without defining the actual number, and a clear question before Canada would be bound to sit down and negotiate separation. Quebec politicians dismiss the Clarity Bill, but they are sure to understand that if the rest of Canada rejects the conditions for separation, our major allies could be expected to reject them as well, given Canada's prestigious standing in various world bodies.

While the rest of Canada must never become complacent, it's remarkable how the political atmosphere in Quebec has remained relatively quiet since Chrétien's time, and there is a fair body of evidence that a majority of Quebecers themselves are exhausted with the old unity and sovereigntist arguments and want to get on with their lives.

Jean Chrétien also stood against the Americans and George W. Bush by keeping Canada out of Iraq, which, from this much later perspective, makes him look like a political genius in the face of what is now widely regarded as a major misadventure. Was Chrétien hurt by the Gomery inquiry on the awarding of contracts to Quebec ad agencies? No doubt. However, unlike his prime ministerial predecessor, Brian Mulroney, nothing stuck to him and he was never personally implicated.

Anyone who follows politics would be aware of the frosty feelings between Jean Chrétien and his predecessor as Liberal leader, John Turner. Turner clearly felt that Chrétien had tried to undermine him, and Chrétien had never shown acceptance of Turner as the leader who should take over from Pierre Trudeau. John Turner was a "hail fellow, well met" sort who had always been charming and chatty whenever we saw each other. He had his problems as leader, but he had an unblemished record as a politician of integrity. Along with many colleagues, I admired the stand he took in 1975 when he resigned as Pierre Trudeau's minister of finance after the government reversed its stand and decided to impose wage and price controls. In the election campaign of the previous year, Trudeau had made his famous "zap, you're frozen" utterance when ridiculing Conservative leader Robert Stanfield's proposal to freeze prices and wages in the face of mounting inflation. The Liberals, with John Turner on the front-row team, trashed the idea and won the election in the bargain. The newsroom buzzed with astonishment at the surprise news of Turner's resignation and marvelled that a politician was actually resigning on a point of principle in a difference with his leader. Years later, after he had stepped down from the Liberal leadership following his second loss to Brian Mulroney in 1988, he called me out of the blue to have lunch with him. When we got together he thanked me: "You guys were always fair with me," he said. "Always even-handed." We saw each other several times over the years, and I was honoured to be asked to act as master of ceremonies for his eightieth-birthday party in Ottawa.

Paul Martin was the last prime minister we were to interview together before Craig stepped aside as Ottawa bureau chief. Martin had won a minority government in 2004. We had been hearing that this very capable man, who was such an all-star finance minister, had trouble making up his mind when he assumed the prime minister's chair. I asked whether he was a "ditherer," as the British magazine *The Economist* had already pegged him. Martin took the question seriously and responded that policies had to be thoroughly worked over and couldn't be decided in a vacuum without sufficient input from many sources and consultations with interested parties. It sounded like the right answer to me, but the "ditherer" label went viral and came to be one of the negative markers of his brief tenure. Martin never managed to emerge from Jean Chrétien's long shadow, and while Chrétien was careful in what he said about Martin publicly, he let the word out, in no uncertain terms, that he thought Martin was "not the right guy" to succeed him.

In the election of 2006, the Conservatives won enough seats to form a minority government, and Paul Martin quickly decided to step down as Liberal leader. Stephen Harper would be in the chair for the next year-end conversation, and I was to strike up a very different relationship with the new head of government.

Craig and I always kept track of the trends and changes in our industry, and in the late eighties and early nineties, change was the only constant in TV. The term "five-hundred-channel universe" was coined in response to the proliferation of cable specialty services, and an increasing number of bright and capable women were coming into the industry. It wasn't easy for them at first. I recall the reaction of one of the old hands who complained about "another broad in the newsroom" when I supported the hiring of a new female assignment editor. Still, we had come a long way from the fifties, when I started in broadcasting and women were consigned to "homemaker" shows and there were virtually none in positions of real power in any of the main broadcast systems. Even at the CBC, there was a general view that women's voices were not acceptable for general broadcast work. And the only woman on the broadcast staff at CJOY in Guelph, which was considered a progressive station at the time, read only menu suggestions on daily meals for listeners.

At CTV in the eighties, Sandie Rinaldo was already anchoring news when the network hired a bright young newspaper reporter from the *Toronto Star* to be a co-host on *Canada AM*. Her easy charm and gracious manner, combined with a steel-trap mind, made her a natural for political interviews with leaders who tried to dodge direct questions. The audience loved her, and it wasn't long before Pamela Wallin, the bouncy intellectual and workaholic from Wadena, Saskatchewan, was a rising Canadian star. Pamela never forgot her roots or the values of the average folks in her hometown who, like her parents, simply tried to make a decent living by working hard and looking after their families. She always understood that connection, and the hometown folks reciprocated by inaugurating Pamela Wallin Way, a street not to be missed if you're in Wadena.

With her formidable intellect and natural abilities, Pamela cracked through more glass ceilings. She was a Womens' Studies graduate from the University of Regina and was to become, along with Susanne Boyce, former president of creative at CTV, and Trina McQueen, now a retired executive from both CTV and the CBC, a true torchbearer and shining example for women pursuing careers in media. At CTV, Pamela became the first woman to head up the Ottawa bureau of a major network. In her latter TV years at the CBC, she established a nightly talk show on its all-news channel that was quickly becoming the Canadian version of *Larry King Live* (without the suspenders, of course). Suddenly, in another of those baffling CBC bureaucratic decisions, the show was cancelled, but Pamela, in her typical fashion, hardly blinked before she was named Canada's consul general in New York. Then it was on to becoming a university chancellor before being appointed to the Senate, certainly one of the wiser choices for that often-maligned institution.

Watching Pamela, Susanne and Trina, I realized that women had to work harder and fight more battles, including overcoming stereotypes and sexism, to gain the ground they've now captured. Too many of my male colleagues had a sense of entitlement about when and how they should be promoted. Some even complained about the new powers women seemed to be gathering. I had to remind them that life, after all, is about balance, and there could be no question that women had some catching up to do. In any case, those three had become trailblazers in moving the game forward for the next generation of women following in their footsteps. It's probably one reason why CTV's choice of Lisa LaFlamme was met with such an overwhelmingly positive response. She had won the job on merit. Her record was there for all to see. The fact that she was a woman was almost incidental.

I am happy to count several women among my friends—apart from Nancy, of course. Sandie Rinaldo is as gracious and lovely as the audience sees her. But she should never be taken for a shrinking violet. Sandie's core strength has helped maintain her poise and professionalism in the face of the early death of her husband and a grim cancer scare several years ago. And there is the indispensable Wendy Freeman, our CTV News president. She is that whirling bundle of positive kinetic energy that drove our daily news system and made my last decade on the newscast, when she was executive producer, some of the best and most productive years of my entire tenure. There is Joanne MacDonald with her "Hey, buddy" greeting—smart, tough when she needs to be, and a senior stalwart in our news division. And there are plenty of others now surging forward to be stars of the next generation.

Does being the father of four girls influence my attitude in this area? Perhaps, but Nancy and I always impressed upon our daughters that they should strive to be independent and not rely on someone else to provide a living for them. We look with enormous pride on all of them. Each is singularly resourceful and successful in her field.

"Don't drop the ball," said CTV anchor Harvey Kirck. And yes, I caught it, just in time for our Grey Cup parade commentary in Toronto, 1976.
CTV NEWS

Harvey towered over me. We had fun with that.
CTV NEWS

You didn't see this on TV. Posing with Harvey's Yorkshire terrier, TJ, on the anchor desk. It was a slow news night.
CTV NEWS

Executive producer
Tim Kotcheff, probably
saying, "Don't screw
this up, Lloyd."
CTV NEWS

CNN's Larry King
comes to Toronto. With
broadcaster Donna
Tranquada, we joke
about his on-air refer-
ence to "Brian Maloney."
He meant Mulroney,
of course.
MILES S. NADAL,
ACTION PHOTOGRAPHICS,
MDC PARTNERS
COMPANY

Journalism school fundraiser
dubbed "Gathering of the Giants."
Front row, from left: Sydney Gru-
son (a Canadian working for *The
New York Times*), Allan Fothering-
ham, Richard Gwyn. Middle row:
Barbara Amiel, Jeffrey Simpson,
Morley Safer, Barbara Frum. Back
row: yours truly, Henry Champ,
Peter Mansbridge, Peter Gzowski,
Peter Jennings, Robert MacNeil.
GRADUATE PROGRAM IN JOURNALISM, FACULTY OF
MEDIA AND INFORMATION STUDIES, UNIVERSITY
OF WESTERN ONTARIO

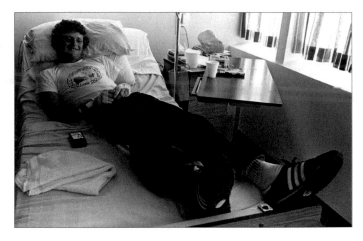

Terry Fox, watching from his hospital bed in Port Coquitlam, B.C., as CTV stages the Marathon of Hope Telethon in his honour. It raised over $10 million to add to his efforts for cancer research.
ANDY CLARK, CANADIAN PRESS

As a reporter, in the inevitable trenchcoat on a wet and windy day at Expo 86 in Vancouver. CTV NEWS

Helping out the children at the Variety Club Telethon in British Columbia.
CTV NEWS

I proudly display the Robertson tartan at the Highland Games in Maxville, Ontario.

Stratford mayor Dan Mathieson, Nancy, me, our daughters Lisa and Lynda, and local MPP John Wilkinson, as we inaugurate the Lloyd Robertson Garden in front of the City Hall, August 2011.

ELIZABETH COOPER

The mayor presents us with the Stratford tartan.

IRENE MILLER

Me with the first leader of
Canada's New Democratic
Party, a beloved man of the
people, Tommy Douglas.

One of several encounters
through the years with the
legendary Henry Kissinger.

MILES S. NADAL,
ACTION PHOTOGRAPHICS,
MDC PARTNERS COMPANY

In conversation with former U.S. president Gerald Ford (left) and Harry
Littler, former president of Universal Speakers, at a Toronto luncheon.
MILES S. NADAL, ACTION PHOTOGRAPHICS, MDC PARTNERS COMPANY

With Prime Minister
Mulroney at the opening of
the Calgary Olympics, 1988.
COURTESY RT. HON. BRIAN
MULRONEY, MULRONEY FONDS,
LIBRARY AND ARCHIVES CANADA/
PMO PICTURE

Prior to CTV's *Conversation with
the Prime Minister*. Laughing it
up with Craig Oliver and Brian
Mulroney. Craig comes dressed
down for the occasion.
COURTESY RT. HON. BRIAN
MULRONEY, MULRONEY FONDS,
LIBRARY AND ARCHIVES CANADA/
PMO PICTURE

A proud moment: receiving
the Order of Canada from
Governor General Romeo
Leblanc, at Rideau Hall,
Ottawa, 1998.
SERGEANT CHRISTIAN COLOMBE,
RIDEAU HALL, 1998

Jean Chrétien in his "don't mess with me" pose, just before my final interview with him as prime minister.

DIANA MURPHY, LIBRARY AND ARCHIVES CANADA

With the influential and charismatic Aline Chrétien, the power behind the throne.

DIANA MURPHY, LIBRARY AND ARCHIVES CANADA

Talking to Stephen Harper prior to a pre-election exclusive at the PM's residence in Harrington Lake, Quebec, in 2008.

JASON RANSOM, PRIME MINISTER'S OFFICE

A chance airport meeting with Canada's charming songbird, Anne Murray.

Happy about the third Gemini Award. With the CBC's Cathy Jones and Rick Mercer.

14

Going, Going ... He's Not Gone!

THE CHANGES TRANSFORMING THE INDUSTRY WERE ALSO
affecting the upper echelons of the CTV network. In 1990,
Murray Chercover stepped aside, and the new president was
John Cassaday, a bright and energetic young business graduate
who was coming off a highly successful executive run with the
Campbell's soup company. "From soup to nuts," the newsroom
wags dubbed the changeover, as Cassaday was to oversee everything we touched, from news to sports to variety and children's
programs. He had little TV experience, but was known as a mar-
keting whiz and someone who wasn't frightened to take the axe
to the redundant or the irrelevant where he saw fit.

John brought with him from his business school days one of
the tenets that is certainly fundamental to running and managing companies: always have a successor ready to step into the
shoes of key people, whether they are heading for retirement
or simply to keep them on their toes. While John was unfailingly polite to me and never mentioned the word *successor,* I kept
hearing from people around him that the idea was something
approaching company policy. Indeed, my pal Tim Kotcheff had
to quickly hire a friend from outside television for a senior news

position. John MacFarlane was a well-respected magazine journalist and would become Tim's second-in-command, a spot Tim
knew he needed to fill before someone he might not have liked
was imposed upon him.

With all of this churning just after I'd turned sixty, and with
two years left in my contract, I knew it might be time to point
to a successor. I was in Normandy in 1994 covering the fiftieth
anniversary of the D-day landings, and network colleague Keith
Morrison was also there as host of *Canada AM*. Our paths crossed
frequently, and I genuinely liked Keith. He had unique gifts as a
writer and broadcaster. Yes, he was considered quirky in many
ways, but that added to his boyish charm. Tall and slim, with
thick, wavy brown hair and a somewhat tentative manner, he
was irresistible to most women, and the rest of us could only
look on enviously as he turned away strings of attractive women
with a smile. His second marriage was to the strikingly beautiful
Suzanne Perry, a former press aide to Pierre Trudeau and the
mother of actor Matthew Perry. Suzanne also had a brief stint
as an anchor on the Global network's evening news in Ontario.
Keith had been a weekend anchor when I first arrived at CTV to
team up with Harvey Kirck for the Monday-to-Friday newscasts.

Keith had moved to the CBC and worked on *The Journal* during the Barbara Frum era, and then was off to NBC in California
to anchor local news. That was where he also won himself a regular slot on the network's weekly magazine show, *Dateline*. Like
so many other Canadian personalities who move south, Keith
was ready to come home for the right reasons. John Cassaday had
found an interested party when he sought out Keith to become
host for *Canada AM* to replace another Canadian, John Roberts,
who had just returned to the U.S. after a stint on the same show.

There was no doubt in my own, or anybody's, mind that Keith had been lured back with something more than a strong hint that he would step into the network anchor chair when I moved aside. John admitted as much to me later.

Indeed, why not Keith? He had been at CTV before and been lauded for his work, and, let's face it, I couldn't stay in the job forever. Also, it was well known that Keith was looking at a return to NBC, and unless he was offered my job, it was likely he would be gone. Even though I was not quite ready, I concluded it was time to make a move. Also, given the vibes echoing through the network on the subject of succession, and considering my age, it was a pre-emption of the inevitable—that if I didn't take this course of action, my contract wouldn't be renewed anyway. Better to do it myself than have someone else do it for me.

When Keith and I arrived back in Paris from Normandy, we met, on my invitation, for a quiet conversation in my hotel room and broached the subject of him taking over the news. Keith was open about his desires, declaring, "There's no job I've ever wanted more." Perhaps it was Parisian euphoria or just the chance to advance a likeable colleague, but I decided to call CTV the next morning. My contract would expire two years later, in 1996, and there would probably be other duties to occupy me for a few years afterward. I paced the floor that night, slept fitfully, and then, when it was time for North America to wake up, placed the call to John Cassaday. I told him Keith should be my successor, and John immediately asked whether I thought he was ready. "I'm sure he can be in two years," was my answer. Agreement came quickly, after just a few hours. It was decided that Keith would do one more season on *Canada AM* and then, in the year before taking the anchor chair, he would become the key national affairs correspondent, covering major events for our newscast. And so it was done: I would be stepping aside in September 1996 and Keith would take over. It never happened, of course, and the surprise waiting for me when I returned to Canada proved ominous for the whole enterprise.

Back from Normandy, I was walking into our offices at Toronto's CFTO, where we originated all of our national news broadcasts, when I was confronted by Douglas Bassett. He was president of Baton Broadcasting, the collection of stations—large and small—that at the time accounted for about 60 per cent of the CTV network. I think Douglas had been lying in wait for me in the hallway, because he pounced hard and fast. He told me in his customary blunt, no-nonsense fashion that there was "no bloody way" Keith Morrison would ever do the news on his stations. I was stunned! So what was I to do? I felt that since John Cassaday, as network president, had made the decision, the matter was out of my hands—I would be bound by the agreement and step aside in September of 1996 and Keith would take over.

All seemed to go well enough during the first year of the accord, but in the spring of 1995 everything changed. Friends were telling me Keith was worried I wanted to stay around, and he was rejecting the idea of becoming a national affairs correspondent, a position that would have greatly enhanced his profile on *CTV National News* and been a natural fit as a lead-up to his full-time anchor position in the fall of 1996. It was the same job Lisa LaFlamme later turned into a launching pad for her run at the anchor chair. In refusing to accept the national affairs role, Keith was effectively out of work, since his *Canada AM* host duties were due to end. What friends and colleagues had been saying for some time led me to believe that Keith was pushing to get into the anchor chair sooner. Eventually, my concerns were justified by Eric Morrison (no relation to Keith), who had succeeded Tim Kotcheff as vice-president of news when Tim returned to the CBC. Eric told me that what Keith wanted in the second year of the agreement was at least fifty percent of all my time as anchor. I was flabbergasted. After handing Keith the job on a silver platter, I was now expected to fade away earlier than planned. It may have been Keith's concerns over the Baton empire's objections to him or his own restlessness, but I was having none of it. My paternal grandparents were from Scotland, and there was a stubborn streak in the Robertson clan that served me well at times like this. We had made a deal, and that was that.

When my agent, Michael Levine, asked whether, under the circumstances, I wanted to renege on the deal and get rid of Keith, my answer was no, but there was one thing that had to be made clear: any chance of Keith and me working together in any way after he took over had just vanished. I couldn't remain with the network. At this point, CTV brass were thrust into an awkward position in which they would have to choose one of us. I was quite prepared to be the one to go—to put myself back on the street and hang out my shingle for availability to other broadcasters.

Eventually, CTV made a choice, and I was asked to stay on. I agreed to a new deal that would take me into the year 2000, and I was fortunate to be around for the launch of a revamped, unified and vibrant private network, consolidated under Baton but keeping the CTV brand. It was to become the most exciting place to work in Canadian television. Keith returned to NBC and the *Dateline* show, a role he continued in even during his time in Canada. In this case, he already had his insurance policy in his pocket in case things didn't work out back home. I still to see him doing interesting work in his distinctive style and wonder what might have been if it hadn't all fallen apart for him. In retrospect, I will always be sorry that the intense machinations of the TV industry ruptured my friendship with Keith. He is a good man and a unique broadcast talent.

When the news of Keith's departure was splashed across front pages in April of 1995, it came as a double whammy. It happened that Pamela Wallin was released from her CBC position at the same time. There appeared to be a connection between the two events, but unless the public relations departments of the two networks decided to unleash their bad news at the same time, it was surely pure coincidence.

The evening the stories broke, I took a call from Keith's wife, Suzanne, asking why I hadn't called her husband to try to straighten this matter out because, she contended, Keith was prepared to stand by the agreement of taking over one year later, in 1996. I had to tell her this was counter to everything I had heard and believed to be true, and besides, since I could have become the aggrieved party in this sad affair, why wouldn't Keith have called *me?* The conversation trailed off and I wished her well. It was over.

A short time later, I was on hand for the remarkable transformation of CTV from a squabbling array of regional affiliates to a streamlined collection of heritage stations that dominated their markets, anchored by a network determined to gain and maintain number one status in the country. It was all brought together by the brilliant Ivan Fecan. He was a true television genius, a tall, intense man with a shock of white hair who always moved quickly, both mentally and physically. Fecan was a true visionary, steps ahead of his competitors and with an uncanny sense of how TV could captivate and inspire as well as entertain.

In the year before I turned sixty-five, Ivan was asked by a Canadian Press reporter how much longer Robertson would be allowed to stay in the anchor seat. He pronounced me "anchor for life" and said I could stay as long as I wanted. I wasn't sure how long I might stay, but I knew it could be for as long as the newscast easily held its own. I also knew that if my luck and health held out, there would be no more thoughts about handing over the job until I was really ready to go.

Nancy didn't complain. She knew that if I went into retirement too early, she'd be stuck with an unhappy husband. I could become distracted and miserable if not kept busy. I would now be on TV for the launch of the new millennium. And, as it turned out, some of the most interesting and dramatic events were still to come.

15

The Halo and the Hair

EVEN IF YOU HAVE A CORDIAL RELATIONSHIP WITH YOUR main competition, it's unlikely they could be expected to hand you a gift-wrapped present that was sure to give you an advantage. That's why our initial reaction to the CBC's move in 1993 to shunt its main news broadcast from ten o'clock to nine didn't mean much at first. They had swooped into our shop to pick off the talented Tim Kotcheff to run the new *Prime Time News* and Pamela Wallin to co-anchor the hour—which would also displace *The Journal*—with Peter Mansbridge. Those two losses at the same time were body blows, to be sure, but we had no idea that the change in the news landscape would have such a positive and lasting impact for us.

After Knowlton Nash departed in 1988 and Peter Mansbridge assumed the anchor chair for the CBC, *CTV National News* continued to do well. But the CBC wanted to change the game completely. The network was undergoing a transformational makeover of its prime time schedule, and news was to be a centrepiece—a noble cause, but would it work? Audience habits, already well established for eleven o'clock and then ten, were challenged again in an overall plan to give the public corporation a much different look from the private broadcasters up and down the dial. The initiative was trumpeted far and wide as "fresh" and "breathtakingly novel"; it was seen as the dawn of a new age for the CBC.

When the new plan took to the air, the response couldn't have been more anemic. The audience simply yawned and, for the most part, proceeded to reject the Corporation's bold idea. No television network, not even one as renowned as Canada's public broadcaster, was going to dictate when people should watch the news. It was a shock to many on the inside, who seemed to believe that if the CBC went anywhere, viewers were sure to follow. But they stayed away in droves, and ratings were so dismal that jokes began circulating that Mother Corp.'s viewers could have been rounded up in a public phone booth. Apparently, the numbers began to look better in the second year, but by then the die had been cast. The move had been judged a failure.

On our side, the fallout from the Corporation's trouble was stunning. Audiences for our eleven-o'clock newscast increased by a remarkable one-third from the year before the change, and CTV News vice-president Henry Kowalski admitted, "The CBC gave us a big boost, but we were already edging up on them." After much internal thrashing about, and after two debilitating years for its news service, the CBC restored *The National* to ten o'clock, split up Pam and Peter, and the bold undertaking was over, leaving many walking wounded in its wake.

CTV National News became the principal beneficiary of the CBC's flawed experiment, and we firmed up our beachhead as the leaders in late-evening national news. It seems that a sizeable group of Canadians who had failed to follow the CBC to nine o'clock came over to try us out, liked what they saw and became regular viewers. A halo suddenly bloomed over our heads. We could do no wrong. Some industry observers contended that the CBC move shouldn't be given full credit for CTV's success. Michael Nolan, an associate professor of journalism at the University of Western Ontario, said, "It [CTV News] has built up a fairly respectable reputation since starting out in 1961." Yes, it takes time to build a franchise, and you'd better be ready when tested. Fortunately, it seems we were.

However, in my view, it wasn't something to crow about. When one news organization has a major failure, it's generally bad news for the industry. We live and breathe in a competitive environment. That's what makes the juices flow, and that's where the jobs come from.

When the CBC returned to ten o'clock, it might have been expected that the landscape in place prior to the change would be restored. Not the case! The CBC's mission statement accompanying its move back to its previous time slot said it wanted "to bring the program [*The National*] closer to Canadians by making it more engaging and more accessible in story selection and tone." It didn't work out, even though some at our place were convinced they planned to copy our more populist style and format. *CTV National News* continued to own the territory in late-evening news. A TV column by Greg Quill in the *Toronto Star* pointed out that, according to the A.C. Nielsen rating agency, CTV's viewership for the week of October 2, 1995, stood at 1,456,000 to the CBC's 1,137,000; three nights later, CTV was pulling in 1,649,000 at eleven o'clock compared to 1,142,000 for the CBC's *The National* at ten.

Two years later, the CBC made another move to increase

audience by throwing a version of *The National* up against us at eleven o'clock. The CBC's vice-president of English television, Jim Byrd, said (somewhat disingenuously, we thought), "We didn't do it to go after the CTV audience." Byrd was hoping the move would give audiences who wanted to watch dramas or sitcoms on CTV or other commercial networks at ten o'clock the option of watching the CBC at eleven instead of us. In any event, there was no effect. The move didn't dent our ratings. The CTV promotion department could brag without qualification that we were "Canada's Number One Newscast" through the nineties and the first decade of the new century.

Our gains in the ratings happened in spite of a controversy that began to circle my head—literally—at the same time. It revolved around my hair—that's right: my hair! There had been some adjustments made to our set that put me at a desk on a wooden riser on the studio floor. The result was to put my head in the direct path of some strong lighting from above—what we call "top light" in TV. Since I was beginning to sprout a sizeable amount of grey hair, it began to shine like the peaks of the Rockies and made me look much greyer than was actually the case. Some of my friends and colleagues started to gently suggest that maybe I should "do something about it."

Given all the jokes through the years about the Harry Hairspray and Linda Lacquer anchor types on TV, you will know by now that hair, makeup, ties, suits, shirts or blouses are the cosmetic factors that often overwhelm the presentation of information. I have had many phone calls and much correspondence over the years from viewers expressing their preferences for certain ties or suits over others, and, in a few cases, requests for the names of my tailor or shirt maker.

It was the dapper Arthur Weinthal, CTV vice-president of entertainment programming, who suggested I start putting a handkerchief in my breast pocket as "a mark of distinction." This seemed to be working fine until a woman in Ontario decided to take on a mission to ensure that tie and pocket puff matched every night. She said, "I'm surprised that the people around you don't give better direction on your wardrobe—what you wore last night was appalling." Although I wrote back only to thank her for her interest, every morning she would send a thumbs up or down on the previous night's choice. Finally, she wrote to tell me that I was probably busier with urgent news matters and that she was sorry if she had taken up too much time, but still, she thought she had noticed an improvement in my wardrobe coordination based on her interventions.

I've missed putting the tiny but distinctive Order of Canada pin in my suit lapel only a couple of times since being presented with the honour in 1998. Recipients are expected to wear the pin regularly, and one night when it was missing, an R. McAdam from Calgary wrote, "It is not only slothful but disloyal of you to ignore your pin." When I wrote back and explained I had simply forgotten, he accepted my explanation and apologized for his "intemperate language." Nevertheless, since then I always kept a spare pin at the ready in my newsroom desk drawer.

But it is the hair that always evokes the most buzz, so I made the fateful decision to try to get rid of some of the grey that the TV lights were accentuating. I was not, after all, employed in a medium where growing old gracefully was part of an accepted norm. I spoke to Joseph de Francesco, my excellent barber (they're all hairstylists now), who had a shop in the Sheraton Centre in downtown Toronto. He advised I use his "colour specialist," a young woman who seemed sympathetic to my plight as I explained the problems with the lights and said that I was not looking for too much change—just enough to wash out some of the grey.

The next Monday afternoon, I showed up in the newsroom with a full head of dark brown hair. I felt self-conscious about it, but thought it might look all right on television. There were sideways glances from some of the staff, and a few suppressed giggles from the women, but I soldiered on as though nothing had changed. When I hit the makeup room in my daily late-afternoon routine, there were some audible gasps and a few who shouted, "What the hell have you done, Lloyd?!" My longtime makeup artist, Elaine Saunders, whom I had first met in Winnipeg in 1957 and had worked with intermittently through the years, started to say, "Oh Lloyd . . ." before trailing off and deciding it was better to ignore the new look. The makeup department hairdresser, our cool and ever-discreet Bruno Malfara, winced slightly when he saw me, but made no comment.

It was after the newscast that the proverbial hit the fan. The hair looked completely different—indeed, it looked black. The desk was flooded with calls about "Lloyd's look." There were emails from across the country the next morning, with some expressing "shock and horror" at the sudden change. I was back to the colour specialist a few days later, asking whether she could bring a little more balance. The result was even more unsettling: my hair began to develop blue streaks, it was orange/copper-coloured for a while and then, after another attempt, I began to turn blond. *TV Guide* commented that "hitting the hair dye bottle is not a crime in itself," but wondered whether Robertson "was having more fun now that he's a blond."

The internal and external fuss had some of us joking that the time we were spending on this silly problem was as much as we'd use up in a major news crisis. To some, it was indeed a crisis. The vice-president of CTV News, Eric Morrison, quietly called Craig Oliver to plead with him to intervene with his friend to get me to clear up the mess over my hair. Craig roared with laughter. "How the hell can I do that? I'm putting stuff in myself." Craig was colouring the fringe around his mostly bald pate, and the columnists were having a field day in referring to him as "Ginger." He would joke it was just "prematurely orange." When Craig and I finally had a mock-serious discussion about our mutual hair problems, he made the point that "women have been colouring their hair for years and nobody gives a damn. It should be the guys' turn now." We both acknowledged that the very idea of hair colouring for news people probably distracted from the image of steadiness of character and decorum that we were supposed to present. Growing old was an accepted reality; why were we, as trusted guardians of truth, trying to change that? It was all a little too much, but it was a testament to the way cosmetics can dominate in television.

Finally, I knew I had to put an end to the ridiculous uproar, and our very own Bruno, who inhabited the makeup room every day, came to the rescue. He is a soft-spoken, handsome Italian who adopts a conspiratorial Sicilian tone when dealing with certain hair dilemmas. Bruno is probably the quintessential hairdresser. He has a subtle and unthreatening way of coaxing his clients to reveal their secrets, which is why he always walks in a sure-footed manner that tells us all he knows what's really going on at the network. He is truly the model for the old advertising tag line, "Only her hairdresser knows for sure." In his muted, semi-conspiratorial manner, Bruno assured me, "I can fix your problem, Lloyd." He insisted I didn't have to let my hair go back to the way it had been, with the lights accentuating the grey; rather he would simply find the right combination to tone it down, to make it look "perfectly natural."

Voilà! After just one session with his unique and still-secret formula, my hair returned to normal and the furor began to die away. That's why I dubbed Bruno "the King," and we had a close relationship that always brought lots of fun and teasing on every trip to the makeup department.

16

Following the Royals: "Evolution, Not Revolution"

NANCY AND I HAD JUST RETURNED FROM DINNER AND A movie one late August evening in 1997 when she called me from the living room. "Lloyd, look." Being an avid tennis player and fan, she had been watching a match when a news bulletin interrupted with an early report of a car crash in Paris involving Diana, Princess of Wales. I watched and listened to the skimpy details, including an ominous reference to "serious injuries," and immediately broke away to a second TV set in the bedroom to tune in to CNN, which, by that time, was becoming a more serious player in the news game after being dubbed "Chicken Noodle News" in its first few years.

Not much that was new was moving there or on any other channels until the details began to slowly seep out later in the evening, culminating in the shocking statement that Diana had succumbed to her serious injuries. The princess was dead! The world was stunned; the death was so violent, so unexpected and senseless that it was hard to grasp the reality that the life of this international beauty, who had so occupied us with the details of her turbulent existence, had been suddenly snuffed out. News organizations were thrown into overdrive; I was on the phone for the next several hours as we firmed up our plans to get on the air quickly on Sunday morning and present extensive coverage leading up to and including the funeral. I was made aware of the impact of the event when talking to my daughters. Lynda told me, "Dad, I found myself crying during the night." Along with throngs of other young people, they were in shock, and all felt a numb sadness. Diana had connected to people in a magical way like no Royal before her. As British author and journalist James Clench wrote, "She captured the world's imagination with her glittering sense of style, her personal warmth and a playful sort of charisma."

I reflect on how many years of my career were punctuated with stories about Diana. There was the glorious wedding on July 29, 1981, when I was in London for our CTV coverage to bring background and perspective for many bleary-eyed Canadians who had roused themselves early to watch the fairy-tale nuptials of "Shy Di" and Prince Charles. They were part of a worldwide audience of 750 million people, many of whom would have followed with dismay, as I certainly did, the ensuing tales of the tumultuous unravelling of the marriage after what was supposed to have been the "Wedding of the Century." The worldwide audience for Diana's funeral sixteen years later was estimated at 2.5 billion—as far as we know, the largest for any live event in television history. I was the lead commentator in London with Valerie Pringle and Canadian royal expert Bonnie Brownlee, who had been personally acquainted with Diana. There wasn't a dry eye for any of us when the caisson drawn by six horses pulled away from Kensington Palace and we could hear the audible gasps and crying of the onlookers lining the streets. Atop the flag-draped coffin there was a simple arrangement of white lilies, and behind, the lasting image for us all: Diana's two sons, William and Harry, solemn and silent, heads bowed, walking in the bright September sun through a London shrouded in grief.

Any encounter with Diana would be a cherished memory, and the time I met her in Toronto in October of 1991 is even more memorable in the light of all that has happened. I was one of the lucky journalists invited to a reception on board the royal yacht *Britannia* when it was docked in Toronto Harbour. The previous night, the royal couple's two sons had flown in from England and the family was reunited. TV audiences had seen pictures of Diana beating a hasty exit from a limousine and bounding up the steps of the yacht, arms outstretched as she ran to greet the boys and smother them with hugs and kisses. Charles was far behind, and his approach was surprisingly matter-of-fact. He was obviously pleased to see them, but there was none of Diana's pure joy and relief. Looking back, the body language said it all; there was a wide gulf between husband and wife, and the stories that had started bubbling to the surface years before about trouble in the marriage and Diana's struggles with anorexia obviously had grains of truth at their core.

On the evening of the reception, there were all the proper "how do you do" exchanges of receiving-line greetings, and as I moved over near some acquaintances, I was startled to see Diana heading straight for me with a faint deer-in-the-headlights look. It's as though she was searching for friendly faces in an unfamiliar crowd. I was on the receiving end of that glamorous smile and those luminous, sparkling eyes as we shook hands and talked about—what else?—the weather. It was a miserable, rainy night in Toronto, and she at least pretended to appreciate my aside:

"We have imported some London weather just for you, ma'am." She replied, "Ah yes, British weather. It follows us around." Since we were not allowed to make notes or record anything, those are my only memories of the exchange, but I do recall how beautiful and vulnerable she was and how she looked a little lost at the same time. A few minutes later, Charles was standing where she stood; he was nattily dressed and smoothly professional, and he gave just the right smile and indication of interest in each guest. His background and training would allow him to present an unruffled presence no matter what turmoil might have prevailed in his personal life.

Having covered countless royal tours of Canada, I've had a chance to meet all the principal members of the Royal Family. The Queen is always impressive. Her diminutive stature may be a surprise at first, but it doesn't take long to realize that here is woman who was thrust into the job of monarch when very young, following the death of her father, King George VI, and she has carefully moulded the role in her own image. Most Canadians will have no memory of anyone else occupying the throne. It is under Queen Elizabeth that the Royal Family began to be known as "The Firm," because it very much took on the character of a smoothly professional, expertly run corporate operation with the Queen as its head, quietly giving her nod of approval or hint of rejection at every aspect of the enterprise. The whole purpose is to present the monarchy as an indispensable part of British life and provide a sense of stability and historical continuity in the various realms, including Canada, where the Queen remains as head of state. It has been said that Canada is the treasured prize of the Commonwealth because it has never seriously questioned the monarchy and so obviously adores and respects the Queen.

There was evidence of this feeling during the visit in 2011 of Prince William and Catherine. It was their first trip outside the United Kingdom after their marriage, a kind of dry run for the new kids on the block before they flew off to Los Angeles.

Royal tours are run with military precision, and while there is a collegial feeling among those who get to cover them, barring slip-ups, there is often not much to report. I've always tried to use the tours to present a panorama of the country, especially in the small towns and more exotic parts of Canada that hardly ever get exposure on national media.

On the Queen's first tours across the Far North in 1970, the majority of the press corps was stuck in Tuktoyaktuk in the Northwest Territories. The royal plane had lifted off just before bad weather came in, but the aircraft carrying the bulk of the news contingent was grounded, and we were put up for the night in a school gymnasium, Canadian reporters and photographers mixing with a few of the hard-boiled correspondents from Fleet Street. Some of the more enterprising members of the paparazzi began taking pictures of this motley collection spread out across the floor on rolled-up bedsheets and borrowed sleeping bags. This brought a loud and furious retort from a female writer for one of the British tabloids as she rounded on one of the photographers: "If you take one more bloody picture, I'll kick you in the balls, if you have any." That ended the commotion, and everyone tried to get some sleep. Canadian lads like me, who had never heard a woman talk like that in public, turned over and pulled up the covers.

The next day, Craig Oliver and I decided we couldn't just sit around and watch other people play cards, waiting for the weather to clear, so as enterprising small-town lads, we sent out a radio broadcast from the shores of the Beaufort Sea to the full CBC network for the program *Assignment*. We spoke of the raw beauty around us, about being marooned up there and how some of our British colleagues were already getting a version of cabin fever and were threatening to charter their own plane out the next day if we didn't get picked up. We were told at the time that it was the first satellite broadcast directly from the Arctic. A few hours later, we were rescued, and for years afterward, there was an enduring camaraderie among the members of the press corps who were "stuck in Tuk." The legendary Charles Lynch of Southam News held a few reunion parties for the group, and reminiscences and liquid refreshment were both plentiful. One of the enduring images from the same tour came when the Queen stopped in Resolute, and there, in the middle of July, we were able to send the country pictures of snow on the low barren sand hills—snow that, at that time at least, dotted the landscape year round in the Far North.

The press reception is always a part of any tour, and while all remarks are understood to be off the record, the members of the royal party are careful, even under those circumstances, not to ruffle feathers. The exchanges are appropriately innocuous. Only once did I get a longer-than-usual audience with the Queen when, knowing of her interest in horses, I began talking about Secretariat, the American thoroughbred racehorse that, in 1973, became the first Triple Crown champion in twenty-five years. Her Majesty commented on him and noted how the large chestnut colt had captured the imagination of so many in Britain as well. She asked if I had ever seen him race in person. I said, "No, ma'am, I haven't." The air seemed to go out of my tires at that point, and she moved on.

The rule on not revealing anything discussed at these affairs is taken seriously, especially by the Canadian members of the Queen's entourage who are usually young, nervous bureaucrats from the Heritage department in Ottawa. On one occasion, I found myself in a long conversation with Prince Philip. He held me in his gaze and continued to ask questions about everything from Canadian hockey to the political personalities of the day. I gabbed away, talking about national events of the time and asking the Duke whether he still held to the view, expressed some years earlier, that if Canadians didn't want the monarchy around anymore and wished to be done with them, they'd happily concur. "Of course," he said in his curt, straightforward manner. After a while, I noticed a bespectacled face peering at me from behind Prince Philip with ears glued to every word. It was Allan Fotheringham, one of the sharpest and funniest writers of our era. Allan used words as rapiers, often sheathed in irony and humour, and the next day he sent me up in a column accusing me of "monopolizing" the Duke's of Edinburgh's time. Did His Royal Highness know of Fotheringham's reputation, and had he been discouraged by his handlers from turning around to talk to him—and was Allan ticked off about that? Or was it all just coincidence? Shortly after the column came out, I began hearing that royal tour types were enraged by the leak of conversations and that Fotheringham would be banned from further receptions. I can't imagine Allan, whom I had come to know and like, being the slightest bit troubled by that.

Of all the Royals, my vote for all-time favourite goes to Queen Elizabeth, the Queen Mother. She was the grandest and most majestic of them all. The great lady combined a twinkling smile and impish sense of humour with a genuine interest in people. Her press receptions were always much-anticipated events. They were relaxed and jovial affairs with the Queen Mum at the centre, wearing one of her frilly-dilly hats, usually with gin and tonic in hand (or so we always suspected), charming everyone in sight.

I carried memories of the first time I laid eyes on her when, at the age of five, my father hoisted me on his shoulders in 1939 as the royal train moved slowly through the outskirts of Stratford with the King and Queen waving from the back of the caboose. They had come to Canada to rally support for Britain as the clouds of war gathered over Europe and the threat from Nazi Germany grew ever stronger.

Conversations with her were always warm and relaxed, with the Queen Mum remembering me from earlier meetings and asking after my health and that of my family and saying how much she loved being in Canada and how she had made so many friends. She once said of her trip to this country with her husband in 1939 that "Canada made us." And how clever of Prince William, during his first post-wedding official tour with his new bride, Catherine, to use the same words, giving Canadians credit for making them feel welcome, and helping them learn about what it means to be a member of monarchy.

The Queen Mother continued her trips to Canada, with the last one coming in 1987, just before her eighty-ninth birthday, and with her last event being the 130th running of the Queen's Plate Stakes at Woodbine racetrack in Toronto. One story about that trip comes from the Queen Mother's official biographer, William Shawcross, and best demonstrates her indefatigable nature and perhaps explains why Canadians were so enthralled with her. It deals with a dinner held at the Ontario Jockey Club, where she met all the club trustees, two by two, over liqueurs and coffee. "With the final pair, David Wilmot and Bob Anderson, a young Aberdeen Angus cattle breeder, she talked about her favourite cattle as she plied them with Drambuie." Then the Queen Mum launched into "an alarming experience she had once had in a landau when the coachmen lost control of the horses on an English racecourse and they ran on for three circuits. What did she do? Wilmot asked. She just gave the spectators a royal wave each time she went past the stands, she replied." That indomitable spirit, always facing down danger with style, as she and the King had done on a grand scale in the Second World War, is why she was so treasured by the people of Britain and the Commonwealth.

On her death in 2002, the British people and those around the Commonwealth confounded the pundits and experts, most of whom felt that because she had lived to 102 and most of her generation had gone, her passing would attract only minimal interest. My colleagues and I watched from our broadcast location near Westminster Abbey as hundreds of thousands of people, young and old, queued up to pay their respects at Westminster Hall and a quarter of a million lined the streets in the damp cold of an early April morning to mourn with the Queen as she bade final farewell to her mother. The pageantry and solemnity of the occasion were a fitting tribute to a woman who had so visibly sustained the spirits of her people during some of the darkest days of the twentieth century. I wrapped up the broadcast that morning by saying, "Thank you, ma'am, for being there when we really needed you."

I've always been tagged as an "erstwhile monarchist" by many of my colleagues, and while I've never objected, it should be pointed out that my attitude toward the Royal Family probably falls in line with that of a majority of Canadians. Queen Elizabeth is simply superb in her role, and there will be no questioning her position as Canada's head of state as long as she is with us. Yes, she's had problems with her family, but it could be argued that those problems have simply made her more human. Too many of us can point to the same kinds of troubles. And there is every indication that the Royal Family has a clear understanding in this multimedia age of the need for rejuvenation and renewal that will assure its survival for years to come. Just look at the smooth rollout of Prince William and Kate Middleton with exactly the right mixture of royal precision, tradition and pop-star hype. These two are now being seen as "in the window" for the next generation of Royal watchers. In the age of celebrity, the Americans, who run the world's biggest showbiz machine, will treat them like iconic movie stars, but Canadians have always had the advantage over Americans in this respect. We can make a fuss over them, but recognize the Royals as part of our family at the same time. The Americans threw off the monarchy over two hundred years ago; we have followed the path of "evolution, not revolution" and can claim the Royal Family as part of our own.

A few years ago, our Commonwealth brothers and sisters in Australia held a referendum on the monarchy, and they ended up keeping the Queen because they couldn't decide how to replace her. They were voting on whether to have a full-fledged president elected by the people, or a head of state appointed by Parliament, a kind of upgraded governor general. Neither idea appealed; the Queen stayed and the question was put to rest, probably for a while.

Can you imagine the fuss of trying to get rid of the monarchy in Canada? It would mean reopening the Constitution, in which the King or Queen is designated head of state, and all ten provinces and territories would have to agree on abolition. The requirement for unanimity was the arrangement put in place when Pierre Trudeau's government repatriated the Constitution in 1982. It would be hard, if not impossible, to achieve. So, can you imagine such a thing happening? "Not in my lifetime," would surely be the first response from most Canadians.

Shedding the monarchy would also cause us to lapse into a kind of national amnesia; the Queen and her ancestors are so embedded in our historical fabric it would take years and countless dollars to erase all vestiges of the Royal presence. Her Majesty is on our money and stamps, and we have to ask ourselves: What harm is it anyway? And what about the Stanley Cup? Lord Stanley was Canada's governor general in the late 1800s, long before Canadians took over the viceregal role, beginning with Vincent Massey in 1949. Would we change the name of the legendary hockey trophy?

Clearly, Canadians are secure within themselves; we are fully independent, one of the best countries in the world and getting better all the time. No one is leading a charge to open up a debate on the future of the monarchy, and barring unforeseen circumstances, it is not coming down the track as an issue in the foreseeable future.

17

Terry's Legacy to Us All

IN THE EARLY NINETIES, NANCY AND I WERE BEGINNING TO enter the empty-nester phase. She had adjusted to my crazy shift patterns and workaholic nature, and our lives looked to be clicking along in an easy rhythm, with the girls all heading out to pursue various careers. Two would end up in behind-the-scenes roles in TV, one had become a teacher, and our eldest had gained her Masters in Social Work and married an American and was living in the U.S. Yes, life was good, but it was about to change. Like so many other Canadian families, we were not to be spared that moment of trauma when we learned that one of the scourges of the times was entering our lives as well.

Nancy called me one day in the newsroom and asked if I was sitting down. "Yes," I answered, holding my breath a little. "What is it?" Her voice began to break and I had a dread sense of what was coming. Our second daughter, Susan, had been undergoing tests and had been found to have a malignant tumour. "The big C," as we used to call it, had hit our family, and it was a stunning blow. I remember the room beginning to spin as I struggled to digest the news. There were days and nights to come when news of events from across the country and around the world didn't seem to matter much.

I went to work every day to keep my mind occupied, and the distraction, if noted at all, was caught only by people who knew me really well. Barbara Frum, who was undergoing her own battles with cancer, called and said, "Lloyd, are you okay? The last few nights I thought I noticed a slight preoccupation in your tone." She had been alerted by mutual friends that there was a family illness, but she couldn't be sure from watching me. I explained the situation, and we found ourselves talking about Terry Fox. He had been dead for ten years by that point, but his legend was growing, as evidenced by the Terry Fox Runs that had started across Canada and would eventually be held all over the world. He had become a symbol for those who believed you should fight until the last breath. Our daughter's tumour was soon removed, and I took a cue from Terry in telling her during those difficult days, "Remember, you're a Robertson. You're tough, you're resilient, you'll come through this." At that moment, I would have given anything to trade places with her—that's when you understand the overpowering bond of love that exists between parent and child.

Susan was ultimately pronounced clear of cancer, and I was proud to serve for a full year as honorary chairman of the Terry Fox Run. I came to know Terry's indispensable mother, Betty, and his warm and unassuming father, Rolly. Rolly was always there to support Betty as the driving force. She was an exuberant presence with her big smile and cheerful "Hi, Lloyd" before we locked in a bear hug. Betty and her team raised half a billion dollars for cancer research and helped wipe away the stigma that contracting cancer was an inevitable death sentence before she herself died—not from cancer but from unexplained causes—in 2011.

I was proud of the role our network was able to play in the Terry Fox story. On September 1, 1980, the day Terry made his tearful announcement that he was stopping his run outside Thunder Bay because his cancer had returned, our vice-president of news, Don Cameron, stormed into the CTV executive offices and said, "We've got to do something about this!" With his innate sense of timing, Cameron realized that the country had become immersed in Terry's story and wanted to help in any way possible. CTV management didn't need much persuading to clear the network the following Sunday night. Cameron then called me and said, "Lloyd, you're going to anchor a telethon to the full network. It'll be called *The Marathon of Hope Continues* and we're not sure how long it will run."

As I sat down in the chair that Sunday night, I had no idea how to start the broadcast. There was no preparation and no script, of course; even the set had been hastily thrown together. I would have to rely on my instincts from years of live coverage to set a tone and carry it forward. Five minutes before the start of the show, I was still trying to work it out in my head. I had never tackled anything like this before. It would have to be done with sensitivity, and yet the broadcast was also a fundraiser. I had to find just the right approach. At that moment, CTV executive Arthur Weinthal, a real pro when it came to the elements of broadcasting, walked up to me and said, "Remember, Lloyd, this is a celebration of courage." I could have leaned over and kissed him. It was exactly the right phrase; it gave me a focus as I led the broadcast from a desk that might have been a reject from a late-night talk show. *The Marathon of Hope Continues* ran close to five hours, and when all the numbers were in it had raised $10.5 million. Every single minute, in almost every part of Canada, 750 people were on the phone, calling in pledges, and every minute the total jumped by $25,000.

Even more amazing was the willingness of Canada's top talent, as well as big international stars, to adjust their schedules to appear on the broadcast in support of Terry's cause. Anne Murray sang a few of her signature ballads in the opening hour and said she was there "for Terry, for Terry Fox, because it's great to have a real Canadian hero." John Denver and Elton John sent videos, and I recall talking with country star Tommy Hunter after the broadcast and apologizing for not being able to get him on the air because of the lineup of talent that had suddenly appeared from everywhere. He said, "No problem, Lloyd. I came here to volunteer and it was great just to be in the same room with such energy and excitement." How very Canadian, I thought.

Terry watched the broadcast from his hospital bed in New Westminster, B.C., where he was undergoing chemotherapy, too ill to appear on the broadcast, but as CTV's Helen Hutchinson told us, "He was moved completely to tears" by the outpouring of generosity from his fellow Canadians. A United Press photographer captured a picture of Terry a little later in the night, spread out on the bed, wearing his familiar running shoes, as he watched the telethon with a big smile.

He died the following June, at the age of twenty-two. At his funeral, I sat in a small enclosed cubicle just off the balcony of the church in Port Coquitlam, B.C., and provided commentary over pictures on a nationwide broadcast. I choked up, barely able to speak, when the hearse pulled away from the church and disappeared through the shimmering mists emanating from fresh pavement on a hot summer day.

Thousands of words poured forth in tribute to Terry, with Prime Minister Pierre Trudeau striking a theme picked up by many when he spoke of how Terry inspired us all "with the example of the triumph of the human spirit over adversity."

Terry Fox looms large in our history. There are thirty-two roads and streets named after him, fourteen schools, and Mount Terry Fox in British Columbia. Terry became the first non-Royal to appear on a Canadian coin. He is on one side, the Queen on the other.

Many have tried to explain the Terry phenomenon. Media personality Sook-Yin Lee, in her presentation of Terry's story for the CBC's "The Greatest Canadian" contest, described his attributes as the perfect mix of compassion, commitment and perseverance. In the voting, he came second only to Tommy Douglas. At the Vancouver Paralympics, where Betty Fox was a torchbearer and Terry's story resonated throughout, athletes were presented with a medal in his name that cited "determination and humility in the face of adversity."

My own take on Terry's profound impact is that he was like our next-door neighbour or the kid down the block who would be upset and angry that they had been hit so early by cancer. Terry took it a step further. He set out to do something about his plight and to make a difference. There was nothing posed or phony about him. He was all gritty reality as he headed out across the country. He struck a chord, reminding us of the toughness and pioneering spirit in so many Canadians whose ancestors came here to open up the land, often under extremely difficult circumstances in a challenging climate.

We are a hardy people at the core. Terry reminded us of that.

18

The Kind of Days They Were

ONE OF NANCY'S DEAR, DEPARTED AUNTS USED TO TURN to me with envy sometimes and sigh, "You sure have an easy job, Lloyd. All you have to do is sit there and talk." I'm sure she wasn't alone in that thinking. After all, most people would simply see me once a day at eleven o'clock at night. It wouldn't necessarily occur to them that I'd be working at other times. In the years before national anchors became involved in every aspect of their broadcasts, the announcer at the CBC would show up in the newsroom at nine-thirty, go through a rehearsal of the broadcast around ten and then read it into the camera at eleven o'clock. When one of the stalwart regulars was asked about the top news story on a certain night, he responded with an echo of Ted Baxter, "Gosh, I don't remember. I was calculating my bank balance at the time." Such was the degree of non-involvement. Well, not anymore!

At CTV, we deliver two, and sometimes more, live broadcasts every night, at ten and eleven. Apart from those key appearances, there are meetings, taping of interviews with reporters and guests, taping of promotions for stories and items coming up on the nightly news, as well as the necessary time set aside for the cosmetics of television, like makeup and hair coiffing. If what you see on television appears easy, any anchor would say "Thank you," because that's how it's supposed to look—but I hope this outline of my days on the news proves it was real work, and more than just talk. As we might say in our program promotions, "All times are eastern, three hours later in B.C., ninety minutes earlier in Newfoundland."

3 p.m.

Arrive in the newsroom and start by dealing with mail and telephone messages. I would have monitored radio or TV newscasts throughout the morning and afternoon, often checking in with our domestic and foreign assignment editors to see what's happening from their perspective.

Chat in my office with executive producer Wendy Freeman. "Hi boss, no screw-ups last night from what I could see." "Right," she says, "but we could have done a lot better on the Ottawa story—too many talking-head experts, not enough real people giving their views." I agree. My veteran makeup artist, Elaine Saunders, delivers tea. "For you, my darling," she sings. I usually drink more tea than coffee. On a bad day, Wendy drinks one too.

3:30 p.m.

The daily editorial meeting, with everyone on board, including our assignment editors, who would have spent the day ordering up stories that are now ready to present to us for review. Wendy chairs the meeting with a thorough look at the night before. On hand are many of my longtime stalwarts on the night shift: senior producer David Hughes; lineup editor and associate producer Mark Borchiver; the show's director, Brian Lebold; the superb wordsmith Bonnie Hewitt; and, for a time, the ruddy-faced classic hard-nosed newsman, Jim Peters. Also present is the only person I've ever described as "perfect" because I've never known her to make a mistake: the indispensable production assistant, Cyan Taylor. Cyan is responsible for keeping us on time while on the air and making sure everything fits into the time slots we've given her. In even the most hectic of circumstances, she has never let us down.

Dave says, "I was really impressed by the way everybody pulled together to gather all the elements on the flood story. Congratulations all around." We check out how we compared to our competition—were there any production or technical flaws in our broadcasts? The conversation continues for as long as it takes to cover these questions, and then we start putting together the pieces for that night's newscast. Some stories of the day are obvious—a major weather calamity, a positive medical breakthrough, the top political story from Ottawa. We set down a rough order that will change according to the flow of the news as the day progresses. What looks like a lead-off story at three-thirty in the afternoon may not be as important later in the evening. We debate whether a story on Paris Hilton deserves space. To me, it's unimportant and irrelevant. We reject it. As usual, we try to end the broadcast with a humorous or upbeat item or, at the very least, something thoughtful. News producers have been doing that for as long as television has been around. It's a way of trying to leave viewers with a smile or something to ponder as we say good night.

4:15 p.m. (approximately)
My first trip to the makeup room for the powder and paint—"to make you look like what you ain't," as Harvey used to say.

I kid with Elaine or the other makeup artists that I'm sorry it's getting harder for them every year. Then into King Bruno's chair for the all-important hair coif of the day. This can take a while, depending on Bruno's insistence that it be "just right."

4:45 p.m.
Conference calls with reporters to work out details of the stories set for the newscast. Dave says, "Let's get a focus on the high-dollar item and make it not just for business buffs, but tell how it affects the average person."

5:00 p.m.
Tape our promos for the affiliates—the short and snappy capsules of the day's news you see on your local CTV stations during the evening's prime-time programming: "Canada's soaring loonie, and what it means for you." We hope these snippets will help bring you to our broadcast at eleven o'clock.

5:30 p.m.
Record an interview with a reporter: "With us is medical specialist Avis Favaro on a breakthrough for multiple sclerosis sufferers. Avis, how soon will the trials on this 'liberation therapy' begin for Canadians?"

6:00 p.m.
Break for dinner. Home with Nancy, and frequently kids or grandkids, as often as possible—otherwise, it's a business-related dinner at a restaurant or in the more utilitarian surroundings of the CTV canteen.

7:30 p.m.

Back in the newsroom for the writing and editing of the eve-ning's broadcast. The pace of the night depends on the way the news agenda unfolds. Ottawa bureau chief Robert Fife calls. He says, "Guys, I have a scoop on the schedule of our troop pullout from Afghanistan." I say to Dave and Mark, "Great stuff. Let's open up some time for that." They concur, and it's done. Dave says, "We should really get this to the top of the show. It's brand new breaking news and it's exclusive to us." Mark and I agree, and the lineup order shifts again.

8:30 p.m.

The "teasers" for the top of our broadcast are recorded. "Tonight: pageantry and glamour as William and Kate are welcomed to Canada." We follow with pictures and sound and quick bursts of information on a few other compelling stories that are designed to "tease" the audience to stay with us through the half-hour broadcast.

8:45 to 10:00 p.m.

More editing and writing of news copy, checking visuals and a talkback with Bob Fife: "Bob, you have some new information on Canadian forces. Walk us through what you've got."

10:00 p.m.

Veteran studio director and longtime colleague John Hurle Hobbs brings down his arm to cue the start of the first edition of *CTV National News*. It goes to the Atlantic region—live to Nova Scotia, New Brunswick and Prince Edward Island at eleven and Newfoundland at eleven-thirty. It is also seen across the country on CTV News Channel.

10:30 p.m.

We determine whether there should be copy changes or updates in stories for the eleven-o'clock broadcast.

I ask for Chyron (on-screen titles) on one segment because an interview subject's voice is hard for the audience to grasp.

11:00 p.m.

Steve Trebelcoe takes the cue from John and starts rolling the teleprompter as I say, "Good evening" for another full edition of news.

This is the show that is usually the "stand-up" broadcast of the night. If no changes are required for the western time zones, it can be replayed intact in each zone at eleven o'clock local time. Frequently enough, though, we will be in the newsroom much later, sometimes till 2 a.m. Toronto time, for breaking stories anywhere in the west, like the 2011 Stanley Cup riots in Vancouver or the 2012 provincial election in Alberta. In that case, we air another full edition of the newscast.

There have been times when we have done five editions of our newscast live to every time zone. It happened after the spectacular crash of a Swissair jet off the coast of Nova Scotia near Peggys Cove, and on U.S. election night in 2000 when it was uncertain whether George W. Bush or Al Gore would be the ultimate victor. That election wasn't decided until several days later and after a complicated recount in Florida.

11:45 p.m. to midnight (most nights)

Head for home and wind down for sleep, which usually comes around 2 a.m.

So, there you are, a sample of the kind of days they've been.

19

Frequently Asked Questions

As someone who has spent over fifty years on television screens across the country, my face and voice have gradually become familiar to millions of Canadians. I've also had the privilege of meeting thousands of people, of all types and ages, in towns, villages and cities, large and small, from sea to sea to sea. Over the last several years, it's been hard to go anywhere without being recognized. When I don a baseball cap and glasses, there is a reasonable degree of anonymity until I open my mouth—then comes the question: "I recognize that voice. Aren't you the guy from the TV news?" When my cover is blown, we engage, and while most just want to say "nice meeting you" in that innately polite Canadian way, others will ask questions, and some can very persistent. Can it be annoying? Yes, at times, but I am well aware it goes with the territory.

As my late CBC friend, Newfoundlander Harry Brown—who described himself as "marginally famous"—once said, "You'd have to be pretty precious to say you didn't enjoy being recognized. Drawing an audience is what you're supposed to do, after all." Richard Bosanquet, who was a newscaster with ITN (Independent Television News) in Britain, understood that it cut two ways when he said, "It's hell being spotted all the time, but if you're not recognized it's even worse. Who's watching then?"

No memoir of mine would be complete without an example of some of my encounters and the questions I've dealt with over the years.

Who's doing the news tonight?

This usually comes from someone who is in shock at seeing this familiar face standing in front of them, or close enough to make contact, and can't figure out how this guy, whom they usually see inside an electronic box, can suddenly be within touching or hailing distance. The line can pop out of someone's mouth almost anywhere. Nancy and I were on vacation in Venice, Italy, one summer, floating along in a gondola, when we heard it shouted from an overhead bridge. "Hey, Lloyd! Who's doing the news tonight?" It's a tough one to answer, so I usually just say, "Not me! I'm right here with you!" or "Why aren't you home watching so you can tell me?" and try to leave it at that.

How come, with you on TV, your wife is driving an old blue Chevy Bel Air?
I was asked this question in the early seventies by a shoe retailer in a mall near our home. I responded, "Well, Harry, it's like this . . . I know you've read all this stuff in the magazines you get from the druggist next door about big money for folks who appear on TV, but those are all U.S. personalities. It's very different in Canada, with our much smaller market and an economy one-tenth the size. Canadian TV people generally, and news anchors in particular, don't make anywhere near American salaries." Harry then asked, "So why haven't you moved to the U.S.?" After I chided him, in good humour,

for being so dismissive of this wonderful country, for which he apologized, I said, "On the two occasions when I've had agents approach me to throw my hat in the ring for an American job, I didn't pursue it."

I've already mentioned the first of these opportunities, when I worked in Winnipeg. The second was a local TV job in New York. This was in 1970, and I'd just started on the CBC's *The National*. I turned the option aside because I was doing well in Canada and preferred to be here. If there was work here similar to what Walter Cronkite, David Brinkley and others were able to do in the U.S., why not stay home and build the same kind of profile in the country of my birth?

As to the money—in spite of what people may have heard or read or seen on the Internet—I never made a million dollars a year.

What was your worst news day?
As a father of four daughters, the story that had me reeling in disgust and trying to control my anger on air was the Montreal massacre on December 6, 1989. Fourteen women students were shot dead by a lone gunman at École Polytechnique; thirteen others were wounded before the shooter, Marc Lepine, took his own life. It was the worst single-day massacre in Canadian history. The details of the killings began coming to us during the course of the evening, and we broke into regular coverage with a grim bulletin on the full CTV network several times as the horror unfolded. Lepine was threatened by the advancement of women into such non-traditional occupations as engineering. Nancy and I had always counselled our girls to find their bliss in whatever fields attracted them. To see the lives of these young women snuffed out so brutally for no other reason than that they

were pursuing the careers of their choice cut too close to home. All tragedies, from tsunamis to plane crashes to school shootings, have their impact on an anchor, but the ones that strike a personal chord teach us never to become immune to any of them.

What is the difference between the network news services?
This question came fairly often during the first few years after I left the CBC for CTV, and I still get it from those old enough to recall my days at Mother Corp. Often enough, this question is related to a perception that the CBC is full of "lefties," with its selection of stories and viewpoint to the left of the political spectrum, while CTV is more market driven.

Well, it's not that cut and dried. Yes, there are people of leftish persuasion at the CBC, and they are certainly more comfortable there than they would be in the world of private broadcasting. But whatever some skeptics may suspect, not everybody at the Corporation is some kind of "bicycle-riding pinko." After all, Don Cherry, who coined that phrase, has appeared on the CBC for years, and as far as we know, only his wardrobe is pink.

And just as there are undoubtedly those of an entrepreneurial bent who happen to have found a niche in a public corporation, there are people at CTV News who believe in the importance of the public realm.

Everybody has biases, of course, but in my experience, journalists at both networks take seriously the responsibility to be fair and balanced in the coverage of public issues. They are not always successful, but they do try.

On both sides, we are far more concerned with building and holding audiences than with pushing any agendas. And in this country—so far, at least—that means presenting the news with as much balance, perspective, and at times humorous detachment as we can muster. I've had NDP supporters tell me that they can watch us and understand we are an "open portal" to the airing of their views just as much as we would be for Conservatives or Liberals. I'm sure the CBC would hope to have the same reaction from the various political parties.

Did you ever come close to missing a broadcast?
On a rainy night in Washington in February of 1998, producer Pat Skinner and I were racing to the White House on a tight deadline for the nightly news. The plan was to anchor a major portion of our broadcast from the famous lawn in front of the pillars.

The Monica Lewinsky scandal was breaking around President Bill Clinton as allegations flew that he had conducted an affair with the White House intern. Having been told we needed only documents showing our network affiliation, we were suddenly brought up short by a tall, friendly southerner at the security gate in front of the residence. "I'd sure like to help out you Canuck folks, but you need a special pass showing today's date to get by me and get in there." We pleaded with him. He wouldn't budge. "I know it's tough, but I had a young anchorwoman from Cleveland crying and making a big fuss over the same thing earlier tonight, and I just had to say, 'Sorry ma'am—no paper, no entry.'" In a flash, Pat and I were back in the street, trying to hail a cab in the pouring rain. By now, it was fifteen minutes until *National News* airtime, and it was only a short ride back to our Washington bureau, where I would now anchor the show—but the darkness and the wet pavements slowed us down. Damp from the rain and out of breath, looking frazzled and with no makeup, I slid into a chair on a tiny news set in our bureau just as I heard announcer Lee Marshall say, "CTV National News . . . with Lloyd Robertson."

By now the script was badly mangled and unreadable. There was no teleprompter and I was improvising all the copy and introductions. The first was to Craig Oliver, dispatched earlier from Ottawa. His credentials as a former Washington correspondent allowed him onto the White House lawn. He started off: "Lloyd, Americans have to be concerned there is a sex addict in the White House."

His startling opening line drew attention away from his bedraggled anchor as I realized this was a night when viewers might have been faced, for the first time, with an empty chair when my name was called out.

What was your biggest scoop?
The one we still wear with pride at CTV dates to February 23, 1993, when Craig Oliver called the newsroom to say he was quite sure that Brian Mulroney would announce his resignation as prime minister the next day. It was an evening that set off a flurry of phone calls and long consultations on whether we should go ahead with the news without hard evidence that it was going to happen. Craig knew something was up when he began calling around to follow up on the hints he'd been getting, and none of his usually reliable sources would return his calls. All of us in the system began calling people who might have information. They either weren't answering their phones or were magically "out" or "unavailable." I managed to dig out longtime Conservative operative and Mulroney adviser Hugh Segal, and in spite of our friendly relationship through the years, he was firmly noncommittal: "Can't say, Lloyd. Don't

know." He quickly pleaded that he had to cut our chat short. What nailed it for Craig, as he points out in his book, *Oliver's Twist*, was a conversation with someone who would *have* to know, a contact he had worked through the years. Craig found a way for this person to reveal an answer without having to volunteer anything. "I would count to five and if he did not interrupt, I would take that as confirmation. The man on the other end waited through the count, and then wordlessly hung up." Craig called us to say he was as close to it as we would ever get. Of the hundreds of reporters covering Parliament Hill, no one else had a whiff of the big news. The one remaining concern was whether Brian Mulroney might change his mind. It was not out of the question; other leaders had changed course when their carefully guarded secret plans found their way into the media. After we broke the news in a major exclusive to the nation, I asked Craig on air, "And what if the prime minister wakes up and decides he's not going to do it?" Craig responded, "If he doesn't go, then *I* will have to." It was CTV News at its best: bold and gutsy, but always up front with the audience. As Mulroney arrived on Parliament Hill the next morning, he shouted to a throng of assembled reporters, "Oliver better start looking for a job!"—giving Craig, as he admits, "a moment of panic" before word leaked out that Mulroney was indeed departing. Once again, Craig earned his spurs in a long career that has made him a journalistic icon.

Why is there so much celebrity news these days?
For those of us in journalism, this is a classic chicken-and-egg question.

Which came first: the supply or the demand?

In the early days of my career, news was serious stuff, but somewhat limited—wars, natural disasters, government pronouncements. People wanted and needed to know about these things, but might well have asked, "Is that all there is?"

Well, no. As news coverage, particularly on TV, became less institutional and more competitive in this country, it occurred to the more alert practitioners of the journalistic trade that other categories of information were being neglected. Rescuing them from neglect might attract more viewers.

Two prime examples are business news and medical news. Both exert powerful—in fact, decisive—influences on our lives. If done properly, both can be presented with the kind of narrative skill that captures the audience's attention and gets the point across. CTV was an early adopter in adding specialists in business and medical news to the reporting roster. I have no doubt these were important and audience-building improvements to our coverage. And that, in a roundabout way, brings us to celebrity news.

In my mind, the pivotal moment in celebrity news happened in 1964 with the arrival of the Beatles on North American shores. At first, they were dismissed as cheeky upstarts with Liverpool accents, funny haircuts and limited talent. But before long, even the smuggest and sleepiest of news managers picked up on Beatlemania. Those screaming teenaged girls had parents who watched the news. Perhaps they would appreciate being alerted to this phenomenon, with its potential to challenge their authority.

As we all know, the Beatles—and the Rolling Stones and the bands that followed—became big news. They were not just a cultural phenomenon, but a business story as well. As one of

Britain's biggest sources of export earnings, the Beatles were invited to Buckingham Palace in 1965 to be invested as members of the Most Excellent Order of the British Empire.

So, did the stories about the Beatles build TV news audiences? You bet. Does the appetite for celebrity news persist? Yes. Is that a good thing? Not entirely.

The Beatles and other artists—and athletes—earned our attention and devotion with their talent. But we have now entered the era of people who are well known just for being well known. With them, what's to report?

The classic example is the American heiress Paris Hilton. She represents a new breed called "celebutantes"—people who rise to fame not because of talent or hard work but because of their inherited wealth—fine subjects for *Lifestyles of the Rich and Famous,* but not for the nightly news.

People make news, absolutely. We will always chronicle the activities of those who are well known because of their real accomplishments. Additionally, everyday people who have become heroes, villains and victims will always find a place in the news.

What to do about celebrity journalism, then? Keep it within limits and apply a high degree of journalistic rigour to the selection of celebrity stories.

What was your biggest gaffe?
I have already recounted a few, but the one that got the most national reaction and was thoroughly embarrassing for me happened about sixteen months after I'd moved from the CBC to CTV. In signing off the broadcast with Harvey, it was customary for us to take turns saying, "Goodnight for CTV News."

If he said the line on Wednesday, I would say it on Thursday. One night, I looked straight into the camera and, from the CTV News studio, announced with an air of complete confidence, "Good night for CBC News." Harvey's jaw dropped, and I scrambled to make it right: "Yes, I finally did it, Harvey." We both laughed and then we were gone as the network logo appeared on screen. How could this have happened so far into my time at CTV? I've only heard one explanation that makes sense for this fairly common mistake by broadcasters. Station calls, sign-ons and sign-offs become routine after a while, and the brain shifts into neutral when you're doing them. That's when the grey matter plays tricks on you.

In Stratford, I worked with an announcer who twice identified CJCS as CKEY, the Toronto commercial powerhouse owned at the time by Jack Kent Cooke, who went on to become a sports and media baron in the U.S. The budding broadcaster eventually got to work there. Stories of these kinds of gaffes proliferate through broadcasting and are always fodder for good talk when the news guys and girls get together.

In my case, I was called to account the morning after by our assignment editor, Dennis McIntosh. As I hit the door of the newsroom, there stood in front of me a chalkboard with the message, "Lloyd will write ten times—Good night for CTV News."

Of all the places you've been, which did you find the most fascinating?
First off, I've enjoyed pretty well all of them. While being an anchor means you're supposed to hold down the home base most of the time, I was able to log several trips overseas to the United Kingdom, to the old Soviet Union and Germany—before and after the collapse of Communism—and down under to Australia.

Travelling as an anchor usually meant dropping in for short periods and never getting a really good look beyond your specific reason for being there. Often I would return to some places on family trips, but there is one TV assignment that stands out. It took me to China in the mid-nineties to film a documentary. It was a place I'd long wanted to visit, and I had the good fortune to be there at a time of great change.

Deng Xiaoping, who had succeeded Mao Zedong as chairman of the Communist Party, was electrifying his country and making headlines around the world. He had uttered the hitherto heretical thought that "it is glorious to be rich" and unleashed the long-harboured inventiveness and entrepreneurial spirit in the Chinese population.

Deng was building what he called "socialism with Chinese characteristics," but the speed of his enterprise meant many were left behind, and the massive Chinese bureaucracy as well as the military and police establishments were still dedicated to their authoritarian ways. They had never experienced any other approach, after all.

We felt the sting of their attitude quite early. Producer Gordon Henderson and cameraman Mike Nolan were at the railway station in Beijing, taking pictures of some of the thousands of migrants who were coming into the city from the countryside to sign up for hard labour jobs during the construction boom. While it's customary to have a "minder" or a "fixer" from the government with you in such circumstances, our ever-present Mr. Wang was not around that day. Gordon and Mike suddenly found themselves confronted by two burly Chinese policemen who demanded they stop work and hand over the tape. Gordon pulled a bold ruse. He took the tape out of the camera and put it in his pocket while removing a blank out of another pocket. None the wiser, the police took the package and escorted the two men into detention in a nearby holding cell. While waiting to be questioned, they saw another detainee try to escape, and as he rushed into the street he was immediately pounced upon by the crowd outside and savagely beaten, leading to the belief that there were many undercover government agents spying on arrivals at the railway station. Eventually, we discovered that the main concern of the police was their belief that we were taking pictures of garbage in the streets, and with the Chinese concern for appearances and saving face in front of the world, this was considered a "serious offence." After a lecture, Gordon and Mike were released, but the incident was clearly designed to send a warning that we were always being watched. There was no doubt about that.

We visited Beijing University, and during a conversation with students there was an awkward silence when I asked whether free speech was important. I got the same reaction, with some tolerant but embarrassed smiles, when I asked about human rights. They brightened when I started talking about their futures; their hands flew up when I asked how many wanted to be millionaires. They were obviously happy about the new wave of capitalism coursing through their country and intended to be a part of it. But the students and so many others we met on our tour of China didn't want to speak out on controversial subjects. They seemed aware of the old Chinese saying, "The bird that flies in front of the flock is the one they shoot."

We followed one of the young labourers in the booming city of Chongqing back to his farm deep in the countryside. He was earning the equivalent of fifty or sixty Canadian dollars per month at his city job, money unheard of in rural areas. To go to his farm home was to visit another era, with his parents feeding the chickens on the dirt floor in the living room and sharing their bedroom with piglets. It was a beautiful, serene setting, with rice paddies stretching for miles over the green and verdant rolling hills. As we saw people use ancient implements to till the soil and maintain the crops, we realized that rural China was a hundred years behind the rest of the world. It took us five hours over rough and deeply rutted roads to make our way back to the city, where once again we were plunged into the reality of the new China, where progress is the only master and all else is secondary.

A few days later, in an interview with the Chinese official in charge of family policies, a firm but pleasant woman in her fifties, the word "progress" was used as a guideline for any change in the government's policy of one child per family in the cities and two per family in the country. Boys were preferred because, on the farms especially, they were considered more useful. Girls were often sold off, killed or aborted. Our guest explained that "with progress, as the farms become more mechanized, there will be less need for strong manpower and there can be more equality between males and females."

Several Canadian companies have been able to take their expertise to China to assist in and profit from the boom. Toronto architect Carl Hall told me, "There's such an audacious spirit here to simply do things—rip it down, dig a hole and push up something new." In all the major cities, the cranes dotted the skylines and millions of peasants laboured, often under primitive conditions, to build the new China.

Like so many visitors, we left enchanted by China. Standing

on the Great Wall, I closed out our broadcast by saying, "For hundreds of years, the Chinese people have been ruled by war-lords and emperors, from the Ming Dynasty to the Communists." They now seem intent on building the kind of society they would like for themselves: a country keyed to their inventive and entrepreneurial spirit, something Mao was worried about. They are creative, good-humoured and practical. There are many of what our native Canadians would call "old souls" in China who understand what has to be done to live in peace and harmony with each other and within the world at large. Let's hope their governments let that happen.

Do you have a favourite recreation?
If I'd been asked that question ten years ago, I would have been hard-pressed to answer. Now there's a quick and easy response: horseback riding. The opportunity for this new adventure cropped up, quite unexpectedly, because of the anchor job.

In the spring of 2002, I was invited to be co-marshal of the Calgary Stampede parade. It has always been considered an hon-our to be asked, and several major movie and media personali-ties, including James Arness, Don Cherry and Ron MacLean had appeared in previous years. My partner would be Canadian gold medal–winning speedskater Catriona Le May Doan. I was given the choice of riding in a car or carriage or getting up on a horse and riding the route like a real cowboy. I hadn't been on a horse for thirty years and was about to say I'd take a carriage when I had a chat about it with Kirk LaPointe, a longtime fan of horses and riding, who was our vice-president of news at the time. Kirk thought I should ride, and the idea began to have some appeal. He suggested that, at the very least, I could get up on a horse and another person could walk in front with a lead line to keep control so that I could interact with the crowds. Another avid horseman, Craig Oliver, scoffed at that idea: "You'll be a laughing stock all over Alberta if you do it that way. Take some lessons to upgrade your skills, be a real rider." Nancy agreed with Craig. "If you're going to do it all, you should certainly ride a horse," she said. Lessons it was, then.

I searched out an excellent trainer near Toronto, Gary Masters, who taught me that horse and rider have to act as a team. "They can be skittish animals," he would say, "but you have to be calm and in control, and once you've mastered a few techniques, you should be fine." In spite of a lot of doubts friends expressed about embarking on this potentially dangerous activity late in life, and realizing it would be only for a short time, I thrived on the challenge and found the experience energizing. I learned when and how to establish a partnership with the horse, when to praise, when to be firm.

Parade day dawned sunny and cool and I met my partner, Catriona, who allowed that she hadn't planned to ride, but "I couldn't let this eastern guy ride a horse all along the parade route while this western gal comes by in a buggy or car." We shared a laugh and I told her, "Thanks, Catriona, but if this were a speedskating competition I wouldn't be doing the same."

There was a great buzz and excitement as the bands and majorettes got set to step out along a wide stretch of 6th Avenue. Ahead of us there was a sea of white western hats, and the morning sunlight caught the tops of the glistening glass business towers that dominate this boomtown of the Canadian west.

The crowds were lined up ten to twelve deep along the sidewalk, ready to witness the opening of the Stampede—"The

Greatest Outdoor Show on Earth"—with a parade that cele-
brates the roots of the region, featuring cowboys and cowgirls,
hundreds of horses and cattle, and western bands and dancers.
Just as I was about to mount my horse, a small grey gelding, the
Canadian Forces Snowbirds roared overhead to signal the start
of festivities and he got momentarily jumpy. He settled long
enough for me to step up and into the saddle as I heard our
CTV cameraman from Calgary, Wendell Tenove, tell me that
he hadn't quite got that picture and could I please do it over
again. Wendell can be a joker, so I shot right back, "Wendell,
I know you didn't get me slipping or sliding off, which might
have been a good shot, but I'm up here and I'll be damned if I'll
do it again." I was aware, of course, that the tiniest mishap on
my part would be recorded for posterity and would certainly
hit the nightly news.

As we set off down the street, the parade marshal had Catriona
and me side by side, but my horse repeatedly tried to run ahead to
catch up with a section of the Canadian Cowgirls riding team just
in front of us. At one point, he did a 180-degree turn, and we were
suddenly facing backwards. An outrider came by, saw I was having
a little trouble and asked, "Lloyd, do you want to get off and take
the rest of the route by car?" I was taken aback by the question.
"Are you kidding? No thanks." And then I recalled my instruc-
tor's words: "Remember, there will be times when you have to take
charge. The horse will even expect direction." I took the reins and
directed my frisky friend to turn around and face the right way,
saying, "This is how it's going to be, buddy, and you'll have to learn
to like it." He got the message and stopped fighting me for the rest
of the walk, enabling me to interact with the crowd. I noted a wall
of cameras ahead as the parade prepared to turn a corner; I waved

and some of the camera folks waved back, a few even shouting, "Way to go, Lloyd!"

The next day, the local papers ran a complimentary story about the Calgary mayor and me making our Stampede parade debut and how comfortable we looked. The bigger story was about Joe Clark's car breaking down. Joe couldn't get traction in those days. He was back again as leader of the Progressive Conservatives, but his party was a small rump in the House of Commons, and a few years later it would merge into the new Conservative Party under Stephen Harper.

Nancy came out to Calgary and was mightily impressed by my riding debut, as was Craig Oliver, who came in from a nearby ranch. I kidded him: "Sorry, Craig, that I couldn't provide you with a news story by falling off the horse and creating a scene." He immediately invited me to join him on an outing at Mac McKinney's Homeplace Ranch, just west of Calgary, the next year, and I have been his riding buddy many times since. As some of you may know, Craig's eyesight has been severely limited by glaucoma and, along with a well-trained horse, I am his guide on these occasions, calling out, "Watch for the low-hanging branch just ahead, pal," or "Water patch coming up—be careful." Craig is remarkable in that he hasn't allowed his marginalized sight to slow him down, and he stands as an example for people everywhere who may suffer the same affliction.

Even though I have been clumsy and badly coordinated in other athletic pursuits all of my life, horseback riding seemed a natural activity for me. Craig said, "You have great balance. It's like you've been up on a horse half your life." And what a wonderful experience to be there in the great Canadian outdoors in the Kananaskis Mountains, savouring the beauty of our surroundings and appreciating once again the glory and topo-graphical variety of this magnificent land. For me, it was a calming experience; I was away from it all and drifting nicely into a reflective mode. In another of his timely quotations on so many aspects of life, Winston Churchill said, "There is something about the outside of a horse that is good for the inside of man." My feeling precisely after every ride.

All right. No more questions. Back to the news.

20

Tuxedos, Ball Gowns
and an Overture to Tragedy

THERE WERE DIRE WARNINGS OF AN IMPENDING APOCALYPSE. Some believers fled to mountaintops to pray; all of the rest of us who kept our feet on the ground were told that, at the very least, we could expect our computers to go wonky. There was so much predicting and prophesying on the eve of the new millennium; the world was looking forward to the midnight hour with a combination of great expectation, fear and dread, or simply dismissive resignation. There were also threads of information from the security agencies that monitor terror threats, reporting that their listening posts were picking up "extra traffic." The experts explained they were detecting signs of terror plots being hatched and that "the world should be on guard."

As a result, those of us in the anchor game in North America and around the world were called to our posts for that time when the numbers clicked over from 1999 to 2000 in each part of the globe. From what I could see, only the British anchors made a fuss and wanted to be paid extra for the assignment; our American cousins were surprisingly quiet on that front, and

Peter Mansbridge at the CBC, Peter Kent at Global and yours truly at CTV, good Canadians all, did our duty.

The signs of trouble leading up to the big moment were becoming apparent, and, unfortunately, one of them had a Canadian connection. Two weeks before New Year's Day, Ahmed Ressam, an Algerian living in Montreal, was arrested at a border crossing in Port Angeles, Washington. Customs officials uncovered a cache of explosives and a plot to bomb the Los Angeles airport on New Year's Eve. Canada was immediately cast in an unfavourable light among many in the U.S., who described this country as a place where terrorists could camp out and weave together their dark plans. It was one of three failed millennium plots by Islamic militants; one targeted a hotel at a Christian holy site near the border between Israel and Jordan, while the third aimed to sabotage a U.S. navy vessel.

These plots were all dealt with swiftly and decisively by authorities, which may have given us a false sense of security as the millennium was born in an uninterrupted swirl of celebrations and big parties attended by classy couples in tuxedos and ball gowns from one end of the planet to the other. In the Eastern time zone, I welcomed Craig Oliver, who was covering Prime Minister Jean Chrétien as he visited Parliament Hill. It was a bitterly cold night, and I kept Craig shivering in his place for several minutes while we enthused about Canada ("It's a great country, Lloyd") and forecast—accurately, as it turned out—that our beloved homeland would become one of the most envied of all in the first decade of the new century. Rosemary Thompson fairly brimmed with excitement—"This is the best assignment of the night, Lloyd"—as the ball dropped at her location, Times Square in New York, and thousands of revellers burst into "Auld

Lang Syne." Then it was on to the Forks in Winnipeg for celebrations with musical legend Burton Cummings, and we ended
the night with music and fireworks in Vancouver. Our broadcast
crew, under the excellent leadership of John Brunton and Scott
Moore, had a warm glow, feeling satisfied that we had helped
Canadians launch the new century with style and excitement.
Indeed, it was a night filled with hope and promise.

But the dark clouds were gathering. Ahmed Ressam revealed
to American investigators that al-Qaeda sleeper cells existed
within the United States—stunning information that was
included in the President's Daily Brief delivered to George
W. Bush on August 6, 2001. That brief was entitled "Bin Laden
Determined to Strike in U.S." The information was taken in
stride by U.S. intelligence agencies, which seemed to think they
had everything under control. They didn't. The world was about
to change. One of the longest anchor marathons of all time was
still ahead of us, and if New Year's Eve was a cakewalk, 9/11
would be like crawling over a deck of fiery coals.

The new century saw CTV become ever stronger. It was
the dawning of a golden age for the network and the huge
Canadian broadcast conglomerate it would become. It seized
a hammerlock on all time periods and was number one across
the board, in all critical slots, all week long. Ivan Fecan and
his brilliantly astute program chief, Susanne Boyce, launched
several new Canadian program projects: *Corner Gas,* with the
inventive Brent Butt leading the cast of talented characters
in the fictional Dog River, Saskatchewan; *Canadian Idol,* which
made Ben Mulroney a household name; and the cleverly exe-

cuted *Flashpoint*, with its expert casting and gripping plots, became an instant hit. *Flashpoint* and *Corner Gas* had brought major international success to CTV, and both had Ivan and Susanne's fingerprints all over them. The two also assembled a list of U.S. shows that would attest to their skills in picking the hits: *Law and Order: SVU, Desperate Housewives, Grey's Anatomy, Criminal Minds.* They were broadcasters and programmers first, as Fecan himself told the CRTC in its review of television policy in 1998: "Programming is my passion, and I'm proud of the fact that I've spent twenty-four of my twenty-six years in broadcasting doing everything I could to enable Canadian programs to thrive both creatively and financially. And the passion remains undiminished."

Both Ivan and Susanne had come up through the ranks. He had started his broadcasting career as a producer on the CBC Radio show *Quirks and Quarks,* and it became obvious to all who met him that he was a quick study. He was soon bounding up the ladder. Although he had never graduated from York University, where he studied fine arts, he described his time at CBC Radio in much the same way as I recall my own period there: it was his "graduate education." But it was television that fascinated him, and he soon conquered that medium. He was a co-developer of CITY-TV's *CityPulse News* before going on to executive positions at the CBC, at NBC in Los Angeles, back to the CBC in an elevated role, and finally to the stations in the CTV network owned by Baton (Bassett-Eaton), where he worked his magic to put together the most successful television network the country has ever seen. Not only was he a superb producer, he was a boardroom wizard as well. He had the knack of making other people understand that his interests were their interests too.

Only Ivan could have pulled off the miraculous amalgamation into one company of all the regional warring factions that made up the old CTV and forge them into a single powerful entity. Soon Baton was buying and swapping properties across the country, until an outline formed of a powerful, unified core under the CTV rubric that would simply blow the doors off all the other Canadian television outlets, private or public, leaving them in its wake. And it didn't stop there. Ivan was a true visionary who understood that to be successful in the new "five-hundred-channel universe" a television company had to feed its bottom line with pieces of the burgeoning cable and satellite properties becoming popular with viewers. He put together deals that would see him and his company eventually own TSN, the richly successful sports cable channel, and the influential Discovery Channel, among others. With diverse holdings in conventional TV, cable channels, sports properties (Maple Leaf Sports and Entertainment) and *The Globe and Mail* newspaper, Ivan became the biggest media mogul the country had seen since Roy Thomson came out of North Bay, Ontario, to gobble up radio and newspaper properties and eventually become Lord Thomson of Fleet. It was a stimulating and invigorating time to be at CTV, and while the news division became a smaller piece of Ivan's larger pie, we benefited from his successes as the company became identified with the best there was to be found on Canadian TV.

Close by Ivan during all this was Susanne Boyce, another true child of the medium. She had produced Jack Webster's show on British Columbia Television (BCTV). It was on every morning—at "nine o'clock precisely," as Jack would bark into the cameras on his promos. I first met Susanne at the Lake Placid Olympics in

1980, when she took a lesser assignment just to learn more about another form of television. During our chats, I got a sense of her natural instincts for what made good TV—"It's got to connect, Lloyd, it's got to be authentic and connect in a real way"—and hoped she might one day be in a position to put her own stamp on an enterprise. Susanne had all it took in smarts, determination and sensitivity to make it work. She moved on to the CBC, where her reputation was further enhanced. Eventually, she met up with Ivan during his second CBC period, and when he was restructuring CTV, he lured her to be his head of programming.

Both Ivan and Susanne had worked in news and related programming and understood the importance of a strong news department to enhance the quality and permanence of both a network and its local stations. They were extremely supportive of me. It may be naive, but I choose to believe it was because they sensed I was a kindred spirit and not just the guy who helped hold the ratings up on the nightly news. Ivan and Susanne were both news junkies and wanted CTV News, with its trusted brand, to be there for the occasions that really mattered to Canadians. Nothing identifies a TV channel more singularly than its local news department and national news connections. Other programs come and go, sports teams and the broadcast departments that follow them may soar and fade, but the news is always there. Ivan knew that the audience would only stay connected to CTV, with its string of heritage stations across the country, if our familiar faces from coast to coast showed that we cared about what mattered to the average viewer every day and we were there for the big events. Susanne and I agreed that, even though some Canadians might choose to watch CNN for breaking news on big international stories, we had to be there to put our own unique perspective on the events and that we should always try to see the world through the Canadian lens. Ivan's line to news managers was consistent: "Spend money on the major occasions when it matters to be there, and make an impact." Sometimes we would argue about the importance of one event versus another, but he could be persuaded, and once he was onside he never wavered in his support, even if it sometimes meant going over allotted budgets.

For years Ivan greeted me with, "Hi, anchor for life." I took that to mean I could stay as long as I was comfortable and didn't have to pay attention to potential successors who were lining up for the anchor job as I moved beyond age sixty-five and into my seventies. He would often appear on the set on election nights and always offered a word of encouragement. He never failed to call on election day to ask, "Okay, Lloyd, are you in the zone tonight?" Ivan understood the complexities of being the helmsman on a seven-hour broadcast through six time zones and keeping straight all of the candidates, guests and issues, as well as working hand in glove with our producers to be sure we missed no cues and stayed ahead of our opposition on other channels. All of this had to be done pretty well off the top of your head. You either knew the file or you didn't, and if you didn't, you wouldn't be back to do it again. When computers took over from old-fashioned calculating machines, the amount of material and the speed of the data increased tenfold. It became necessary to know the ridings and the candidates as they popped up on the screen. There was no time to consult files during the actual broadcast; you had to know as much as you could by the time you sat down on the set on the big night in order to guide the audience through the often-confusing maze of people and numbers and be able to direct the conversation as the story unfolded.

Election nights always take me back to the basics of TV that I learned in Winnipeg in the fifties. They are simply old-fashioned live TV, updated with all the modern technology, and brutally unforgiving to the hesitant or unprepared. They never fail to get the juices flowing, and when you know you've won the night, there is little else in an anchor job that can be quite so gratifying.

Ivan Fecan had left CTV when I anchored my final election broadcast on May 2, 2011. While he never missed being on hand for election nights and other major broadcasts, there was one occasion during our times together when he found himself stranded and frustrated. It was September of 2001, and Ivan and his wife, Sandra Faire, were taking some rare time off overseas. Nevertheless, his network restructuring, his high standards and the green light to go big had equipped us to cover an earthshaking tragedy that would reshape the habits of a generation.

The phone rang and rang on the morning of September 11, 2001, and a frustrated Nancy, who had been watching TV at our daughter's home, was unable to wake me. There was a second round of calls just after nine o'clock that finally jolted me out of a deep sleep. On the other end of the line was the urgent voice of CTV News vice-president Dennis McIntosh: "Get moving, turn on the TV, get a handle on what's going on and get in here as quickly as possible." I bolted out of bed and grabbed the TV remote. There was the picture, by then being seen everywhere, of the World Trade Center with smoke pouring out from the upper levels. As I skimmed the dial, while trying to get dressed and pick up all the latest information at the same time, I came upon Peter Jennings, and I recall the first words I heard from

him, now recounted in a book compiled by his widow, Kayce
Freed, and ABC news correspondent Lynn Sherr.

"There is chaos in New York at the moment," Jennings was
saying. "There is chaos." Then this exchange with a reporter
from the scene:

> DON DAHLER: It has completely collapsed.
> PETER JENNINGS: The whole side has collapsed!
> DAHLER: The whole building has collapsed. The building
> has collapsed . . .
> JENNINGS: My God! The southern tower—just collapsing
> on itself.

Then, a little later, this exchange:

> PETER   JENNINGS: Let's   look   at   the   north   tower
> quickly—quickly.
> JOHN MILLER: The north tower seems to be coming down.
> JENNINGS: Oh, my God!
> MILLER: The second—the second tower.

I was now tearing through traffic, trying to make what is normally a fifteen-minute drive to work in the shortest possible time. I
had the radio blaring as the all-news stations did the best they could
to get on top of a story that was moving with lightning speed. I was
stunned by the enormity of what was being broadcast—the towers collapsing with thousands of people either inside them or in
the immediate vicinity. When the car was finally parked, I trotted
into the newsroom, which was alive with activity—people barking
orders and phones ringing nonstop. Producer Tom Haberstroh,

who would spend the next several hours working with me on the other end of my earpiece, said that we were calling our special broadcast *Attack on America*, and he went over what video we had to show once I got into position. Then I was off to makeup to get ready for a day of encountering the unknown. Dennis told me that Lisa LaFlamme and Rod Black, hosts of *Canada AM* at the time, were holding the fort until I was ready. Trina McQueen, whom Ivan had hired to head up the CTV portion of his ever-expanding empire, came in to tell me that everything was cleared to go up on the network for as long as we needed. Trina and I had known each other for years as former CBC News colleagues; now we were together at CTV. We discussed the impact of the story and agreed we were heading into uncharted territory.

All systems were go when I got on the air. We were showing tape of the crumbling towers and gathering more material about the latest incident of a plane striking the Pentagon in Washington. I talked to eyewitnesses and experts and tried to sort out the story of another flight that had been hijacked and had crashed in Pennsylvania. We had established remotes at major airports in Toronto and Montreal as our reporters talked to travellers on flights that were turned back from U.S. destinations. We were also hearing about U.S. airlines landing in Gander, Newfoundland. At a certain point, I stopped, looked into the camera and said, "The magnitude of this disaster is truly breathtaking." It hit me that this was nothing like anything encountered since the Kennedy assassination, and clearly it was going to have a greater impact on the lives of all of us worldwide.

The U.S. government had basically shut down for several hours, believing that the best approach was to say nothing for fear of getting it wrong. We were left with wildly fluctuating speculation and gossip. Would there be attacks in Chicago and Los Angeles or elsewhere? Would there be an attack on the U.S. Capitol building? What about the White House? And what about Canada—could we be immune from attack? There were reports about a fourth plane being hijacked, another about a train being taken over . . . Time and again, I told our viewers, "Now, remember, this is information from one source only. We're checking—we'll have to get it confirmed." It was difficult to try to keep the newsroom calm that day, but my erstwhile floor director John Hurle Hobbs was doing his best and also making sure that one of my favourite snack foods, banana bread, was handy when needed. John was also aware that I fortunately possessed one quality that is quite useful in an anchor: the greater the pressure, the calmer I become. However, there was one point where my face clouded over. We knew there were Canadians in the tower, and I learned that one of them was the son of my longtime acquaintance Hans Gerhardt. Did he make it out? Sadly, he was among the twenty-four Canadians who lost their lives that awful morning. Hans and I had greeted one another for years when he was *maître d'* and manager at hotels in Toronto, ending up as the key man at Sutton Place. He always had a smile and asked about my health and family. The news of his son shook me as the reality sank in that the al-Qaeda terrorists had struck so close to home.

Dennis McIntosh was working feverishly to get our reporters in place at key locations. With U.S. airspace closed, he was sending people to New York from Toronto and Montreal by car; mobile broadcast trucks were commandeered from across the country to head south. With Washington covered off by our regular correspondents, he was trying to get someone in place as quickly as possible in New York, but to get them on the air he had to rent a mobile locally. Since Manhattan was sealed off, the closest available truck was in New Jersey. He was on the phone almost constantly.

> DENNIS: How much to rent by the hour?
> NEW JERSEY MOBILE OWNER: Eight thousand dollars [a huge amount by conventional standards].
> DENNIS: Book it!

Dennis was spending money lavishly, but he knew he had to. It was a time when money didn't seem to matter much. Late in the day, when I was talking to one of our business analysts and said, "In light of all that's happened, it may be unseemly to spend too much time worrying about the falling markets," several calls came in complimenting my approach.

Dennis was a million and a half dollars over budget by the end of the third day of our special coverage. Only at that point did Trina say, "Maybe we should slow it down a little bit."

By the end of the afternoon on 9/11, we could be pretty certain the nature of the story was changing from a rush to get more information to an assessment of the terrible toll. I found myself switching into a more reflective mode around eight-thirty in the evening, when I said, "It's time to pause and think about what really happened today—how, in the space of a few brief hours, thousands died, and how our world will change as we adapt to what's already being called the new normal." At two-thirty the next morning I signed off after fourteen hours on duty and went home to find Peter Jennings still at his desk at ABC.

Three days later, at one o'clock on a sunny Friday afternoon, Canadians joined hands in a fellowship service with their

American neighbours as a hundred thousand people quietly filled Parliament Hill, and the massive Gothic structure provided the outline of a chapel for those gathered under the Peace Tower clock and the mass audience on television. We all cried that day, including me. My voice quavered a little as I provided commentary on this intensely emotional event.

A few weeks later, I was in New York and got close enough to the burned-out shell of the World Trade Center towers at Ground Zero to see that the site had now become a shrine to hundreds of New Yorkers who could only stand and stare in silence at the blackened sentinels of the buildings as they recalled the horrors of the day.

While in New York I went over to ABC to see Peter Jennings. There was intense public interest at the time in how the anchors, on air for long hours during those difficult days, had coped with their own emotions. Dan Rather of CBS News broke down in tears when discussing with talk show host David Letterman the heroics of the firemen during the frantic first few hours on 9/11. Some who had never liked Rather saw them as crocodile tears, but the more charitable felt he had cracked because he had tried to be stolid and steady for so many hours during the crisis and was genuinely overcome with emotion when he talked about those hours in the more relaxed setting of the Letterman show.

I asked Peter for his view. He had been on the air for sixty hours between Tuesday morning, just before nine o'clock, when the first plane hit the towers, to Friday at midnight. He told me he thought "we could be allowed an absence of emotion in such situations" and went on to say pretty much what was later recorded in the book by his widow.

One of the roles, I think, we can play is to give people information and perspective in a quiet, reasonably sober sort of way. Television is very inflammatory at times and can, at the same time, be necessarily calming. When we have a national tragedy, we all turn on our television sets to be reassured that our lives are intact and have meaning. I have the privilege of sitting at the centre for periods of time. I don't want to be pushing my emotions on other people. My opinions, my analysis, my sense of context about why something is happening, yes. But I don't want to be pushing my emotions on people. I think it's important to keep it together.

If we don't keep it together, who's going to?

With his typical elegance, Peter had just presented the classic definition of the traditional anchor role. Walter Cronkite had established it at the time of the Kennedy assassination almost forty years earlier, and on September 11, 2001, we were all consciously or subconsciously following his lead. Walter showed a trace of emotion when he announced the death of Kennedy, and then he steadied up and continued. It's fine to be human and show emotion at the appropriate moment, but it's also important to understand the context of the event, and if it is a time of chaos and uncertainty, as opposed to a memorial service, the audience needs to see the anchors composed, giving us the most reliable versions of the obtainable truth and presenting a balanced perspective.

I had now been in broadcasting long enough to participate in the coverage of two tragic events after which people would talk about where they were and what they were doing when they became aware of what was taking place. While the Kennedy story gripped the world, I would agree with most anchors and commentators who have experienced both events that 9/11 had a greater impact, given the deaths of three thousand people and the lasting consequences for the everyday lives of millions around the world.

The impact of the 9/11 attacks on Canadian life—and even the Canadian self-image—cannot be overstated. The graphic recollections of that day lingered in the minds of most of us. And, of course, the attacks unleashed forces worldwide that inevitably drew Canada in. This was an attack breathtakingly close to us all, and we could be vulnerable too. This country was soon involved in the U.S.–led "War on Terror," which turned out to be Canada's longest war ever.

It's one of the great regrets of my career that I never got to Afghanistan to cover any of that time with our soldiers. I almost made it in 2008, and then a federal election campaign intervened and I was chained once again to the home front.

Coverage in the field for *CTV National News* was left in the capable hands of our staff correspondents—including, in the early stages, Lisa LaFlamme, who would later succeed me at the anchor desk. Lisa would never court danger, but I felt obliged on most occasions to remind her to "take care" as we signed off our frequent nightly chats on air.

Week in and week out for a decade, I had a hand in pulling our coverage together and, to borrow a military term, "debriefing" the various correspondents and commentators who contributed to our understanding of what the mission involved and what it hoped to accomplish. It was always a stab to the heart when I had to read the names of those who gave their lives in our behalf. It was the first conflict since the Korean War in which Canadians were involved directly as combatants. It gave me pause to reflect that we really were living in a changed time.

Canada's military contribution was to root out the al-Qaeda forces behind 9/11 in the volatile Kandahar province and, in this respect, Canadians succeeded beyond everyone's expectations. As the battles and roadside bombs proliferated and the casualties grew, so did the Afghan place names that will remain part of Canadian history: Kabul, Tarnak Farms, Kandahar, Helmand, Ma'sum Ghar, Panjwai, Arghandab, Spin Boldak and more.

These were places where, in all, 158 military personnel and four civilians died in the service of Canada and Afghanistan, and many more were grievously wounded physically and/or psychologically.

When I think about that war, I think of the casualties and the impact their sacrifice had here at home. Though they grew weary of the mounting costs in lives and billions of dollars spent, Canadians honoured the military as they hadn't done since the Second World War. We showered them with praise for their efforts, with respect and symbols such as the Highway of Heroes. No more were Canadians in uniform seen solely as peacekeepers—nice guys in blue helmets. They were tough, disciplined warriors who put their lives on the line to do the job they were given. We—and the world—could not have asked for more.

21

Wonderful Wendy and the New World

SURVIVING IN TELEVISION IS AN ART UNTO ITSELF. WHILE news and sports people generally have a longer shelf life than talk show hosts and quizmasters, we still have to be aware of the changes constantly driving our industry, and just keeping up requires constant adjustments. I had started out in black-and-white TV with a limited number of channels, followed the move into colour and still more channels and then into the five-hundred-channel cable and satellite universe and high-definition television. As the new century unfolded, technology was moving ahead at a blistering pace.

Media observers and critics had been forecasting the demise of the daily mainstream newscasts ever since the twenty-four-hour channels began sprouting, and their predictions of our early death had become more intense with the launch of many new sources of information on the Internet. The traditional evening newscasts in Canada and the U.S. were still drawing respectable audience numbers, but we all knew it was going to take more effort to remain relevant enough to keep people tuning in for this old-fashioned "appointment television" while also maintaining integrity and credibility. At CTV, we had already introduced some special segments to differentiate ourselves from other networks, including "Goldhawk Fights Back," in which Dale Goldhawk pursued scam artists and stood up for the little guy, and "Success Story," to draw attention to people who are making a positive difference—stories to inspire or motivate. Still, we had to keep adjusting and moving forward. We were coming into extremely challenging times. The anchor may be strong enough to stay in place, but you need key people around you to help keep the team fired up on the big stories and understand how to drive an entire news system.

As in most endeavours of life and work, it's the people who make the difference. That's why, when Wendy Freeman took the job of executive producer of *CTV National News,* I knew I had a buddy to go the distance. During coverage of Pierre Trudeau's funeral in 2000, Wendy was the producer marshalling our reporters outside Notre Dame Basilica in Montreal, trying to get to important guests first. The CBC's Jason Moscovitz was heard to say, "Wow, who is that woman over at CTV? She really knows what she's doing. We should hire her." "Not so fast, buddy," I said to myself, and I determined that we could never let that happen.

Wendy is a little over five feet of mini-bulldozer, whip smart and with a voice that cuts through glass. She can be tough and fiercely competitive, but she has a big heart and sound integrity. She is someone you can trust with your life. Her husband, Elliot, is wonderfully calm and very funny, and they have two children. Wendy is from Montreal and came to CTV after attending Columbia's journalism school and doing stints at CITY-TV in Toronto and U.S. stations in New York and Detroit, where she worked as a writer, editor and producer. She had moved up quickly through our system and took seriously Ivan Fecan's commandment: "Keep Robertson in that anchor chair as long as you can." She was never far from my elbow, making the last eleven years at the desk some of the most productive times in my career, doing the same for the newscast and for all who had the good fortune to be a part of the operation.

I knew almost instinctively from the outset that Wendy would be the one to keep us moving forward. She was in tune with all the new trends in television and technology and was not bound by conventional thinking. Still, she was tentative at the beginning, reluctant to let her own opinion stand. I took it to be the natural stance of a woman in what had been a boy's world, so I started calling her "boss." Pretty soon the title caught on, and everybody was calling her the same. Her natural confidence kicked in, and soon she was soaring—pushing, prodding and pulling people along with her.

They were also times laced with great fun. Wendy is a genuine character with a magnetic personality that draws people to her as she appears to bounce through life two feet off the ground, always waving, smiling and telling everybody, "It's all good," which often meant it really wasn't so good at all. Her other mantra was, "It is what it is," and in any given situation, she was always right. Travelling with her was a combination laugh riot and three-ring circus.

On one occasion in Washington, we had to hold an editorial meeting in which she yelled to us through a crack in an elevator, where she'd been stuck for more than an hour— "Make sure those items come in on time, Lloyd," and "Don't let Roger Smith [a senior Ottawa correspondent] sell you on more than one minute and fifty seconds." On the same trip, I learned Wendy was afraid of heights. A tall platform with steep stairs topping out at about fifteen feet above the ground had been constructed to give us a great background shot of the Capitol dome at night. President George W. Bush was about to read his famous "axis of evil" speech. CNN was using the same facility, and I exchanged greetings with Wolf Blitzer, a mainstay of that channel, just as he was leaving and I was moving into position. Wolf is from Buffalo, New York, and was familiar with many Canadian news people. From below, I heard, "Lloyd, Lloyd . . . I have something to tell you." Wendy proceeded to yell complicated instructions about when items would be ready and changes that had to be made, while Wolf waved goodbye and looked a little puzzled at the peculiar way these Canadian TV people communicated. Wendy finally came up to the platform on the second day but, white as a sheet and unusually quiet, she was there for less than three minutes.

In 2005, on the death of Pope John Paul II, CTV News president Robert Hurst, who had returned from a management position in Vancouver a few years earlier, decided Wendy and I should fly first class to Rome via London and have access to the big fold-down beds as far as Heathrow Airport. By that time, we had spent several days working around the clock as the Pope lingered near death, including jumping on the air at five-thirty one morning after a false report from a reliable source that the Pope had died. Bob had logged several years as a correspondent in various parts of the world and knew about the wear and tear of long and complex broadcasts.

On the plane, Wendy settled into her position right next to mine, went to sleep and immediately began sniffing loudly. Between the muted buzz of the plane and her loud snorting and sniffing, I hardly had a moment's sleep as we winged our way across the Atlantic. She was all apologies when she woke up, blaming her allergies, but the incident was so funny and she was so contrite, I quickly forgave her.

Landing in Rome, we raced straight to our location in Vatican Square, overlooking the Pope's apartments, where a set that was barely ready for broadcast was soon in place for us to begin delivering our first newscast back to Canada. Our erstwhile technical chief, Bill Strain, was there, surrounded by loose wires and operational chaos as Wendy began barking orders at him about the need to speed up and get things done. Bill is a gentle, taciturn man who has seen it all when it comes to crazy TV scenes, but this time a raw nerve had been touched. Bill said, "Now, look here, young lady . . ." and then trailed off before he could do more damage.

The short outburst didn't faze Wendy as she kept on pushing to get us on the air back home—which, with a lot of scotch tape and baling wire, as we say in the business, we managed to accomplish with relative ease and no sign that the situation was spinning out of control all around us. A short time later, Bill and Wendy were laughing and chatting like old friends, and it was obvious once again that no one who cared about being professional could stay angry with Wendy for very long.

By the time I got to bed that night, I was seriously overtired. The Pope's funeral was still a full day away, so I warmly contemplated the opportunity to get some sleep. Trouble was, I seriously overslept. We still had a broadcast to make to Canada the day before the funeral, and I was placing it in jeopardy. I quickly showered and began to get dressed when Wendy called. I asked why she hadn't tried to wake me earlier, and she sheepishly admitted to running down the hallway seven times before she heard my shower running and felt comfortable about calling. The guilt from the sniffing episode on the plane was still lingering.

Our hotel was a converted monastery about a five-minute walk from Vatican Square. It was sparsely furnished but comfortable, and we were congratulating ourselves on finding such a place so close to the central location. The morning of the funeral, we got a shock. The gates to the square were locked, and as we headed out into the street that led directly into the square, it was filled wall to wall for six blocks with the faithful lining up to get inside. "Oh, my God" was our reaction as we plunged into the crowd, realizing we were going to have to elbow our way through to get to the news location in time for the beginning of our broadcast to Canada. Wendy and I started shouting, "We're from CNN!" thinking all would recognize the call letters of this international cable and satellite broadcaster. Some made way, but others weren't so accommodating. I had a staring match with a large gentleman who seemed on the point of giving me a hard push, but he ultimately backed off. Lisa LaFlamme, who would be an on-location reporter for us in the square, found her way blocked by four nuns in grey habits. They showed no sign of giving way until Lisa, the Catholic girl with lots of spunk, said politely but firmly, "Out of the way, sisters, I'm coming through." They quickly parted their ranks. Travelling with us was a tall, handsome young priest from London, Ontario, Father Michael Bedard. He fell far behind us as so many members of the crowd wanted to meet him and receive his blessing.

It wasn't until we reached our broadcast location that we learned that our own CTV call letters would have moved us smartly through the crowds—we happened to share a call sign with Vatican television. By this time, the gates to the square had opened and the vast crowds surged forward to be part of the momentous occasion. It was a five-hour broadcast that April morning from in front of St. Peter's Basilica, and some members of our crew were getting very tired. When the CBC's Adrienne Arsenault, who was sharing broadcast space just next to us, came through, she motioned to catch my attention and, with a smile, pointed to the CTV executive producer. Wendy was sound asleep, head tilted back in the chair. I kicked her gently and whispered, "Stop sniffing. The cardinals will hear you." Then, as Father Bedard started to giggle, I continued to talk quietly over the proceedings being picked up by the cameras. It may have seemed like a little episode of insider irreverence to some, but it was the shot of adrenalin we all needed to get us through another long day. I can imagine the late John Paul, with his keen sense of humour and humanity, having a little chuckle himself.

On these major international broadcasts, all the world's TV networks usually share pictures from a central source—in this case, Vatican television—and will frequently supplement with their own cameras trained on their hosts and reporters or set up to display different angles of the scene in front of them. The U.S. networks regularly put up more of their own pictures than anyone else. Their people are usually booked into the most expensive hotels, and they are always the dominant presence. I kept looking over to the ABC News booth to try to catch sight of my friend Peter Jennings. There was no sign of him. Charlie Gibson and Diane Sawyer anchored the broadcasts, and I thought it very peculiar that the principal network anchor had not been brought in for an event of such magnitude. It turned out that Peter had been away on holidays, and when I asked about him I was told that he had undergone some medical tests when he got back. The next day brought the grim news.

In a raspy voice, Peter appeared on his own news broadcast to say, "Some of you have noticed in the last several days that I was not covering the Pope. While my colleagues at ABC did a superb job, I did think a few times I was missing out. However, as some of you now know, I have learned in the last couple of days that I have lung cancer. Yes, I was a smoker until about twenty years ago. And I was weak and I smoked over 9/11. But whatever the reason, the news does slow you down a bit. I've been reminding my colleagues today that almost ten million Americans are already living with cancer. And I have a lot to learn from them. And 'living' is the key word." He promised to continue to do the broadcast on good days. "My voice will not always be like this."

He would never appear on his newscast again, but he was in constant contact with the newsroom and his friends and colleagues. Fiona Conway, who had worked with me at CTV before moving to ABC News in New York, where she was often Peter's producer, talked with me again about getting the Order of Canada for him. We had been pursuing the award for months before his illness, but there were the usual delays. No one in American broadcasting pushed for more exposure for Canada than Peter. He always made sure the big stories out of this country—federal elections, the Quebec crisis, the different medical system—received a thorough airing in front of his U.S. audience. Finally, after many phone calls, as we both furiously worked our contacts, he received the honour on the weekend before he died.

In August, only three months after Peter announced that he had lung cancer, the ABC network broke into regular programming.

ANNOUNCER: From ABC News, this is a special report.

CHARLIE GIBSON: Good evening. From ABC News head-quarters in New York, I'm Charles Gibson. And it is with profound sadness and true sorrow that I report to you Peter Jennings has died tonight, of lung cancer. Peter died in his apartment here in New York. With him was his wife, Kayce, his children, Elizabeth and Christopher. His sister Sarah was also there.

Then came a family statement: "Peter died with his family around him, without pain and in peace. He knew he had lived a good life."

To me, Peter was the best of our anchor breed. He was the true heir to the Cronkite mantle, and had become the template for the generation that followed Walter. He was erudite, elegant and deeply human. He was a perfectionist—some would say he cared too much, but Peter would scoff at the thought. He was a superb broadcaster and a great reporter because he never lost his awe of the life experience. He wondered about things—he had a boundless curiousity.

I knew very early how restless he was. Peter and I worked together at the CBC in Toronto in the early sixties, and we struck up a solid relationship as two kids who had caught the broadcast bug early, worked in small radio stations, and were eager to move on and make our mark. Peter came from a more sophisticated background; his father, Charles, was a vice-president of the CBC and had done on-air work as well. One day, Peter called me: "Come on up to the announce booth. I've got something to tell you." He was doing station breaks for the Toronto CBC station, CBLT, and was bored with some of the mundane tasks a CBC announcer was expected to perform. Peter was six feet tall, and he had his long frame stretched out with his feet up on the desk, next to the talk switch that would put him on the air.

"I've had a call from the guys over at the new CTV and they want to talk to me about doing a national newscast for them." I asked him how his dad would feel about it. He admitted surprise: "He's very supportive." When he asked my opinion, I told him, "Well, Peter, we're both the new guys on the block here. You've done more than I have so far, but doing a nightly national newscast could be a big break." A few weeks later, his handsome visage was appearing on CTV.

We had kept in contact over the years, and then one night, when I was watching Larry King interview him, I suddenly heard my name. They were talking about Canadian newscasters, and Peter said, "Lloyd Robertson—he's a very accomplished anchor who is with my old network, CTV." I wrote and thanked him. He replied, "I was happy to do it." That was Peter: if he liked you, he never forgot you.

I was honoured to be invited to his memorial service at Carnegie Hall in September, a month after his death. It was classy and eloquent, a fitting tribute to the man. Two Mounties flanked the stage. Even though Peter was an American citizen by then, he had never forgotten his roots. He loved music, and it was a large part of the service. Yo-Yo Ma played the cello, and jazz maestro Wynton Marsalis filled the old hall with the many strands of emotion in his versatile repertoire. Peter's daughter, Elizabeth, recalled some advice he had given her when speaking at her high school graduation ceremony: "There is nothing worse than sliding through life with conventional wisdom. We have to remind ourselves that every day we step off the cliff into very large questions about life. Have a good trip." Peter was never fearful of stepping off that cliff. His was indeed a life well lived.

And this from his colleague Lynn Sherr: "He was magical. There was a radiance about him. With Peter not on this earth, the universe won't be as much fun."

In my own case, I was just immensely proud to have had him as a friend, and stood in awe of his enormous talent.

The Siren Call of Politics

MANY TV NEWS PEOPLE HAVE BEEN APPROACHED TO ENTER politics. Some have only flirted with the idea, while others have jumped in. There was my old friend Bruce Rogers, who ran for the NDP when we were both young CBC announcers. As noted, TV correspondent Ron Collister ran for the Conservatives when Robert Stanfield was leader. Neither of these two made it into the House of Commons, but there are other examples of successful runs by broadcasters: Don Jamieson, who was a well-known newscaster and commentator in Newfoundland and went on to become a major force in Pierre Trudeau's cabinet, and John Harvard from Winnipeg, who was in Jean Chrétien's cabinet and ended his public career as lieutenant governor of Manitoba.

Broadcast organizations are always torn when their news people decide to run for public office. It's appreciated that reporters and anchors who cover public issues every day are probably some of the best qualified to allow their names to stand. Their profiles also give them easy name recognition and a perceived "leg up" on their opposition, even if it is no guarantee of electoral success. But once a news person runs for elective office under a party banner, their objectivity is forever called into question by the partisans of the parties opposing them. That's a moot point if they're elected, perhaps, but what if they are defeated or win one term and then lose the next? While it's understandably hard to convince the partisans, members of the general public may have a problem too. In today's ever-present media world, where every joke and gesture, every word and overheard whisper can become the image of the hour, the campaign of a high-profile media type is likely to receive more than its share of public scrutiny. It could be difficult, then, for the average viewer to simply wipe out any memory of what a candidate, who may have been known for fairness and accuracy when reporting the news, let fall from his or her lips when scrambling for votes. Many biting, unkind and unfair comments can splash into the public record. They may be used as quotes or quick pictures in reports, despite occasionally lacking the proper context, but they find their way into the public domain nevertheless. Take the comments that come quickly to mind from well-known politicians. Pierre Trudeau's challenge to western farmers—"Why should I sell your wheat?"—and Brian Mulroney's comment about one of Trudeau's patronage appointments, "There's no whore like an old whore," have stood the test of time. John Turner supposedly patting his fellow Liberal Iona Campagnolo's bottom is also the stuff of legend. It's enough to make an average person think twice about public office, let alone a media personality.

I have had to encounter the question of whether to run for public office a few times myself. In the spring of 1984, a long-time acquaintance, William Jarvis, who had been a cabinet minister during Joe Clark's brief interregnum in 1979–80, decided to leave politics. Bill was the Progressive Conservative MP for the riding of Perth-Wellington in Ontario, which included my hometown of Stratford. He took me to lunch and set out his wishes. "Lloyd, I'm asking you to consider running for the nomination to replace me as the Conservative candidate. I'm sure the riding association would be delighted, and I'm also pretty sure, barring the unforeseen, that you could win the seat."

I was flattered and had to admit, given my long interest in politics and public issues, the idea had some appeal. After a day or two of thinking about it, I called Bill and told him that while I was very honoured to be considered, I was deeply involved in my TV journalism career and wanted to stick with it. In fact, I had just accepted the position of senior editor after Harvey's departure and realized that a move into politics would have snuffed out what I had always wanted to do: be totally involved in the preparation and presentation of national news. In the ensuing election, Brian Mulroney's Conservatives clobbered the Liberals under John Turner, and the well-respected Conservative candidate for Perth-Wellington, Harry Brightwell, was easily elected to succeed William Jarvis. It could have been me, I knew, but I also had not a sliver of doubt that I'd made the right choice.

Eighteen years later, Liberal Party president Stephen LeDrew approached me with a request to run in the same riding. The Liberal MP, John Richardson, was retiring for health reasons, and there was to be a by-election. Paul Martin was on the verge of becoming the Liberal leader, and I could probably have played a role in forming a new team. The invitation had a little more appeal this time because I was nearing the end of my television career. I was approaching age seventy and knew that there were many more TV years behind me than ahead of me; this could be a chance to give something back to the citizens of my home constituency. Mind you, I have been very concerned about giving back through charity efforts for the city of Stratford and support for the world-renowned Shakespeare Festival over the years.

As to the issue of party labels, I've long considered myself an independent, one of those centrist Canadians interested in a strong economy that creates jobs in a society that looks after its dispossessed and downtrodden. I would not be one of those people who tells others how to live their lives, and I understood that governments can't do everything and there are times when you have to make tough choices about what ideas to support and what programs to cut. I have no doubt that my years in news and the continuing mission to keep our broadcast in the centre when covering politics contributed to my reaching this position. To me, taking up political life is about public service, trying to make the right decisions in the interests of the people and not being slavishly dedicated to one party banner or another. Parties have to organize themselves into groups of like-minded souls in order to make the system work, but the excesses of hardline partisanship can be pretty unappealing.

Again, I listened to the offer to run for office, and again I rejected it, telling LeDrew, "Thanks, but no thanks."

I thought that would be the end of it, but a short time later there was a total surprise. The Prime Minister's Office was calling me in the CTV newsroom late one Thursday afternoon in the fall of 2003. It's not that unusual to get a call from a press secretary to clarify some important point in the course of daily news coverage, but it wasn't a press aide this time. The call came from the office of Jean Chrétien's appointments secretary, asking if I would consider allowing my name to stand for the Senate. The Senate! There was stunned silence at my end, during which the caller must have thought the line had gone dead.

When my response finally came, it was "Let me get back to you on this." Chrétien was nearing the end of his time in office and was filling some vacancies in the Red Chamber. There was no apparent reason why he would want to appoint me, except that I was considered a friend and someone who had tried to be fair to him through the years. Often, prime ministers will make a high-profile choice to allow other questionable appointments to slide by unnoticed. However, I knew the prime minister was sincere; he felt it would be a good choice.

When I told network CEO Ivan Fecan about the idea, he chuckled and was enthusiastic at first—"Why not a senator doing our newscast?" Since there was no rule against senators holding outside jobs, except in clear cases of conflict of interest, we talked about how it might work. I could travel to Ottawa for votes and we could work out an arrangement to bring me back to our Toronto-based national newsroom, maybe do the news from the capital on some of those nights, and certainly always have a replacement at the ready. I had an uneasy feeling about it all, and both Ivan and I thought we were getting ahead of ourselves, so we agreed to talk about it more the next day. That happened to be the Friday before a Saturday night press gala in Ottawa that I was scheduled to attend. The prime minister would be present as well.

At Ivan's Rosedale home, we hashed over the idea some more and realized that letting me continue on the newscast as a senator would be impractical. While senators are generally considered more above the fray than members of the House of Commons, I would have still had to join the Liberal Party. Even if it were agreed that I could sit as an independent, there was still the matter of accepting an appointment from a Liberal prime minister.

Ivan noted that former *Globe and Mail* editor Richard Doyle, who had become a Conservative senator after he retired, performed no role on the paper after he entered the Upper Chamber. He also underlined the point that he didn't want me retiring any time soon, even though my contract was about to expire. "Remember," he intoned, "you're anchor for life." It struck us both at the same time that the question about the Senate appointment had given me some leverage in extending my contract another five years. I told Ivan I didn't want to go there at that point. It was important for me to be fair to the prime minister and give due consideration to an offer of public service. I could give the Senate more than five years before reaching the mandatory retirement age of seventy-five.

The next evening at the press gallery event in Ottawa, I was having a quiet chat with the prime minister when he said, "Lloyd, it would be great to have you in the Senate." I thanked him and smiled noncommittally, and we had a few minutes of idle chit-chat in the presence of the petite and beautiful Aline Chrétien, whose legendary influence on her husband could, for all I knew, have had something to do with his interest in me for this appointment.

As I scanned the room filled with members of the media who knew nothing about my little drama, I could only imagine what some of them might have thought if they had been in the same position or been called upon to give advice on what to do. A few had, only half-jokingly, tried to get the attention of various prime ministers to consider them for the Senate. My CTV colleague Mike Duffy would have been shocked that I wouldn't immediately jump at the chance; others would have wanted to know what I had done for Chrétien to cause him to look to me;

and still others would warn that my image of even-handedness and independence would be tarnished if I were to accept any appointment offered by a prime minister.

The next afternoon, a Sunday, I called my old friend and colleague Jim Munson. "Jimmy" had landed on his feet to become Chrétien's press secretary after being laid off in a CTV News downsizing a few years earlier. He had held several correspondent positions for the network, including two terms in China, and had ended his news career in our Ottawa bureau. I knew that he would understand the message I now concluded would have to be sent to the prime minister on my behalf. I told Jimmy that, while it might be fine for a reporter or other media type to cross over to the political side, it was next to impossible for an anchor. The anchor has to represent the very essence of what a national network news division is supposed to be about. I had worked hard for years to cultivate CTV News as an open portal for all positions and shades of opinion. Even if my appointment were viewed as benign and maybe even good by most people, some would have been suspicious, and that was enough for me to turn away from the idea. Every major network anchor in North America would understand the dilemma. While some, like Walter Cronkite of CBS and Tom Brokaw of NBC, were courted to enter politics, and apparently pondered the possibilities, they never went forward.

Jim Munson passed along my message to the prime minister, and I was delighted that a short time later, just before Jean Chrétien resigned in late 2003, our Jimmy landed in the Senate himself. With his knowledge of his country and its place in the world, he is a worthy addition to the Red Chamber.

Around the same time, I settled on another five-year deal with CTV. I would be working through my seventy-fifth birthday, not in the plush and sedate surroundings of the Senate chamber, but in the hurly-burly of daily news, where there would be no dozing off.

A few years later, Jimmy Pattison, the west coast billionaire and one of the sharpest business minds I have come to know, asked whether I had ever been approached to stand for politics. I admitted I had and I had rejected all comers. Without asking for details, he said, "Smart move, Lloyd. Once you've established your reputation for independence in the public's mind, you don't do the slightest thing to sully it." His words were like a benediction. If I had been left with any yearnings for the game of politics, Jimmy Pattison wiped the slate clean.

23

Connecting with a Prime Minister

I FIRST MET STEPHEN HARPER IN 2002, JUST AFTER HE had been chosen as leader of the Canadian Alliance party and become head of the Official Opposition in the House of Commons. He had arrived for an interview and to meet Ivan Fecan at CTV's sprawling suburban headquarters in Agincourt, in Toronto's east end. There was no reason to believe at the time that I was about to strike up a trusting relationship with another political leader and a man who would become a major force in Canadian politics.

Harper was a tall, somewhat shy and slightly physically awkward man who showed no signs of being the master strategist who would soon apply shock therapy to the Canadian political landscape. He was about to bring together the various elements of the right-of-centre political persuasion across the country: those seen as rabidly right-wing members of the Reform Party from the west that had morphed into the more moderate Canadian Alliance, along with the members of the still-more-moderate blue Tory elements of the Progressive Conservatives from Ontario and the eastern provinces.

Harper was an easy target of criticism for the governing

Liberals. They had been busily building a file on him, and he had left them several openings. During his years as a Reform Party MP, and later as head of the National Citizens' Coalition, he was on record as opposing same-sex marriage; while speaking to a gathering in the U.S., he painted Canada as "a European welfare state in the worst sense of the term"; and just after he was elected Alliance leader, he told Maritimers they were trapped in "a culture of defeat." Even though he was roundly criticized for his remarks, he never apologized and even went on to say that too much of Canada had a "can't-do attitude." While many Canadians may have agreed with him, the Liberals were soon branding him as a "scary guy," a clone of the much-maligned George W. Bush, and warning that he would push Canada closer to the United States. Depending upon where you sat on the political spectrum, this was either someone who knew his own mind and wasn't afraid to say his piece, a refreshing change to many, or a total alien who had dropped from the sky into the always-moderating waters of Canadian politics and would eventually be banished into the obscurity from whence he had arrived.

All of this was buzzing through my mind as I met Harper and he announced, "My father watched you on the news regularly, Lloyd." He said that in the deadly earnest manner for which he's become known. And it was not the first time he would mention it. The remark didn't mean much to me at the time, but as I look back, it takes on a new dimension. Was there a subtext there that would give me an advantage in dealing with him later? Was he in fact saying, "If my dad, whom I adored and respected, thought you could be trusted, then you're okay with me?" In any case, whether he was campaigning as Opposition leader or after he became prime minister, Harper's door was always open to CTV

News. The easy access caused anger and bitterness among some of our competitors.

One evening, a former colleague from the CBC's French-language network, Radio-Canada, went so far as to make the ridiculous charge that our better location for an event in a government building was because we were "the Conservative network." It was an uncalled-for cheap shot, and anybody who had bothered to monitor our daily coverage over any period of time would have found us to be scrupulously fair to all parties. Perhaps we were hearing from parts of the media stung by charges from Harper and his friends of small- and large-L liberal bias. It was a time when Conrad Black was about to launch the *National Post* and purchase a string of newspapers from the Southam chain. Harper had regarded these as positive developments that would bring what he called a more "pluralistic" approach to news, in contrast to the "monolithically liberal" bent of the previous management.

More specifically, in our own case, Harper's longtime assistant and director of communications, Dimitri Soudas, told me that whenever he had taken a personal request for an interview from me to the prime minister, it had never been turned aside. He noted at the same time, "That wasn't the case with a lot of others." There was no reason for Harper to regard me as a pushover and he had to know that there would be some hard and direct, if never nasty, questions put to him as leader. While I acknowledge that the high ratings profile of CTV News helped draw in politicians, Dimitri agreed with me that it probably all started with the prime minister's father, Joseph. I was from his dad's generation and was someone the son could trust just as the father had done.

In Quebec writer William Johnson's book *Stephen Harper and the Future of Canada*, there is a reference to the prime minister's regard for his father. Harper says, "My father was not merely honest; he had flawless integrity. In spite of his ambitions, he jealously guarded the interests of others as if they were his own." And Stephen Harper is big on integrity. Only once did he call my own into question. It was on the eve of Remembrance Day in 2010, and I was granted an interview with the prime minister, who was travelling in South Korea. There were many questions at the time about what would be the composition of the Canadian contingent in Afghanistan after our combat troops pulled out, which, at the time of the interview, was scheduled to happen in July of 2011. From the anchor desk in Toronto, I asked him about this directly, and without hesitation he told me that Canadians would remain in a "non-combat" role and would help to train police recruits and carry out other humanitarian tasks. The answer had given us a scoop, much to the annoyance of other media travelling with the prime minister. Shortly after we finished, my email box was buzzing with questions from Dimitri.

Apparently, it appeared to him and Harper that we had been granted the interview under false pretences. "Lloyd," he asked, "what happened to the questions about veterans and Remembrance Day?" I had asked one question about that, but I wasn't aware that an earlier communication from CTV to the prime minister's office had given the impression that Remembrance Day would be the only subject of the interview, so he wouldn't have expected to be questioned about Afghanistan policy. That information never got to me and, even if it had, I would have rejected it, since we couldn't agree to put conditions on the interview. Telling Harper this would have killed the exchange, but that's how it works. As it turned out, it was a simple miscommunication all around, and once I explained this to Dimitri, he advised the prime minister and the whole matter quickly evaporated. It might have been different and caused a more permanent rupture if we hadn't been dealing with Prime Minister Harper and his people for several years by that time.

The first year-end *Conversation with the Prime Minister* with Stephen Harper in the chair had come in 2006, after he had defeated Paul Martin's Liberals and formed a minority government. My new CTV partner during these events was Robert Fife, who had been appointed Ottawa Bureau chief after Craig Oliver elected to step down from that position but continue as our chief political correspondent. Craig's problem with glaucoma had severely limited his eyesight, and while CTV would have been quite happy to have him continue in his managerial role, he wanted to lessen the pressure of his workload. Thankfully, he was still highly visible to our audiences; Craig continued on the air with his usual gusto, and many of us observed that it was as though he'd been granted a second wind. He was as good as, or better than, ever.

It's hard to think Craig could have chosen better than his handpicked replacement for the job in the person of Bob Fife. Bob had been in Ottawa for fifteen years, working for various publications and with several scoops to his credit. Like Craig and me, he is a product of small-town Canada. He grew up in the northern Ontario town of Chapleau, where folks worked hard and honestly to earn a living and look after their families. Bob told me that he frequently used his mother back home as a gauge to determine whether his stories were populist and made sense. "If she gets it," he said, "then I know I'm on the mark." She was his model of the average Canadian. I've jokingly played that back to him over the years when he was trying to communicate a particularly complex Ottawa piece in the newscast. I would ask, "Bob, do you think your mother will understand the meaning of all those numbers and regulations in the environment story?" We would both laugh, and he'd be back later with a more compact and perfectly clear version of the same item. Bob was successful in Ottawa because politicians and bureaucrats alike knew that if he was made privy to inside information from them, the source would never be revealed. Bob was an impenetrable vault in that respect; he could be counted on to protect the person who gave him the scoop.

During this *Conversation with the Prime Minister*, all three of us—Harper, Bob and I—were nervous going into the interview. Harper was formal and not very talkative before the program got started, unlike Chrétien, Martin or Mulroney. He asked, "Do you really think we have enough to talk about to cover a whole hour?" We assured him we had, and then we were underway. These interviews last one hour and, in television terms, they are "live to tape," which means they have to run like a live discussion with no editing except occasional trims for time. The editorial content has to retain its integrity to protect both parties. Yes, there can be start-overs if there is a production or technical problem or if someone can't hold back a long cough or there is a physical emergency. Otherwise, it's like a live show.

We had combed through our stories of the year and had come up with several questions on a number of topics. Harper was thoroughly impressive. He answered all the questions directly, with little obfuscation and in detail and depth. Here was a smart, well-briefed prime minister. He knew what he wanted to say and said it with intellectual force.

The next year, during the *Conversation*, Harper, a trained

Hi, y'all! Back in the saddle, as co-marshal of the Calgary Stampede parade in 2002. Yes, I stayed on the horse.

My favourite horse, Monty. I think he likes me, too. Mike Nolan

Craig Oliver and I cowboy up before setting out on another ride in the foothills of the Rocky Mountains. Mike Nolan

Canadian news togetherness is bliss. Three national anchors in two languages—Peter Mansbridge, CBC; Bernard Derome, Radio-Canada; and me, CTV—after a charity event at the National Arts Centre in Ottawa. Mike Pinder, Courtesy National Arts Centre, Ottawa

Bob Fife and I scored the first TV interview with Laureen Harper, who joined our year-end *Conversation with the Prime Minister* in 2010. Jason Ransom, Prime Minister's Office

With members of the
faculty after receiving my
first honorary Doctor of
Laws degree, at Royal
Roads University in
Victoria, B.C.

Dan Anthon,
Royal Roads University

Carrying the flame in Sidney,
B.C., on October 29, 2009, the
first day of its journey back and
forth across the country for the
Vancouver Olympics.

Darryl Dyck, Canadian Press

Accepting the Queen's
Diamond Jubilee Medal
from Ontario lieutenant-
governor David Onley,
in February 2012.

Tessa Buchan

The day before she takes the chair, Lisa LaFlamme says, "No, I'm not really washing my hands of this guy." CTV News

A final touch-up for the last newscast from long-time make-up artist Elaine Saunders. CTV News

Wendy Freeman (the Boss), president of CTV News, gearing up for the final show. CTV News

Phew! It's over. Sixty seconds after the final broadcast.
CTV News

On set with my pals and Canadian news starlets—Sandie Rinaldo, Lisa LaFlamme and Senator Pamela Wallin—after the final broadcast, September 1, 2011.
CTV News

With Nancy, looking relieved, moments after I signed off the news for the last time.
CTV News

Ivan Fecan, the TV genius, says, "Thanks for all the good years, Lloyd." CTV News

And Wendy's still in charge as I take a call at the after-broadcast party. CTV News

Up and away in B.C.—on location filming with producer/daughter Lisa.

A birthday for youngest grandchild Jesse, with mother Lisa, Deanna, Raymond and Rebecca (top).

Nancy and me on our fiftieth anniversary in 2006—with all seven grandchildren.

All smiles, please, for the family cruise photo (from left): Nanci Lee, Susan, Lynda and Lisa, with Mom and Dad.

economist, warned us accurately that troubles were on the horizon because of the housing bubble in the U.S. In 2008, as the Great Recession loomed, he introduced his government's plan to deal with the coming storm through a series of stimulants to the economy.

Harper was never a media-friendly type but, like him or not, the majority of longtime observers of the Ottawa scene will admit unanimity on one point. As one veteran journalist said, "Harper is the smartest prime minister to come along since Pierre Trudeau." This prime minister also knows what he wants: to stamp the Conservative Party into the Canadian consciousness in a more lasting way. Protecting the Canadian flag could be seen as a part of that plan. The bright red maple leaf had become almost a secondary Liberal brand. Now it's the Tories who are telling patriotic Canadians that, under the law, they will be able fly it wherever they wish, and if others don't like it, too bad. (An Ontario couple that was forced to remove their flag from the front of their garage in a retirement community can now tell their neighbours to go fly a kite and make it stick!) It's a clever way of co-opting some Liberal territory, and there is nothing the Liberals can do to fight back. They would be branded as "unpatriotic," after all.

There is an irony here which is not lost on those of us who were around for the raging flag debate in the early sixties. The big Tory hero and leader of the time, John Diefenbaker, fought furiously to keep the Red Ensign, which combined the British Union Jack with Canada's coat of arms. Diefenbaker compared the maple leaf unfavourably to the flag of Peru. He railed that "it shows nothing of our heritage . . . Far from distinctive." Interesting historical point, maybe, but irrelevant in this age, in which the maple leaf has become the proud rallying point for Canadians of all political stripes and the Conservatives know that the public will enthusiastically support any move to protect it.

There was a fascinating sidebar from our first hour-long conversation with Stephen Harper that few people but the producer and our makeup woman noticed. Very seldom is TV makeup applied to the hands—it can be uncomfortable and it messes up clothing. About halfway through the taping, producer Anton Koschany turned to our director, Brian Lebold, and asked, "Are those scratches on the prime minister's hands?" Peering into the monitors in front of them, they agreed they were. Should makeup be applied? It was decided to let it go, but it remained a puzzle until close to end of the interview when, in a lighter segment of the program, the prime minister told us that he and his wife, Laureen, had taken in hundreds of stray cats over the years. And so it was revealed to the nation that the new prime minister and family had a real love of animals, and that the leader of the government had occasionally been scratched by some of the pesky little creatures they were trying to bring to safe harbour.

At the end of 2010, coming up to my last *Conversation with the Prime Minister* before leaving the anchor chair, we asked for Laureen Harper to participate. She had never agreed to before, but this time she did. After a long wait, the answer came back positive and we were also able to secure the invitation to conduct the interview at the prime minister's residence in the beautiful Gatineau Hills just north of Ottawa, a favourite retreat for busy prime ministers and their families.

When CTV sent out a press release about the TV event, the sneering from some quarters of the media and political world was almost palpable. Indeed, Bob Fife had to explain that we had been granted this unusual access because it was my last *Conversation* broadcast and the Harpers felt it was an appropriate gesture for a journalist they had come to like and trust. Even my longtime acquaintance Karen Redman, a former Liberal MP and an effective caucus chair and government whip under Jean Chrétien, asked, in a friendly but slightly suspicious tone, about Laureen Harper's appearance. I reminded her that Jean Chrétien's wife, Aline, had also been a guest on one of the year-end broadcasts. "Ahh, Lloyd," she responded, "It makes sense then."

It was hard to tell if Mrs. Harper was nervous when the cameras focused on her as she arrived on set for the last segment of our program. She appeared a little tense, but after I asked her the first question—"Tell us how you choose which activities and charities to support"—she settled down and talked easily about selecting charities that are meaningful in the world. She also talked about how the Harper children had adjusted to living at 24 Sussex and being the son and daughter of a famous father. She made the point, "We try to create a normal setting for them" by letting them have friends over for visits and encouraging them to lead the same kinds of lives as other kids. Near the end of the hour, Bob Fife asked, "Have the pressures of high office had any negative effects on your relationship, or have they brought you closer together?" The prime minister hit that one out of the park. He spoke warmly and with pride about his wife's activities and accomplishments and ended with "Laureen has been my rock through all of this. I couldn't have got this far or done this job without her. I owe her a lot." If opposites truly do attract, that has to be the explanation with these two. He is stolid and serious while occasionally, with her apparent encouragement, showing his lighter side; she is gregarious and full of fun.

In the election that came five months later, Mrs. Harper was the prime minister's constant companion as he campaigned across the country on his way to a majority government. It was the perfect image of the happy family at Conservative headquarters in Calgary on election night, with the PM and his wife and children, Ben and Rachel, basking in the congratulatory glow of the big win the Conservatives were at last able to pull off.

I was left to ponder the extraordinary animus directed toward the Harper people by some members of the media during his first four years in office. The bad feelings even extended beyond those who worked for media organizations that supported the Liberals, where you might expect hard-edged attacks on the Conservatives at every turn. The editorial support of newspapers or other media for one party or another has always been a part of our politics, and it provides spark and interest to debates over public policy. In questioning colleagues about the anti-Harper phenomenon, some put forward the thought that it was the prime minister's "divide and conquer" strategy that bothered them most of all. "It's just like his politics," they contended. "He likes to set people and groups against one another." Maybe so, but surely we don't believe others have not employed the same tactics in the past. It's just that when Harper, with his reputation for a controlling personality, tries it, he is judged more harshly.

It will be some time before we are able to judge him on his record, but if early signs are any indication, his so-called hidden agenda will not materialize. Harper is far too clever to allow himself to be boxed in on arguments about same-sex marriage, abortion or capital punishment. In spite of what his more hardline MPs may feel, the chances of any of these issues being reopened are slim to none. Many Canadians will hail the Conservatives' success in placing more emphasis on the victims of crime rather than sympathy for the perpetrators, while others will lament the government's law-and-order agenda that calls for more incarceration but doesn't say much about rehabilitation. And while the country is getting used to the idea of weaning itself off Big Daddy and Mommy governments, we don't want to look to a permanent "leaner and meaner" future; the challenge will be to find a way of trimming back while keeping in place the kinder, gentler side of our caring national community. That's the Canadian way.

24

Clocking the Countdown

STEPHEN HARPER WOULD HAVE KNOWN WHEN HE MET Ivan Fecan that the CTV chief was a supporter of the Liberal Party. Our head honcho had stated his political preferences publicly on several occasions. What he would make clear to Harper and all the other political leaders, as well as to the key people in his news department, was that his political stripe would never be allowed to interfere with the way our newscasts were put together. He respected his news people as professionals and, as a former newsman and a businessman, he knew it would wreck the credibility of the entire division and certainly affect the ratings for news programs if we suddenly became a house organ for one political party. He stayed the course with that attitude even after he told me, "They [the Liberals] were coming after me with complaints about coverage and expecting special treatment" during the 2006 election, when the Liberals began to slip behind the Tories in popular support. This was one of several reasons why those of us who worked closely with Ivan respected him so much and remained loyal to him throughout.

Not only was Ivan the quintessential television genius, he understood exactly what he had to do to protect his network and its people from those with outside agendas. Ivan began to pull away from his support of the Liberals after 2006, and told me he was very disappointed in their choices following Martin's time. By the 2008 general election, his support was lukewarm if anything at all.

Having lunch with Ivan was always a special occasion. I had deliberately limited my contact with him over the years, avoiding running to his office with every little complaint and asking to see him only on matters deemed important to the ongoing health of the news division. We had developed a special relationship; he could come to me to discuss important matters, like the choice of the next president of the news and current-affairs department, or ask about any specific problems or issues with personnel. I was expected to call on him if there were matters that couldn't be solved at a lower level. My approach on every occasion was to be deadly honest and discreet. He appreciated that.

In 2008, it was contract time for me, and Ivan invited me to lunch with him at the Toronto Club, an established, stolid bastion for business people in the downtown core of the city, full of polished wood panelling, chandeliers, linen table cloths and discreet staff. To be a member of the club spoke to your standing in the community, and you were mightily impressed to be invited as a guest. You had made it if you got inside the Toronto Club.

Another of my five-year contracts had expired, and while Ivan continued to commit himself to the "anchor for life" idea, I would have to decide what I wanted. At the age of seventy-four, I wasn't looking for another long-term commitment, but knew I wanted to be in place for the Vancouver Olympics in February of 2010. The Games would give me the chance to be around and on the air for the third Olympics staged on Canadian soil, after Montreal and Calgary. The Games could be bookends. Montreal in 1976 was my last major anchor assignment for the CBC. I moved to CTV shortly afterward, was there for Calgary in 1988, and could now look forward to hooking up with Olympic host Brian Williams for the broadcast of the opening ceremonies in Vancouver. Ivan really wanted me to stay for the 2010 Games, so we quickly agreed to two more years and said we would look at the future again in 2010. At this point, the future looked limitless.

And who was to say I couldn't go on forever? Nancy wouldn't be happy about it, but she wouldn't push too hard. I could also be sure that my closest old buddies, like Craig Oliver, Tim Kotcheff and former producer Del Archer, wouldn't hesitate to give me the order to get out when they saw me deteriorating. Del had made it almost his mission to let me know regularly by phone or email when he thought he saw some slippage. "Why are you slurring your words tonight, Robertson? It's not like you to drink before you go on the air." I would plead simple fatigue or might tell him he was hearing things, even if I realized he may have been partly correct. Certainly, I didn't want my friends to have to tell me the time had come. I was becoming aware, though, that the nightly workload was beginning to exert more pressure. Coming in at three in the afternoon and being at my best at the end of the long run at eleven o'clock, and sometimes well beyond midnight, was becoming more difficult. How far was I prepared to push it? I still enjoyed the work, but acknowledged it was getting harder.

I had been lucky with my health for a long time. The bleeding ulcer had healed over years before, but a few indications of post-seventy ailments, such as more severe osteoarthritis, were surfacing. My attitude was to push forward in the face of these minor challenges and laugh them off.

I have often been asked, "So, what made you decide it was time to pack in the nightly newscast?" There is one moment that stands out. In January of 2009, Wendy was leading our team to Washington for one of the biggest political events of a generation: the inauguration of Barack Obama, the first black president in U.S. history. I was looking forward once again to being a part of something that would be a marker for a generation. I would be at the centre of a day when the whole world was living an important event and leading our CTV coverage for Canadians. We had acquired space for our broadcast team on a balcony at the Canadian embassy with a view of the steps of the U.S. Capitol building, where the ceremony would take place. We also had access to the wide lawn in front, which would make the perfect background shot for viewers of our coverage. The show producer, Jana Juginovic, and I talked excitedly about the lineup of guests for the program, including Canada's former ambassador to Washington, Frank McKenna.

The weather in Washington was brutally cold, and I was fighting a nasty flu bug that had been floating around the enclosed quarters of the CTV newsroom days before. I thought I had beaten back the bug, but the moment I opened my mouth to talk to Sandie Rinaldo on Sunday night, at the beginning of inauguration week, I felt my throat seize up and had to fight hard to maintain just enough voice to finish the talkback. Wendy was standing off camera to my right and was shocked to see how quickly the colour drained from my face and how my shoulders slumped visibly while on air. The flu had finally overtaken me. It was the eve of my seventy-fifth birthday, and I was too sick to sample a birthday cake Wendy and Lisa LaFlamme had bought for me; it was back to the hotel and into bed. I began ordering up gallons of tea and honey from room service as I called CTV News president Robert Hurst in Toronto. Hurst was always straightforward and practical at these times. After expressing sympathy, he said, "Well, you'll remember I had this two weeks ago, and I was down for about four days. You can expect the same. We'd better get a backup plan in place right now." Our Washington bureau chief, Tom Clark, was immediately assigned to anchor the newscasts the next day on the eve of the inauguration and put on standby to take over commentary duties for me on the Tuesday morning ceremony if necessary. Lisa LaFlamme, who had come down to do items for our newscasts on Monday and Tuesday nights, was told to be ready to take Tom's place on the lawn among the crowds to conduct interviews with those gathering to view the big event on Tuesday morning.

I was devastated and miserable. There I was, flat on my back on Monday, January 19, 2009, my seventy-fifth birthday, with friends calling to wish me well while I whispered into the phone that I couldn't talk for long because of the laryngitis that had hit me along with the cold and fever. Wendy was buzzing about with hot soup and whatever else she could muster up, but she was also very busy with the thousands of details that go into planning major coverage. My old friend Fiona Conway, of ABC News, suddenly became an angel of mercy. She arrived for a visit, and after gasping and laughing about my hotel-issued leopard-skin bathrobe, admitted she'd never seen me so sick. Fiona ordered the hotel to keep up the flow of a constant supply of various forms of herbal teas, pots of honey and what had to be the widest selection of throat tablets in the universe. A doctor the hotel called was of little help. She prescribed a strong throat medicine and said, "You'll just have to stop talking and wait this out." She refused to even consider giving me a steroid shot.

How appalling! Was I about to miss my first big special-event broadcast in more than forty years of doing this kind of thing? As the morning of Tuesday, January 20, Inauguration Day, arrived, I began testing my voice at 5 a.m. I could get about forty-five seconds' worth of sound out before it began to crackle and fade. I was facing a broadcast that would run for three hours, with long sections during which I'd be expected to talk or control the conversation. Wendy, who had been monitoring me throughout while running the production schedule, called at five-thirty to put the critical question to me: "So, how are you feeling?" She got the answer she expected, and told me later she knew it was the right one. In deep frustration, I mumbled into the phone, "I don't think it's possible. Go ahead with plan B." A few minutes later, Susanne Boyce called. Her Highness, as I had dubbed the head of all CTV creative, was ordering up a special soup concoction from the hotel kitchen, and she thought that if I rested my voice all day, I might have just enough vocal strength to anchor that night's newscast.

For the first time, I uttered in a croaking voice something that must have sounded like a revelation: "I'm not invincible, nobody is, and no one in this world is indispensable." There was a long pause before Susanne replied, "Oh Lloyd, of course you're invincible. Now just drink the tea and sip the soup." The harassed but always pleasant hotel employees, who by this time must have had enough of room 420, were soon delivering mugs of a hot beverage that tasted good and went down smoothly. I settled back into bed, told the desk to hold all calls and tuned in to watch the inauguration broadcast. Canadian networks were not available, so I had to watch CNN, among others, while Tom Clark led the commentary for CTV and Lisa LaFlamme worked the crowds. Both were potential successors for my job, and they did well from what I heard after the ceremony. After remaining silent and drinking Susanne's secret recipe all day, I had just enough voice to appear on site at the Canadian embassy to anchor the national news that night. Our longtime lighting wizard, Adrian Goldberg, quipped, "Good thing you showed up, Lloyd. After this morning, the audience might have thought you didn't like Obama." This was a good enough reason to work hard to get back on camera, but I told Adrian, "Shh. Don't make me talk or laugh." There were a few anxious moments on the newscast when my voice began to fade at the end of some sentences, but I got through, and that was triumph enough on one of the worst days of my professional life.

Happily, I was in good health a month later and able to handle all of the commentary when the new American president made Canada his first foreign stop after his swearing-in. But his inauguration in Washington had brought what I believe was an epiphany: I wasn't invincible and shouldn't risk pushing my luck on the nightly news too much longer. I suppose I could have tried to keep going as long as possible—"as long as they keep paying, you keep playing," as some baseball oldtimers used to say. But hanging on to the desk by my fingernails until someone pushed me off had no appeal. I wanted to leave at or near the top. My life heroes were always the people who had the grace and good sense to go out at the top with their record intact: the former Liberal premier of New Brunswick, Frank McKenna, who won two majority governments and stepped down rather than try for the uncertain three-peat; the legendary hockey greats Wayne Gretzky and Jean Béliveau, both of whom left on a high; and the Denver Broncos quarterback John Elway, who won two Super Bowls and went out with class.

Our newscast had been number one in the country for eighteen years. It was in an almost unassailable position, but we would have to start thinking hard about the person who would step in to take my place, and we undoubtedly needed some kind of succession plan. I quietly began saying to close friends, "I will be looking closely at leaving the chair in the weeks and months after the Games in Vancouver." I started to warm to the idea, wondering what I might do after stepping away from the news. Full-time retirement was not in the cards. While Nancy would appreciate seeing more of me, she also knew I'd be like a caged lion with nothing meaningful to occupy my time. Golf would not be the answer. So the plan would be to move over but not out, to lift anchor but not dock the boat. By mid-2009 I was actively thinking about it.

25

And That's the Kind of Day It's Been

W HEN THAT LITTLE CATCHPHRASE WAS FIRST UTTERED
at the end of the news in the mid-nineties, some folks
liked it, others sniffed at it as being "too pedestrian," but most
colleagues and viewers didn't seem to notice—until, after a time,
they did. The day and date had always been a part of the sign-
off for the nightly broadcast, as in, "And that's the news for this
Thursday, September 17." There was a reason for making what
seemed at the time an insignificant little addition.

By the late 90s, twenty-four-hour news channels had proliferated all across the television landscape. The Americans had
CNN, Fox News Channel and MSNBC going strong; the CBC
had signed on with Newsworld, and CTV had been granted
a licence to operate a national all-news channel on cable and
satellite. It was to be up and running by 1997. This meant that
access to television news was no longer limited to the evening
newscasts on the various networks, whether at the supper hour
or later. On the eleven o'clock news side, we had to distinguish
ourselves from the all-news outlets the public would have had
access to all day. We wanted the audience to understand that our
mission for the late-evening national broadcast was a special one.

As always, we would take the day's events and, as professional news people, look hard at what had happened in this country and across the globe and assess what mattered to Canadians as part of our national community and of the worldwide human family in an interconnected world. The only real difference from what we had been doing previously would be that we were attempting to give people a little more on a story than they might have seen during the day and to add context, analysis and possibly a brief interview with a principal player if time permitted. It was a prescription to leave viewers feeling they had been brought up to the minute with all the important news, not just of the last hour but of the last twenty-four, and that we had presented it in an interesting and meaningful way. Everyone agreed that this moderately readjusted approach would drive the new mission, and I was left to contemplate how to state it in a subtle and unobtrusive manner within the body of the show. That's when the idea sprouted for the little tag line at the end of the news. We were telling people this was more than just another national and international news program; this was the "final word"—but we always reminded viewers that local news was to follow. Local news directors can become apoplectic if the network tells people to go to bed or gives them a pass to tune in to the late-night comedy shows on American networks instead of staying tuned to the local news. As far back as the 1950s, Larry Henderson was told to stop saying "Good night, everyone" on *CBC National News* because there was a fear at the local level that the audience would think the station was about to sign off. A compromise was struck by having Larry sign off for the CBC news only.

I had no idea that "And that's the kind of day it's been" would take on a life of its own. Soon, people would be saying it back to me when I was out across the country, and when I experimented with dropping it, there was an immediate response. It was 2000, and on a whim, I decided maybe we needed a change with the new millennium. But it was clear the audience didn't think so. Two nights after I dropped my catchphrase, CTV News vice-president Henry Kowalski phoned me. "Lloyd, what are you doing? I'm getting calls from people who miss your closing tag. Would you please reinstate it?" I was getting the same calls and email correspondence from viewers, so I quietly slid the phrase back into the closing, without comment, after only a few nights' absence in 2000. Those who hadn't noticed it was gone weren't aware of any change, and those who missed it were happy again.

Ten years later, when Lisa LaFlamme was announced as my successor, she was bombarded with questions about what she would say to close the show. Columnists wrote about her dilemma of choosing a phrase, and some members of the public told me it was what they would miss the most when I vacated the chair. Lisa handled the matter with style, saying it had been many years before I had crafted any special closing for the broadcast, so she felt there was lots of time to decide and for now would probably just say, "See you tomorrow."

My pals at the *Royal Canadian Air Farce* on the CBC put some music to my catchphrase, and I joined them to sing a gospel music rendition, all gussied up in our choir gowns, on their New Year's Eve broadcast at the end of 2010. It was always so much fun when I was able to be a part of their show. Don Ferguson, Luba Goy and the late Roger Abbott stand as true legends among the outstanding talent across the Canadian television spectrum. They deserve the recognition they receive as a group that truly understands the unique humour this country appreciates. We like to make fun of ourselves, and we enjoy watching our politicians and major personalities join the fray and let their hair down.

The attention drawn by the little closing catchphrase proves what those of us who work in broadcasting know to be the case and ignore at our peril. Most members of our audience are creatures of habit; they have their routines and don't like them to be interrupted. Even something as simple as a sign-off for a TV newscast becomes familiar if it's said every day and becomes part of a nightly ritual. People have often told me they would reply, "Good night, Lloyd." Change is always a challenge, and especially so in television, which is a very personal medium. The public makes judgments and hard choices on a whole range of factors—including, apparently, how a broadcaster says goodbye. "And that's the kind of day it's been" served its purpose in helping to make our late-evening broadcast distinctive.

As we prepared for the launch of our own all-news channel on CTV in 1997, we spent the year searching the country for talent to work as anchors, interviewers and reporters. Ideally, they should be people who could perform all three functions or at least had the potential to grow into them. That was the new reality in our business and, most especially, in our twenty-four-hour news channel, which would be operated on a tight budget. It couldn't be allowed to put too much strain on the entire CTV News system, which was already servicing the national newscast and our affiliates across the country.

For some time, I had been tuning in to the CTV affiliate in Kitchener, CKCO, which was doing a commendable job of serving all of southwestern Ontario, including my hometown of Stratford. It kept me connected to my roots, and it was through this outlet I first noticed Lisa LaFlamme. She was constantly popping up on the station's newscasts and seemed able to do it all. As an anchor, she had poise and authority; her interviews were always smart and sharp; she knew how to cut to the heart of the matter in her questions; she showed promise as a reporter and storyteller; and she presented as warm, natural and unpretentious. Lisa had the magic; she knew how to connect with an audience.

Thinking of her as an excellent prospect for our all-news channel, I called Henry Kowalski: "Hey, Hank, you've got to take a look at Lisa LaFlamme in Kitchener. She has the stuff—would make a good hire, I think." Henry started monitoring her work and was impressed too. On a bright spring day in May of 1997, Lisa was invited to CTV's head office—located at the time in the Eaton Centre in Toronto, where a gold-plated sign with the network's insignia led visitors to an upper floor. Stepping out of the elevator, she was ushered into a boardroom to meet Henry and his deputy, Robert Hurst, who would later succeed him, and CTV president John Cassaday. If the southwestern Ontario sweetheart was intimidated by the steel-and-glass magnificence around her and the aura of the big time, she didn't show it. CTV brass were clearly swept away by this smart, poised and charming young woman. She was hired on the spot.

There was a final hurdle, however, one that often gave network executives bouts of indigestion. Since CTV at the time was still owned by its affiliate stations in those years, local management had to be contacted and told that one their top talents was being scooped up by the network. These were often tense conversations with high-powered station owners and managers, who were quick to remind the network that they were the ones who were really in charge. In this case, there was some grumbling from one of the CKCO executives, who said, "She is one of the very best we've got," but there was also the realization that Lisa could not be denied her big break. She was clearly so loved and respected by her Kitchener colleagues and bosses that no one wanted to stand in her way.

While executives worked out the details of the plan, Lisa was zooming along the 401 back to Kitchener in her little green sports car, over the moon. She called her family to say "Hey, guess what? I just got the big job with the network!" Lisa's emotions are never far from the surface, and that day she was probably bursting into song, as she does at times like these. When she walked back into the CKCO building on Kitchener's King Street, the staff and management were lined up to greet her; there was applause and hugs and tears of joy all around. She was their girl, they loved her, and some were no doubt forecasting Lisa would soar to the top in the next chapter of her life. They would be right.

In the autumn of 1997, Lisa started as an anchor on what was then known as CTV News 1, now called CTV News Channel. She also handled consumer affairs for *CTV National News.* Her talents were so obvious to all that her rise through the system began shortly after she got her foot in the door, moving up to a job as a parliamentary correspondent in our Ottawa bureau, then to co-host on *Canada AM* and eventually to the position that would give her profile and stature and display her wide-ranging talents as a reporter and communicator. After no more than six years at the network, she was handed the plum assignment of national affairs correspondent.

Suddenly, Lisa LaFlamme was everywhere: in Afghanistan, with Canadians troops; on the scene of natural disasters in

Central America and Asia; and back home on the election trail, covering federal party leaders. If big news was breaking anywhere, Lisa was on it. She developed a healthy rapport with her colleagues in the field and on the desk on the home front in Toronto. While Lisa would try valiantly to extend the length of her items with passionate arguments about the worth of certain elements in her story, it was our job, in a fast-moving half-hour broadcast, to keep the reports tight and seldom over two minutes. When I spotted something I thought we could tighten down without losing any of the flavour of the story, she would respond, "Bingo, Lloyd!" and the debate was over. Lisa was a delight to work with because she cared so deeply about everything she did and wanted it to be the best. Yet there was never any rancour in the midst of debates about content and form, and if she lost an argument, she never held a grudge. During these times, some of my co-workers would say, "You really like her and respect her, don't you?" Without hesitation, I agreed, and found myself on the same wavelength as some of my other close friends who were saying, "When you decide it's time to go, maybe she's the one." At the very least, we all agreed Lisa should be on the list of candidates for the anchor chair. She would join a stellar collection of mostly male colleagues, including longtime CTV correspondent Tom Clark; Kevin Newman, who anchored *Global National* at the time; and John (JD) Roberts, the ex-Canadian broadcaster who was working in the U.S. All were well qualified for the job, and as the 2010 Olympics approached and my own preference about leaving after the games started to sink in within management ranks, the more serious sifting for a successor began. Focus kept shifting publicly, but in the end, from the network's perspective, there were only two prime candidates: Lisa and Tom. Tom had made no secret of his long-held desire to take the anchor chair, and both he and Lisa had been filling in for me during vacations and other time off for several years. Tom had proved himself and was an excellent correspondent and anchor, and while I encouraged him to keep the job on his radar, he heard me say several times that no one could expect a guarantee. Network brass was adamant on that point. They wanted to be free to make the choice they saw as the most appropriate when the time came.

The race to the finish was underway. Still, Ivan Fecan never wavered from his mantra: "Lloyd, you're anchor for life." It was comforting to know the decision was indeed my own, but at the same time I felt responsible for doing the right thing at the right time. What happened over the coming months would nudge me forward to an orderly exit.

26

Carrying the Flame

IN THE HISTORY OF THE TIMES I'VE COVERED IN THIS country, there was one major event that captured the Canadian imagination over a period of months like no other. We can all feel common cause when our national hockey teams beat the big guys from Russia or the United States, but for a sheer, long-lasting expression of joy in who and what we are, nothing topped the Centennial celebrations of 1967—that is, until the Vancouver Olympics of 2010.

The brilliant idea of running the Olympic flame out of Vancouver and back across the country over three and a half months, the longest such trek in the history of the Games, captured Canadians' imaginations as thousands volunteered to take part in the relay over 106 days. They lined up in Blind Bay, British Columbia; Canadian Forces Base Alert in the high Arctic, the northernmost settlement in the world; and in dozens of communities, large and small, across the land.

I was anxious to be a part of it all, and as host broadcaster and Canadian rights holder for the Games, CTV wanted me out on the trail early. That is not to say others in Canadian media weren't given a chance. The CBC's Peter Mansbridge and personalities from various outlets were invited and took part. The torch run was a national celebration, after all, not something to be cornered for the benefit of one organization. My turn came in Sidney, B.C., on the day of the flame's arrival at the end of October 2009. As I hopped on the bus with several others to be dropped off at our various locations along the relay route, people were just beginning to tell stories of why they wanted so much to run with the torch.

A woman spoke movingly about dedicating this moment to her mother, who had died two months before and was a passionate Canadian who had been looking forward to Vancouver's moment to shine on the world stage. A man who had just conquered cancer said he was running because he wanted to give thanks for his life's renewal and, as a second-generation Canadian, celebrate the country that had given him so much. I shared a seat next to an aboriginal teacher from northern British Columbia who told me her whole community was thrilled that she was there representing them and able to share this unique experience on their behalf. When I was let off the bus, torch in hand, ready to run, there was soon a cluster of folks around me, asking questions and wanting to touch the torch. It was like no other Olympic torch I'd ever seen: white aluminum with smooth, undulating lines to portray the Canadian winter landscape. One wag had said it looked like a marijuana joint—a cheap shot, I thought. To me, it was modern and innovative, just like our country. Soon, I was "kissing the torch" of the previous runner and the orange glow unfurled as I lifted it high and started the easy jog, about six blocks, through Sidney's downtown. What an exhilarating time! Residents shouted, "Go Lloyd!" Others waved the maple leaf through upstairs windows. Some decided to run alongside, kept back a respectful distance by the relay's security people. When

I handed off the torch with a hug and a kiss to the woman from our bus who was the next runner, a cheer went up as though I'd completed a marathon. For weeks afterward, our little group exchanged pictures and notes and Christmas cards. Other participants did the same, as this bonding around the flame became the experience of a lifetime for so many. Wendy Freeman, who was out west to guide our newscasts and who kept pace with me that day, said, "I can't believe you ran the whole way." I told her, "Okay, boss. I may be two months from my seventy-sixth birthday, but I'm not a piece of ancient porcelain that's about to crack open."

A few months later, when we were three days into the Olympics, the state of my health came up in a strange way. After our broadcast out of Vancouver one night, Wendy drew my attention to an Internet blog written by Howard Bernstein, a former CTV producer I knew well who had moved on to work elsewhere, including Global and the CBC, many years earlier. Howard claimed he was in possession of a "very trustworthy rumour" that other reliable TV industry sources could repeat but not confirm as fact. It alleged that I would rather not have gone to Vancouver to anchor Olympic news coverage because I was finding the travel and workload difficult. What's more, the rumour held that I had called a meeting with CTV bosses for March 3, just days after the end of the Games, at which I was expected to resign as CTV anchor. My first reaction was to laugh it off and not bother about such stuff during a busy time. But suddenly, it was out of my control; I was about to be thrust into the world of a modern media phenomenon: the non-story that breaks across the Internet and Twitter and bursts into life through gossip and mischief-making.

The next morning, CTV News president Robert Hurst called me early.

"Lloyd, do you know about Howard's blog?"

"Yes."

"Well, it's now gone viral. It was picked up by David Akin [another former CTV employee then working for Global, who had put it up on his blog]. It also appeared on Macleans.ca in a piece by [national editor] Andrew Coyne. CTV public relations is now getting calls from the Canadian Press, and I'm told the *Toronto Star* is on the line."

"Wow, must be lots of space available, even if the Games have started. You and I both know we'll be having contract talks in the spring, but the March 3 date is hilarious. I'm anchoring our network budget coverage that day. I can't believe this would take on a life of its own."

"Well," he said, "we'll have to put something out in the form of a denial. We don't want this hanging over your participation in the Olympic coverage."

I was appearing later in the morning on a popular radio talk show with Bill Good on Vancouver's CKNW. Much as I didn't want to shoot down my old friend Howard, there was now little choice. He had always prided himself on journalistic purity, and yet he had never bothered to call me. I would have been delighted to hear from him again. Of course, if I pulled apart the rumour and told him the real story of my intentions, it would not have created as much buzz and therefore as much attention for him. It's hard to ascribe motive behind Howard's story, but it could have been floated to him initially by someone trying to smoke me out to get a commitment on a departure date. Bill and I treated the whole matter lightly, as he agreed

my health and attitude seemed fine and I was actually ener-
gized by being at the Olympics rather than tired. The Canadian
Press and other outlets printed parts of the exchange between
us under the general heading, "Lloyd Robertson not ready to
retire—just yet." Factually correct!

Those opening few days of the Olympics had CTV stewing
for other reasons, too. The damp grey weather and melting snow
near the city had become an issue. But first, there was the shock
of disaster just before the Winter Games of 2010 were set to
launch on Friday, February 12.

As Brian Williams and I were leaving our hotel for the opening ceremony at BC Place Stadium, we heard the stunning
and horrifying news: a twenty-one-year-old luger from the
republic of Georgia, Nodar Kumaristashvili, was dead after an
accident at the end of his final ninety-mile-per-hour training
run that morning. This was a nightmare scenario. As longtime
special-events broadcasters, the two of us had been in tight
situations before, but this one presented special difficulties.
Brian and I knew this would be one of the biggest broadcasts
of our respective careers. Millions would be watching across
the country, and our work had to be as perfect as possible—
there could be no mistakes in identifying prominent people or
teams from all over the world, and the mood of the occasion
had to be reflected in our commentary. We knew the program
planned for the opening was set to be a moving and dramatic
pageant of the Canadian experience, with historical references
set to music and dancing, as well as traditional elements of
an Olympic unveiling, including the parade of athletes from
eighty-two nations, the most ever for a Winter Games. But the
tragedy of the morning loomed large and had to be acknowl-

edged in a sensitive and thoughtful manner. We drove to the stadium in silence, pondering how to deal with it.

After consulting the producer of the TV broadcast, Brian said we would confront the subject head on. I liked that approach and appreciated working with Brian. He is an excellent broadcaster and sports journalist who has perfected the difficult balancing act of promoting our amateur athletes while never becoming an obsequious mouthpiece for the sports establishment. Our co-host for the opening was gold medal–winning speedskater Catriona Le May Doan, my former co-marshal at the Calgary Stampede and now a commentator for CTV. Brian asked her how the athletes would cope with the tragedy of the young man's death. She said, "All athletes bond at times like this," and went on to say they would pause and reflect and then move on because Nodar himself would have wanted his teammates and colleagues in sports to continue with the Games. As Brian turned to me, I said, "Like so many of our viewers, I was shocked and deeply saddened today. It's one of those moments when life, at its most raw, intervenes. We slow down, think about the fragile nature of who and what we are and realize we have to move on, and that's what we'll do tonight." Our Olympic executive producer, Rick Chisholm, told me later that he breathed much easier after those exchanges because he thought we had effectively dealt with a delicate situation with as much class and style as could be mustered.

And then, the opening ceremony splashed across TV screens around the globe with an electrifying entry that saw a snowboarder racing down a high alpine run. He came closer and closer, to the undulating beat of musical accompaniment, until he was seen soaring through the Olympic rings and into the stadium in front of sixty thousand awestruck and cheering spectators.

I confess to enjoying these spectacles, and that night brought lifetime reflections for those of us who get a little choked up at the sights and sounds of togetherness among peoples of the world. When the Georgian team marched in wearing black arm-bands, the entire stadium, including all of us in the broadcasts booths, rose in unison to honour the fallen Olympian.

There were so many high points: Sarah McLachlan sing-ing her enchanting "Ordinary Miracle"; k.d. lang, moving gin-gerly around the stage in bare feet, singing Leonard Cohen's "Hallelujah"; and Canadian opera star soprano Measha Brueggergosman, her voice caressing the stadium and touch-ing millions across the world with the haunting melody of the Olympic Anthem. Canadian rap poet Shane Koyczan took to the stadium floor, captivating the audience with a new work called "We Are More" that spoke to the glories of our landscape and the hardiness of our people.

Given the traumatic start to Opening Day with the young luger's death, all went well with the spectacle at BC Place—that is, until the end. It was one of those "breathless moments" for organizers as Canadians covered their eyes in embarrassment. Brian and I were doing only sparse commentary, simply allow-ing the ceremony in front of us to play out, culminating in the lighting of the indoor Olympic cauldron. Our microphones were closed as wheelchair-bound Paralympic gold medallist and humanitarian Rick Hansen carried the flame on the last stretch of its journey into the stadium, handing off to Catriona Le May Doan. We had been tipped minutes before that she would be slipping away from our broadcast booth to turn up at the cen-tre of the pageant. With her were other sports heroes of the age, including B.C.–born basketball star Steve Nash, Canada's female athlete of the twentieth century, Nancy Greene, and hockey superstar Wayne Gretzky, each taking the flame to their torches. The show's producers had designed an arrangement that would see four pillars rise from the stadium floor, and each athlete would light the tip of a pillar to form the flaming cauldron. But the fourth pillar malfunctioned, and our Catriona stood with an increasingly tense smile as the pillar she waited to light stuck stubbornly to the floor. The seconds ticked by like long minutes as orchestral music vamped in the background and the audience began to realize, "Uh-oh, there's something wrong. Could the grand plan be screwing up?" In fact, it could. Brian and I, who had been sitting back, arms folded, watching the spectacle, both leapt to our talkback switches to the producer at the same time: "Open our mikes! We've got to explain this!" we shouted, almost in unison.

Brian talked about the hydraulic system failing, and I commented on the anxious mood of the stadium spectators. Finally, the suspense broke when the producers acknowledged that the fourth pillar was not going to rise. Catriona's face lit up with a wide smile as she saluted the crowd with her fiery torch and the tension quickly evaporated. Wayne Gretzky went outside to light the outdoor cauldron that would burn for Olympic visitors throughout the Games, and the evening was over.

There was a delightful moment in the closing ceremony when we displayed for the world our appealingly self-effacing Canadian humour. A technician crawled out from under the stadium floor to show us that the malfunction that had plagued the opening had been fixed, and Catriona reappeared to finally get her chance to light the cauldron before the flame died for the end of the Games.

It was a young Quebecer, twenty-two-year-old Alexandre Bilodeau from Rosemère, who lifted the gloom of the opening days and caused pandemonium to erupt by capturing the first gold medal for Canada in an Olympics staged on our home soil. I was standing with colleagues, watching his run in the men's moguls, and when he was announced as winner we literally jumped and yelled for joy. It was the first of many such outbursts. Alex himself said, "It's just the beginning, I think." Was he ever right about that! Magic descended on Vancouver. The sun came out and shone for six straight days. Canada went on to win fourteen gold medals, more than any other country, as happy crowds wound through the streets of downtown Vancouver, singing, cheering and chanting. The CTV gold medal theme song "I Believe," sung by Nicole "Nikki" Yanofsky, was played over and over all across the country and Canadians had it running through their heads during the Olympics and for days afterward.

The joyous atmosphere settled over our broadcast teams as well. On the news side, we were busily pumping out two or more nightly broadcasts every day of the Games, under the supervision of Wendy Freeman, with our solid senior producer David Hughes and director Brian Lebold backing her up. One night, Wendy approached me with a strange and strident demand. "Lloyd, open your mouth." "Whaaat?" I responded. "Open your mouth," she came close to yelling the second time. "Damn, they're right," she said, and ran back to the phone. I had just finished our first newscast, and the wife of CTV president Rick Brace had called from Montreal with the suspicion that I had something stuck in one of my front teeth. Wendy spotted a tiny piece of sugar candy and confirmed the news to

Rick, who had been standing, peering into the TV monitors at Olympic headquarters with CEO Ivan Fecan. She came running back to the desk, pitched a bag of ju-jube candies I'd been eating into the garbage and demanded I clean my teeth. Then the whole crew collapsed in laughter. The image of network head honchos, faces pressed to a TV screen, trying to determine whether an anchor had something stuck in a tooth, told us all the broadcasts were going well. We sailed through the rest of the Olympics incident-free—and with Wendy's candy ban in effect at the anchor desk.

As the sights and sounds of the Games drifted eastward beyond the Rockies, across the Prairies to Ontario, Quebec and the eastern provinces, most of us again experienced the bonding that brings us together as a country. It's something television does better than any other medium.

Vancouver 2010 was a triumph for our athletes, for the people of British Columbia and for the CTV network. Our people led the way in presenting broadcasts that were technically perfect, with inspired production elements through music and visuals to maximize the excitement and elevate the importance of the occasion. They were much more than a string of sports events cleverly strung together; they had heart and soul and touched Canadians wherever they were. Did the experience change us? Did we feel better as a country after the Olympics? Yes, I think so, just as we did after 1967. Back then, we learned to love ourselves and determined that Canada was worth saving from separatist pressures in Quebec. The same feeling enveloped the land in 2010. The red maple leaf was seared deeper into our collective consciousness.

Olympics are always regarded as a high-profile window for broadcasters. The event draws audiences that cross over the lines of dedicated sports fans who tune in regularly for hockey, baseball or football; they go beyond news viewers or soap opera buffs and reach people of all ages, right across the cultural spectrum, at all times of the day. Viewers become addicted to the Games and will keep TV sets on from morning till midnight to follow the fortunes of their favourite competitors and feel connected to an event that dominates the entire planet.

If you're a broadcaster, it's a thrill to be asked to be a part of the Olympics, but you know you'd better be good. If you do well, the shine can last for a long time, just as the consequences of a poor or mediocre performance can linger too long, and perhaps even leave a lasting legacy that stops a budding career in its tracks.

For Lisa LaFlamme, the Olympics vaulted her into an even more prominent position as an accomplished Canadian broadcaster. Lisa was co host of *Olympic Afternoon* with the excellent James Duthie, an anchor on TSN's first-class hockey coverage. As a news person, Lisa was venturing into a potential lion's den. Some of the hard-nosed writers in the sports fraternity have no time for news people who dare to traverse their sacred turf. I suffered a lashing in print in the summer of 1992 for my hosting work on the opening of the Olympic Games in Barcelona. Al Strachan, who worked for several different newspapers in his heyday and was a regular on *Hockey Night in Canada,* complained, "If you use a newscaster as the mainstay of your opening ceremony coverage, it stands to reason that the whole production will sound like a newscast. Had there been any news, that would have been fine. Unfortunately, there wasn't. So Robertson pretended there was." He went on to accuse me of "regurgitating" handouts from Olympic organizers. It's the kind of subjective opinion that forces an anchor to grow a thick skin. The barbs can sting and often hit the intended mark; you just have to move past them and focus on the task in front of you. I later told Al I'd enjoyed his column and had had fun spending time in the sports playpen.

Lisa tackled the Olympic assignment with her usual determination and laser-like focus. She learned all the rules of Olympic winter sports and the backgrounds of the athletes so well that the head of CTV Research told me, "She knows almost as much about these Games as Brian Williams." To her credit, she never tried to show off her depth of knowledge, but kept it quietly in reserve until needed and concentrated instead on the compelling stories every Olympics produces. These run the gamut from young people suffering hardship in the quest for great achievement to displays of grace under pressure, and often to dealing with crushing disappointment before the entire world. Lisa had already established her news credentials to be in line as my successor; now she was proving she had the stuff to move beyond, onto the broader stage, while never losing her poise. Her natural warmth and easy charm flowed freely through her performances, and her emphasis on the human dimension of what was happening brought home her sensitivity to the concerns and emotions of the athletes.

She showed great empathy when interviewing Joannie Rochette, who won the bronze medal in ladies' figure skating less than a week after her mother, Thérèse, died of a heart attack. "I know my mother would have wanted me to continue," said the charismatic young athlete. Few in the audience were aware that Lisa was dealing with her own grief. Her father had died a little more than a month before she launched into the Olympic coverage. Her parents were both huge supporters of her work, and her father called every day when the globe-circling correspondent was off on a major assignment. All of us in the CTV family were aware of Lisa's situation and made sure we did what we could to boost her spirits. To her credit, she carried on with professional aplomb, never showing any signs of distraction.

Timing often counts for a lot in life, and Lisa understood the critical importance of the assignment she had drawn as a host of the Olympic broadcasts. Her performance erased any doubts that she might not have the range to be the network's prime news anchor, which extends well beyond the eleven-o'clock news and includes, among other things, the need to conduct interviews across the cultural and political spectrum, navigate the editorial flow through news specials on events like election broadcasts, and be a believable public spokesperson for the news department and an appealing representative for the CTV network. By the end of the Games, she was widely regarded as the prime contender for the anchor chair, just as I was on the brink of making a decision about moving on. Lisa had followed the advice about timing uttered by the words of the bard immortalized just a half-hour's drive from her Kitchener hometown. As William Shakespeare wrote in *Venus and Adonis,* "Make use of time, let not advantage slip."

27

The Lingering Goodbye

ALL OF US AT CTV WERE ON A HIGH AFTER THE VANCOUVER Olympics. The audience had watched the programming in record numbers, and the complimentary emails and letters flowed in to our affiliates for weeks afterward. Ivan Fecan and his team had led what was widely acknowledged as the best television coverage of an Olympic Games the country had ever seen. We all felt buoyed by the response, and I was beginning to think about staying on until after CTV's coverage of the London Summer Games in 2012, to which we again held the broadcast rights. Another part of me was saying I should go sooner, not push too hard in my late seventies, accept a lighter load and leave on a high before my hand was forced by health or other circumstances. Also, Lisa LaFlamme and Tom Clark had been in the anchor bullpen for a very long time and, this late in my tenure, I didn't want either of them departing the fold because the current occupant of the chair was once again going to stay longer than expected.

It was in this atmosphere that in mid-April 2010 management offered me a contract for two more years, which would have taken me to September of 2012 on *CTV National News.* The need for a decision was hurtling toward me, and procrastination had to be set aside. I said to Nancy, "Let's go away and talk about the future." She had expressed concerns about me working so hard and would prefer an earlier rather than later departure from the daily news. I also owed this steadfast woman more of my time. During a warm April week in Florida, we walked the beach, read books, went to movies and generally mellowed out. I worked through a plan that she thought was a good one. Nancy continued to say that the decision had to be my own, but after more than fifty years of marriage, her body language and voice fluctuations said it all. She liked what she was hearing. There would be one more year on the news, and then I would gear down to an easier schedule for year two. Nancy knew it would be impossible for me to stop completely. Indeed, a few months later I made the following comment: "I couldn't suddenly hop off the daily news treadmill that had been running at 140 kilometres an hour on two networks for four decades—both legs would fracture." Also, the autumn of 2011 would take me to thirty-five years at the CTV desk; it was a substantial number and, when added to the preceding six years on the CBC's *The National*, it totalled forty-one, more years as a network news anchor than anyone in North American history. It was an appropriate time to bow out.

We headed home with the plan in my pocket and a week later heard some surprising news from inside the Canadian anchor world. Kevin Newman, who had been the helmsman of *Global National* for ten years, was stepping down for a period of "rest and renewal." In spite of Kevin's statement that "there is no other job in broadcasting waiting for me," my email and those of my colleagues began to buzz with speculation that he would be taking over from me. When the Canadian Press called, I simply said, "Kevin Newman is a great news anchor and I wish him well in whatever he chooses to do next." The chattering classes within the TV universe had apparently concluded that Kevin was on his way to the CTV anchor chair. It wasn't true, but that didn't matter—it made for great water cooler talk. My friend Craig Oliver, with whom I'd been sharing thoughts about stepping away from the desk for some time, told me, "Lloyd, I'm not asking for your timetable, but you have to know this move by Kevin sets the whole anchor successor question in flux." He was right. What's more, as Christopher Waddell, director of Carleton University's school of journalism and communication, pointed out, "It creates an opportunity for the network [Global] to think about doing something different when they replace him." Would they consider a woman as the five-day-a-week national news anchor? What if they came after Lisa LaFlamme? We knew they would be interested.

Under Kevin, Global had been snapping at the heels of CTV's number one national news position. They had pushed the CBC into third place in the nightly news ratings. Even though we didn't feel it was legitimate for Global to compare themselves to us, since the CBC and CTV were the true late-evening newscasts and Global's national broadcast was at the supper hour, it gave them bragging rights, and advertisers and journalists still read the basic numbers regardless of the time slot. While no one was pressing me for a quick decision, Kevin's sudden move, though not entirely unexpected by insiders, had complicated my carefully formulated plan and plunged us into the fascinating but always murky waters of network anchor politics.

Apart from Global's expected pursuit of Lisa LaFlamme, Tom Clark was still in the picture. Tom's always professional performances were being eclipsed by the flurry of encomiums flowing to Lisa for her work at the Olympics.

The situation made some of us think of the Walter Cronkite–Dan Rather scenario from the early eighties. It was a very different set of circumstances, but it reminded us how volatile the politics of these changeovers can become. The reliable CBS correspondent Roger Mudd had been the good soldier as Walter's backup for years and expected to be rewarded with the top job when the time came. However, when the "most trusted man in America" announced his retirement, Rather pulled a fast one. He encouraged a feisty rising competitor, ABC News, to make him an offer, placing his CBS bosses in a dilemma. Rather had been a star player on the Sunday show *60 Minutes,* and while his brusque, tense style was not altogether suited to the evening news, CBS management decided they couldn't afford to lose him and offered him Walter's chair over the loyal and more watchable Roger Mudd. Tom Clark, on the other hand, had already amassed impressive credentials as an anchor, and if his contractual arrangement had allowed an approach and an offer from Global, he too could have been in play.

This heated speculation spurred me forward. At the end of May 2010, the time had come to lay out my intentions to network management. Starting off with CTV News president Robert Hurst, I explained the plan for one more year on *CTV National News* and then proposed a lighter assignment in other CTV programming for the second year. Bob was immediately engaged and seemed relieved and excited that we were finally getting down to something we both knew had been coming for a long time. We discussed an expanded role in the network's long-running current-affairs show, *W5.* I had been co-hosting and doing occasional reports for them for several years; now I would have the chance to work on longer-form journalism at a less hectic pace. More urgent, though, was the need for a quick decision about my replacement. In the interests of everyone involved, especially Tom and Lisa, we had to make the choice and move the person into a more prominent position on the anchor desk. Bob said, "Okay, I'll take this to the big guy [Ivan Fecan] and get back to you." Ivan's reaction was that he respected my choice but wanted to hear from me directly. It was time for another lunch.

Anchor transitions can be tricky. They can get messy if the central character, the departing anchor, doesn't want to go. Dan Rather's sour exit from CBS is an example. Rather had been under heavy criticism for a report that alleged the military record of former president George W. Bush was a sham. It turned out the information had come from a biased source and it was quickly discredited. Rather eventually apologized, but the damage had been done. He had also been running third among three in the U.S. network news ratings for several years, and his bosses had finally found an excuse to get rid of him. He left under a cloud, suing the company and oozing bitterness.

Charlie Gibson, one of Peter Jennings's successors at ABC News, woke up one morning and decided he didn't want to be the anchor anymore and left as soon as he could. The network got lucky with their hasty choice of Diane Sawyer. The most orderly transition on the U.S. side was Tom Brokaw's departure from NBC. He gave two years' notice, and the company eased in the experienced and capable Brian Williams, with his all-American looks and presence. NBC's ratings held steady at number one.

In this country, it had been quiet on the national anchor front for several years. Starting in 1978, when the CBC finally settled down from its earlier machinations over union jurisdiction, Knowlton Nash managed to put in a record ten years on *The National* before passing the torch to Peter Mansbridge in 1988. Peter now looks to be heading for the quarter-century mark, an unheard-of number in an organization where anchors were sent flying on the slightest of whims. Who will come after Peter? Who knows? When I moved to CTV in 1976, I readily accepted the dual-anchor role with Harvey Kirck before settling in on my own. Now, in what was sheer coincidence, two key front positions were coming open at the same time—at CTV and Global.

This time, lunch with Ivan took place on a warm and sunny day in late June, at a classy outdoor café at another elegant downtown business stop, the York Club. The tables, under stylish umbrellas, were far apart, so intimate conversations could take place without being overheard by surrounding patrons. Ivan looked me straight in the eye and asked, "Are you really serious about this?" I again set out my plan and didn't alter the proposition I'd presented to Hurst. "Lloyd, you're a tough guy," Fecan said. "I see your mind is made up." We moved quickly to the next phase. I would stay on the news into late 2011, one more year, during which a date would be set for formally stepping aside. Lisa had been confirmed as my successor, and she would become my primary backup effective immediately. There was no rush to make a public announcement, but Ivan felt the news wouldn't stay under wraps for long once we started talking to the principals involved. I thanked him for his unyielding support through the years, and we parted on a reflective note, talking about the good times we'd had making television that audiences seemed to like. I felt so fortunate to have been able to spend the last fifteen years in the company of such a communications wizard. Ivan reached for greatness and took chances and, more often than not, the result was a superb quality of television programming, the like of which this country had never seen before. I watched pensively as he clamped on his sunglasses, stepped into his sports car and, with the wind blowing his grand mop of grey hair, waved goodbye. We were not parting forever and would continue as friends and associates, but the main game was coming to an end.

Early in the morning on Thursday, July 8, long before we had expected to be making a public announcement about my eventual departure, Ivan emailed me with a terse comment: "Lloyd, I don't like this." He was commenting on the now-hot rumour sent to him by news division president Robert Hurst, and copied to me, that Dawna Friesen, a Canadian working in Britain for the NBC network, was on her way home to become anchor of *Global National.* The information came from reliable sources close to us.

Dawna Friesen and Lisa LaFlamme had started out together as anchors and reporters at the launch of CTV's twenty-four-hour news channel thirteen years earlier. After other stints in Canada, Dawna had signed on with the American network and was posted to London, where she covered news originating in the United Kingdom and Europe for several years. Her return to Canada would be big news for Global, and Ivan chafed in the knowledge that it would also put them first out of the gate with the announcement of a woman anchor. If there was one consistent marker in his time at CTV, it was the burning desire to always be first in every way. After contemplating his email, I called him with a suggestion. "So, let's go. Let's roll out our plan right away." He was intrigued, but said he'd get back to me. We had no idea as to the timing of Dawna's announcement, but understood the deal was done, so it could come any time. By noon on July 8 the decision was made to go ahead, knowing we would benefit from a quick surprise announcement and hopefully scoop the Global folks. Very carefully, and under strict secrecy, we unveiled our strategy.

1:00 p.m.

CTV News president Robert Hurst, who had been in touch with us from his Muskoka cottage, begins his three-hour drive back to Toronto. Executive producer Wendy Freeman, on vacation in New York State, is called back but has car trouble. To her everlasting frustration, she doesn't get to Toronto until early the next morning. I call our Head of News Administration, Joanne MacDonald, to ask whether we can dig out the tape of the beginning of the first "Harvey and Lloyd" newscast from October of 1976. "I think we can find it," says the always-helpful Joanne. "What's the reason?" "Tell you later," I respond.

3:30 p.m.

The night desk of *CTV National News* assembles for the daily meeting on what's available for the nightly broadcast. They note a meaningless feature piece I've asked our assignment person to slot into the last segment of the show. "What's that about?" asks Mark Borchiver, the night producer on this occasion. I say, "Oh, you know, it's a slow summer day. It will do until we can find something better as we go along."

4:30 p.m.

I bring Joanne into the loop. She's already sensed something important is up, but when the news sinks in she expresses surprise and sadness. There is a brief hug, and then it's back to business.

6:00 p.m.

I write and structure the last segment, which includes a clip from the opening of the 1976 newscast, to be followed by a roughly forty-five-second announcement from me.

7:30 p.m.

Joanne and I assemble a few more people who can now be brought into the "need to know" group. Some old friends enter the room, and I get a little misty-eyed before explaining the drill to Mark Borchiver, Brian Lebold and production assistant Cyan Taylor. There is a reflective pause as I finish, we shake hands and move on.

9:30 p.m.

I address the newsroom, giving writers, editors and crew the basics on the coming announcement of my departure from the newscast, to take effect the following year. There is silence, a few sighs, and then a plea from me for a cone of silence around the information until after our initial broadcast to Atlantic Canada and CTV News Channel at 10 p.m. "Please . . . no emails or tweets, and no phone calls to friends." Everyone respects the request—there are no leaks.

9:50 p.m.

Ivan Fecan and Susanne Boyce arrive in the newsroom, champagne in hand. These two understand that television history is about to be made, as a long-running anchor who has brought news to Canadians on two of this country's original television networks is about to announce his departure.

10:00 p.m.

The broadcast rolls out as usual until the last segment, when the audience sees a tape from October 18, 1976.

> ANNOUNCER VOICE OVER: Lloyd Robertson . . . Harvey
> Kirck . . . with the *CTV National News.*
> HARVEY: Good evening. Lloyd Robertson joins us tonight for
> CTV News, and he couldn't have come on a busier news day.
> Lloyd?
> LLOYD: Thank you, Harvey . . .

At this point, we fade to the studio, where I explain what's happening.

"Yes, that was in 1976. So why are we reminding you of this tonight? Well, I thought it was an appropriate way of letting you know that I have agreed to stay on for another TV season, to make it thirty-five years at CTV. But that will be the final year. That means I'll be stepping aside in the latter half of 2011. So I'll be around for a while yet. To me, here's the big news on this night: tomorrow, CTV will announce the name of the anchor who will become my immediate backup and will take full-time possession of the anchor chair later next year . . ."

10:30 p.m.

The champagne corks pop as Ivan and Susanne lead the toasts. The phones start ringing, and I hear from my senator pal Pamela Wallin, who jokingly complains that she hadn't been consulted about this move. I remind her that senators retire at seventy-five, and I'll be seventy-seven before leaving the desk. There is one more broadcast, and then, at midnight, the lonely drive home, my head swirling, over the monumental event of the day and the coming change in my life. The one downside is that the early announcement means it will be a long, lingering goodbye—not what I would have preferred. However, I agree with Ivan that it's important to get our news out first. There is little sleep that night, and the calls from media begin early in the morning. There is still much speculation that Kevin Newman will be the choice to succeed me. I give no hints and head for work early.

Just before noon on Friday, Lisa swept into the newsroom. We had a long embrace, and I turned to the assembled throng. "Ladies and gentlemen, it is with great delight I present to you the next anchor of *CTV National News*." There were whoops, cheers and clapping. They all knew and liked Lisa. There was acceptance and appreciation that someone who had worked so hard and displayed such a wide range of talent was the deserving choice. At noon sharp, I appeared on CTV to reveal Lisa as the next anchor and say how proud and happy I was for her. Immediately after, there was an email to me from Ivan. "Ha ha," he chortled, "Global has just said their announcement of a new anchor will come next Tuesday." It was a clear coup for CTV.

The newsroom was soon flooded with reporters and photographers. Lisa and I spent our afternoon being interviewed for TV, radio, newspapers and the Internet. There was blanket coverage of the story on Friday, and the weekend papers played it big, in many cases on the front pages, with stories on the future of TV news and the rise of women anchors, and there were interviews in the papers and on the Internet with Lisa, with news executives and with me. The whole effort was a public relations triumph.

On Monday, there was a note from Ivan: "Dear Lloyd: Over the last few days, you have conducted a master class in how to successfully stage a transition. Congratulations!"

On Tuesday, July 13, Dawna Friesen was put forward as the next anchor of *Global National*. Dawna is charming and graceful, and all of us who know her have great affection for this accomplished woman. Her return to Canada, however, received minuscule coverage when compared to the news of the CTV anchor transition a few days earlier. It may be unfortunate, but in the high-stakes television game, it's all about getting a leg up on your competition. Ivan Fecan had pulled off another win for the CTV network—it would be one of his last. News of the anchor transition seemed to set the dominoes tumbling, with major changes coming swiftly at Canada's most prominent private broadcaster.

I was sad to witness the departure of Tom Clark from CTV. Tom claimed no bitterness over not getting the anchor job. He and management could not reach agreement on his future at the network, and there was an eventual parting of the ways.

There was a major ownership change, too. Bell, which had held about a 15 percent share in the network, bought out the other owners to take full control. This signalled a change at the top of our administrative structure, since BCE (Bell Canada Enterprises) already had a chief executive officer. It meant the key leadership in place under the previous ownership would take their leave when the new group took over. In September of 2010, Ivan Fecan announced he would depart the following spring, and his principal program chief, Susanne Boyce, would not be far behind. Then, Robert Hurst, who had guided our fortunes as CTV News president so successfully for ten years, took retirement. He was succeeded by Wendy Freeman, who would become the first woman president of the CTV news division in its close-to-fifty-year history. It was a deserving reward for one of the best and brightest in Canadian television.

For me, the last busy year from the summer of 2010 until the latter part of 2011 flew by. Lisa continued trekking everywhere, with on-the-scene reports of a joyous rescue of miners in Chile, to the Arab Spring in Tahrir Square in Cairo. She also assumed a more prominent role as principal backup on *CTV National News*. She was CTV's lead commentator for the April 29 royal wedding of Prince William and Kate Middleton. With the Canadian federal election two days later, on May 2, I stayed back to help a new producer through the complications of the always-frenetic election night coverage. The outcome, a majority government, also played well into my plans. It would bring less focus on the daily agenda of Ottawa politics, since the pressure of a minority Parliament collapsing at any time was now off the table. It would mean at least four years of stability in the nation's capital, with Stephen Harper's Conservatives firmly in charge. It was now a clear march through the summer to the finish line of the Robertson anchor era.

Craig Oliver, Tim Kotcheff and I took a week to reminisce at our favourite ranch getaway in Alberta. We talked of old friends, good times and the catalogue of people and events that had helped change Canada and made our broadcast careers so fascinating. Craig was about to tell CTV management that he would step aside after one more season as host of the Sunday morning political affairs show *Question Period*, while continuing as a political commentator, and I was into the final countdown to departure from *CTV National News*, set for September 1, 2011.

The day dawned sunny and warm. I was in a mellow mood through several media interviews and calls from colleagues, politicians and close friends. The final drive to the studio seemed surreal. I'd been working from midafternoon until midnight for the last forty-one years. Could this really be the last day?

The routine of the daily editorial meeting, talks with reporters and chatting with folks in the makeup room took place as usual. All asked how I was doing, and there was one common response: "I'm really comfortable with this decision. It is the right move at the right time." Wendy was close by throughout the day and into the evening. She was determined there must be no hitches in our plans for a classy and orderly turnover.

In a nearby studio, a group gathered to view a documentary on my life and times. CTV had scheduled it for a full network broadcast at 10 p.m. Eastern time, in the hour preceding the final newscast. It was put together with loving care by my daughter Lisa, an experienced filmmaker and producer, and it was a stunning success.

While the show could have been a simple review of the news stories I'd covered over time, it morphed into much more. Playing off my sign-off, it was titled *And That's the Kind of* Life *It's Been* and covered the unlikely rise of the young Stratford boy, first in small-town radio; traced his path through the joy and tumult of growing pains in the TV industry and followed the fortunes of this young country as it blossomed into adulthood and expanded its influence. The show was a ratings winner and a triumph for Lisa who, under the supervision of *W5* senior producer Brett Mitchell, dug into every corner of my life to unearth material that even I didn't know existed. In the closing of the documentary hour, I was seen heading down the hallway toward the exit door, saying, "To find something you love to do and spend your life doing it—it just doesn't get any better than that."

Then it was eleven o'clock and time for the final newscast.

> ANNOUNCER VOICE OVER: *CTV National News,* with Lloyd Robertson.
> LLOYD: Good evening. One last time for *CTV National News.* And we begin with a story you'll only see here.

After that brief nod in acknowledgement of the final broadcast, I introduced a report by Lisa LaFlamme that included an exclusive interview with media baron Conrad Black as he prepared to return to a U.S. federal prison. Viewers were then led through the normal run of stories of the day, including a report on a review of the Stanley Cup riots in Vancouver, an item on NHL hockey enforcer Wade Belak, who was thought to have taken his own life, and a story on how Canada planned to help rebuilding efforts in Libya after years of oppression under Moammar Gadhafi.

I insisted that this broadcast had to be a news show like all the others, and that only the last segment should be dedicated to saying goodbye to the anchor. The news, which is always the first draft of the history of our times, must take precedence over all else. Anchors come and go, but our lives and the news they create hum along. It is the daily drumbeat of time for all of us.

Nearing the end of the broadcast, we saw a videotaped message from Prime Minister Stephen Harper, who noted that I had been delivering the news since he was "barely more than a boy." The interim leader of the Opposition, the NDP's Nycole

Turmel, and the Liberals' Bob Rae sent best wishes—and then came the last commercial break in the broadcast before the final goodbye. There was a tiny knot in my stomach, but I was otherwise calm; my time as anchor of the *CTV National News* was now ticking away quickly—less than five minutes left.

As the picture returned to the studio after the break, I took a deep breath and, with a sense of serenity, launched into my prepared closing remarks.

> And so we come to the end, and it couldn't happen at a more fitting time than the beginning of September 2011. It was thirty-five years ago this month that I agreed to come to work for CTV, and Harvey Kirck and I teamed up for a successful seven-and-a-half-year run. During that period and since, we have had the usual ups and downs in the news cycle, from natural disasters to royal weddings, and I am deeply grateful to the many of you who have stayed with us through it all.
>
> For me, it's been a rare privilege to have been able to serve in this position for so long. It's been a front-row seat to history. If someone had told me sixty years ago this would be my life, I would have said they were crazy. Most of all, it's been fascinating to watch our country grow in confidence and stature. We have developed a unique place in the world. We can brag—in that modest Canadian way, of course— about our triple-A credit rating, about the success of the Vancouver Olympics, and look forward with some assurance that we won't have to undergo the near-death experience of another Quebec referendum.
>
> Thank you a thousand times over for all of your touching messages, some that speak of watching through the genera-

tions. There is the woman from Ontario who tells me that as a student, our familiar opening music would take her from studying at eleven o'clock to join with her parents for the newscast and to discuss the events of the day. She now does the same with her own children. Without her, and people like her, I would not have been around for so very long.

And it is not false modesty to say that I am only the most visible member of a highly skilled and thoroughly dedicated team of news, production and technical professionals [*gestures*] all around me here and out beyond. I can never offer them praise enough.

The *CTV National News* with Lisa LaFlamme begins on Monday. I will see you along the way.

And that's the kind of day it's been this Thursday, September 1. For all us at CTV News, good night.

At the end, there was a tingle of emotion, but I held it together. My image faded from the national news set for the last time, and we saw photos of me with close colleagues as a special rendering of "Thanks for the Memories," sung by Canadian Cal Dodd, played out to the end of the newscast.

There was applause from the newsroom. Old friends and family, as well as CTV's new president, Kevin Crull, gathered around the anchor desk for a few moments of reflection and pictures. I was elated and relieved. The final night had gone well.

Do I sometimes miss the daily rituals? Yes—but there is always opportunity for me to look back on those times through the thousands of letters and emails that flowed for days and weeks afterward. The amazing response from so many Canadians was humbling, and it speaks volumes about the power of broadcasting and its ability to touch people's lives in so many meaningful ways. It was a revelation for me to see that a daily news program, followed through the generations by the very young and the very old, allows us to chronicle how our own lives and the lives of relatives and friends have been shaped and changed through the years. Your messages spoke of comfort, companionship and inspiration. They all touched me at the core.

I share these few with you.

> "As my parents watched your programs and I watched from the end of my bed through a partially closed door, I was encouraged to ask the question 'Why?' long before I was old enough to understand the answer." —Lawrence

> "I would snuggle up with my grandmother and watch the news before going to bed. It was a moment in the day I cherished so. My grandmother died ten years ago, but every night I sit on the couch and feel like that little girl snuggled up on the couch with my nanny." —Jennifer

> "As much as the warmth from the household fireplace, or the glow of the kitchen lamp, or the soothing noises of home, you gave me the feeling that all would be okay." —Maxwell

> "As a little girl, I was never afraid to watch you tell the day's events from near and far . . . . CTV News is like part of the family, and the tradition carries on with my eldest son as well." —Anonymous

"My fourteen-year-old daughter has decided to take broad-cast journalism at college when she graduates from high school, and her goal is to one day work at CTV and be a news anchor, 'just like Lloyd Robertson.'" —Judy

And good luck to your daughter, Judy. If she thinks it through and possesses a natural curiosity about life and how the world works, she may find her bliss. She will be challenged, fascinated, occasionally frustrated, often gloriously happy—and never, ever bored.

For me, through six decades behind the microphones or in front of TV cameras in local, regional and national coverage of Canada and the world—That's the Kind of Life It's Been.

And What of the Future for Media?

*P*rotests *appear to break out spontaneously in the streets of previously tightly controlled countries—and the man and woman in the street post the evidence online.*

A Vancouver website promotes protests in North America against "corporate greed," and thousands turn out on Wall Street—and in Canadians cities too.

Meanwhile, newspapers shut down because the Internet has scooped up the classified advertising—the "want ads"—that had kept many of them afloat.

Broadcasters rack their brains to find new ways of sustaining the financial burden of covering the news in the face of the Internet onslaught.

Does this mean the end of media as we know it?

In my opinion, it's more like the end of the beginning. Over the last few years, social media have become more and more popular, but it is too early to throw out the television sets and silence the radios.

I have been around long enough to remember when the professional hand wringers were crying that television—yes, it too was once a new medium—would make radio obsolete and bring about the end of the movies. It didn't happen, of course. Painful adjustments were made, and the various media learned to get along—and in fact become interdependent.

I believe that will happen again, though again the adjustment will be painful. For one thing, the revenue-chasing ingenuity of media executives everywhere will be severely tested. As the old advertising systems start to break down, new models must be found. Already, media companies have learned that owning more than one property is critical; you have to get your content out there in front of as many eyeballs and ears as possible. For example, all of Canada's major TV players with traditional channels, like CTV, CBC and Global, have sprouted new properties on cable and satellite and are making certain they have websites to push their content and advertising—and some are even getting back into radio and newspapers. The more outlets, the merrier the chase for those precious advertising dollars.

In a newspaper article in which he had kind things to say about my career, a former CTV colleague, Mike Nolan—now a professor emeritus at the University of Western Ontario—took a look at the often-bewildering images changing the media landscape and concluded, "The network anchor has become a redundant messenger." On this point, I have to disagree.

Tweets may provide early alerts to potentially world-shaking events. YouTube and Facebook posts may give us the beginnings of documentation. Wikipedia may be a starting point for background research. But this kind of "crowdsourcing"—to use a current buzzword—is not an alternative to traditional coverage, or a replacement for it. It is a supplement, providing important, but at best fragmentary, glimpses. It certainly gives the impression of making the world run faster. All information moves with lightning speed, bouncing from one country to another with instant opinion and often spotty interpretation and biased analysis running along with it. However, your traditional, dependable sources are able to make good use of it. Reporters and editors within our system are able to take these nuggets and get to the scene of the action faster and hook up with information sources earlier, based on what real people are saying. We can then deliver the news to our audiences based on our own professional assessments of the nature of the story.

This new dynamic in information gathering is actually helping traditional media. For one thing, it is driving people to their television sets in greater numbers. During the mass demonstrations in the streets of Cairo, for example, news viewership soared as the general public became fascinated by the phenomenon and were looking to their established news sources to provide them with more context, verification and analysis.

I believe that people will continue to look to the news professionals at CTV and elsewhere to pull the day's events together— at least for the foreseeable future. Anchors and hosts of talk programs will continue to be the contact points for the audience. With hundreds of channels now available across the dial, making it more difficult to establish long-term relationships with audiences, anchors and interviewers may not have the influence they once had, but they will continue to serve a critical purpose. The audience expects them to be their guides through the maze of often-confusing times; viewers, listeners and readers still treasure credibility.

This conclusion is supported in a survey by the Canadian Media Research Consortium. It found that "information provided by traditional news media is judged to be reliable and trustworthy by nearly nine out of ten Canadians." Only one in four thinks information from social networks is reliable.

I certainly would not presume to predict the future of media. But I note some promising trends. Hopefully, the various forms of media—amateur and professional—will continue to find ways of stimulating and reinforcing each other, making news coverage both more participatory and more complete.

When the current revolution—and it is a revolution—shakes down, we may find ourselves living in a more liberated world. Twitter and Facebook are enormously useful resources in those parts of the globe where whole populations still live under oppressive regimes. It's almost impossible for police states to totally control these media. People will be better informed than ever through social media—more will be engaged in the politics of their countries and in the process of holding their leaders to account. And that in itself is reason enough to hail this brave new media world and not be fearful of it. These are new times; we should embrace the challenge and celebrate the refreshing openness they present.

Acknowledgements

Nancy and I come from a time when talking about yourself in public was considered boastful and rude. You were to go through life keeping your head down, working hard and minding your own business. I had spent my career covering other people, and while being in the spotlight as a news anchor and public personality came with the territory, the thought of trotting out my own life, warts and all, onto the public stage was not an attractive proposition.

My instincts snapped into place, then, when agent Michael Levine started pushing me to do a book and daughter Lisa said, "Dad, when you finish your time on the news, we should do a documentary on your life and career." "No way," was my reaction to both. Who would be interested anyway? My response didn't stop either of them from continuing to press on, and I finally relented just enough to consider their ideas.

Harvey Kirck and Knowlton Nash had both written books late in their careers, and the nonfiction lists have been flooded through the decades with the life stories of U.S. news personalities, from Barbara Walters and Mike Wallace to Tom Brokaw and Walter Cronkite. Also, we were in the age of Oprah, when the

comings and goings of all manner of celebrities and TV personalities were fodder for the endless appetite of TV talk shows and
were breathlessly documented over and over. These days, everybody talks about everything—the pendulum has swung totally
in the other direction. Perhaps my thinking was old-fashioned
and too confining.

While not ready to jump into the deep end of the pool and
make a firm commitment, I started tinkering with the few first
chapters of this book. I soon began to get into the story, and
it didn't take long before I was happily banging away at the
keyboard, dredging up my past and digging for anecdotes that
spanned sixty years of broadcasting and covered my journey
through early television.

Writing a memoir is a critical test for the soundness of the
author's memory. While much of what precedes this is from
recall, I've had extensive assistance from friends and family.
Their patience and willingness to help without reservation have
made it a fascinating journey into new territory for me.

Most valuable were Nancy's files of clippings, notes and pictures from my entire career, dating to the first time I anchored an
election on television: it was the Diefenbaker sweep of 1958, and
I received a "fine job" mention in the Winnipeg *Tribune*.

I am also deeply indebted to daughter Lisa for her superb
work on the documentary on my life, which brought forth even
more material that was useful in structuring the book.

My editor, Jim Gifford, of HarperCollins Canada, kept
me on track with his gentle prodding to reveal myself on a
personal level, as well as his regular prompting to look harder
or longer at the events that dominated my time at the anchor
desks of two networks. And my patient and precise production

editor, Allegra Robinson, looked after the many small details involved in the final stages of the editing process.

I'm grateful to editor and writer Don Cumming, a longtime colleague who provided intimate knowledge on the formative stages of news departments at both CBC and CTV. His assistance and insights at important junctures in the six decades covered in this book were essential and much appreciated. The same applies to my friend and writer Ken Bagnell. Thanks to former CTV News vice-president Dennis McIntosh and my longtime nightly news producer Larry Rose for providing ideas and suggestions. Emily Young Lee, our always-helpful communications manager at CTV News, kept me on track while I wrote the book and performed several other tasks for the network at the same time.

My eldest grandchild, the bright and vivacious Jessica Hester, cast her astute university-trained literary eye over certain portions of the text and presented worthwhile ideas. She is now one of seven grandchildren, including Cameron, Max, Deanna, Rebecca, Raymond and Jesse, all of whom are filled with promise and expectations as they launch themselves into the world. My California nieces, Bonnie and Mary, were helpful in providing early photographs and information.

And a salute to those TV colleagues behind the scenes who were not connected to structuring the book but provided fodder for stories. Some have already been mentioned, but there are others who helped create the atmosphere that allowed me to thrive. Many of them I am happy to call my friends: the erstwhile principal director Brian Lebold and his predecessors Mike Hooey and Jim Mellanby, are key among them. John Levantis is a longtime fixture at CTV who performed his various tasks as studio director and teleprompter operator with diligence and patience; cameramen Roland Gerig, Wayne Summers, John Clifford, Dale Moore, David Silliker and Glen Mowat, among others, always made me look good and we had fun together. Mark Kaiser and Peter Hodgson were two of the editing wizards who helped keep our broadcasts looking sharp. As an audio man, Chuck Reinhardt, with his finely tuned ear, is unsurpassed in his field, and my warm thanks to technical producer George Baker, who performed miracles in holding all the bits and pieces together on so many of our big broadcasts through the last several years. Thanks also to Elaine Saunders, Linda Bradley and all in makeup who worked their magic on my behalf; to Anne Dinely, whose shining studio teleprompter presence made us all feel better, and Dave Norris for his steadiness and good companionship in several different roles. There were many others across the country and around the world who passed through my professional life, some on a daily basis, and some I'm still working with. It's impossible to list them all, but they know who they are and they also know their imprints on my journey will always be with me.

By the way, you may have noticed I have only weighed anchor on the news and am still active in various program areas. Canada's longest-running current affairs show, *W5*, is a great vehicle for stories that make a difference in people's lives, a mission that counts for a lot at this stage of my life.

My friend Tim Kotcheff once speculated that our first marriages had survived because our partners had "let us do our thing." It's not that simple, of course, but there is no doubt that Nancy had that much figured out quite early. Through it all, she has been my rock, and her prominence speaks for itself throughout the book.

Our treasured daughters, Nanci Lee, Susan and twins Lisa and Lynda, have provided constant inspiration and encouragement. They and their patient spouses, Mark, Ron and Don have heard me blathering on about this book for more than a year. I hope the result shows it was worth their time and attention.

Most of all, my immediate family has brought the balance so critical in a busy life. The next chapter for me will be about giving back as much as I can—to family, to friends and to the country I came to love and cherish through these last many years.

Index